The Secrets Of

BODY LANGUAGE

BY THE SAME AUTHOR

La synergologie (*Synergology*)

Les codes inconscients de la séduction
(*The Unconscious Codes of Seduction*)

To contact the author:

Email: philippe.turchet@synergologie.org
Blog: http://blog.synergologie.org
Website: http://www.synergologie.org

The Secrets Of BODY LANGUAGE

An Illustrated Guide to Knowing What People Are Really Thinking and Feeling

Philippe Turchet

Skyhorse Publishing

Published originally under the title: *Le langage universel du corps*

Skyhorse Publishing books may be purchased in bulk at special discounts for sales promotion, corporate gifts, fund-raising, or educational purposes. Special editions can also be created to specifications. For details, contact the Special Sales Department, Skyhorse Publishing, 307 West 36th Street, 11th Floor, New York, NY 10018 or info@skyhorsepublishing.com.

Visit our website at www.skyhorsepublishing.com.

10 9 8 7 6 5 4 3 2

Library of Congress Cataloging-in-Publication Data is available on file.
ISBN: 978-1-62087-072-3

Printed in the United States of America

To Jocelyne,
For your attentive eyes.

"Science is not 'organized common sense' at its most exciting, it reformulates our view of the world by imposing powerful theories against the ancient, anthropocentric prejudices that we call intuition."

—Stephen J. Gould,
Ever Since Darwin: Reflections in Natural History

"Language must fulfill several different tasks. If one were to rank them, it is surely the emotional aspect that would come first, well before any communication about the external world, so important is it for the material survival of the individual and the species: animals get along well."

—Dominique Laplane,
Le pensée d'outre-mots

TABLE OF CONTENTS

PART THREE

WHEN THE BODY THINKS OUT LOUD

Preface

This work is illustrated with visual sequences demonstrating concrete forms of emotions. In some cases the images are taken from actual video footage, and a technique has been used to allow the subjects to retain their anonymity without altering the physical characteristics being analyzed. Taken from real situations, these images are firsthand. If by any chance you feel that you recognize a face at random through a disguised emotion, as we look at certain emotions together, don't forget that this person's turmoil is not entirely unlike your own when you struggle with the same contradictions . . .

Introduction

Body language is universal. Some of you will be taken aback by this statement, believing in your heart of hearts that it is actually a cultural phenomenon. Some of you can even point to a particular symbolic gesture, specific to a group of people, in order to prove that body language is cultural. And you know what? You'd be right! But we simply aren't talking about body language on the same level.

Culture transforms us every day and it has an impact on our behavior. We are immersed in it and we are its products, so all our interactions are cultural. But in this book we will not be focusing on the cultural level. We go deeper than that.

Universal body language was gradually established sometime between the emergence of bipedalism, seven million years ago, and of spoken language, thirty-five thousand years ago. This time period is so broad that the very substance of body language had time to become a major genetic component of human evolution. We are not asking if a person living in Manhattan makes the same gestures to communicate with children as someone who lives in a hut in New Guinea. If they are both human beings, it is through their common genetic makeup that began forming seven million years ago—or 350 million years ago, when the modern human brain first developed—that they both acquired the necessary knowledge to recognize and understand each other. In fact, if they met each other today, they would be able to recognize and understand each other.

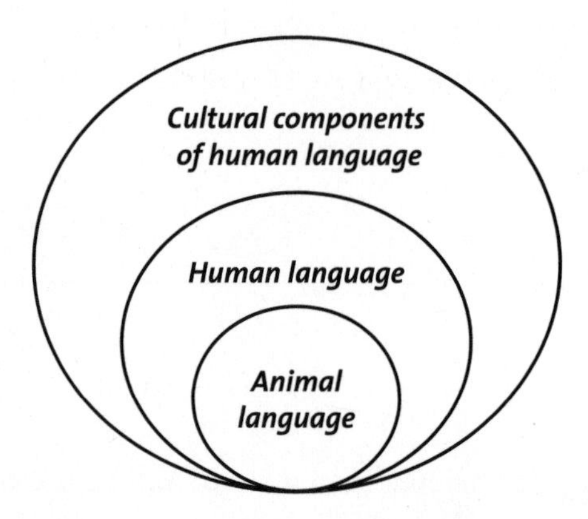

The universality of body language is a prerequisite for our purposes. This work demonstrates it through illustration, in every sense of the word. Practically, it shows the body in action more than it theorizes about its universal character. Of course, these issues will be addressed, but let's take universality as an assumption for now, knowing that by the time you finish this book you will fully accept that body language is universal.

Body language expresses all of our emotions: those that we wish to keep to ourselves and those that we wish to transmit. From there, we extrapolate billions of different body postures, but they never stray from these three simple rules:

1. Every emotion can be read on the face and the body.
2. When we keep our emotions to ourselves, our hands have a tendency to wander over our faces and our bodies.
3. When we want to convey our emotions, our hands move toward the person to whom we are speaking.

Body language will give movement to this book, which will describe as accurately as possible these three realities:

1. Body language is a language of *imprinted* emotions.
2. Body language is a language of *repressed* emotions.
3. Body language is a language of *expressed* emotions.

"Emotion . . . everyone knows what it is until the moment they are asked to define it."

—Joseph LeDoux,
The Emotional Brain

"When I say that I am angry, I might be, but I could also be mistaken.
In fact, I might be scared or jealous or both at the same time. Outside observers are more qualified to judge my mood than I myself am."

—D. O. Hebb

PART ONE

Body Language, A Language of Emotions

CHAPTER 1

Body Language: Nonverbal Language and Emotions . . .

Emotions hold a fundamental place in our lives as human beings. They are at the root of all our decisions, yet they are, paradoxically, largely ignored by mainstream science. This is all the more astonishing because they have an unequaled advantage in the world of human sciences: They can be seen! Emotions are concrete and can be measured and recorded. They are expressed by the human body, and transform it. That is why we call it "body language." However, the academic community often prefers the expression "nonverbal language," which is more sterile. In reality, these two expressions clarify each other, one embedded in the other, thereby contributing to a better reading of the body.

You Said "Nonverbal Language"?

Body language is not an invention of the mind. More than 80 percent of our exchanges pass through channels other than words.[1] There is no serious (or even fanciful) doubt about this fact, but, astonishingly, no rigorous investigation has found, even today, a way to classify nonverbal human exchange.[2] Nonverbal language is enigmatic, a true gap in our knowledge, almost as if it didn't exist! You don't agree? Take a classic academic definition from any common French dictionary, like *Larousse* or *Robert*. While looking for the antonym of the word "verbal," you might think you would find an expression similar to "nonverbal." Well, you will have wasted your time and money. The words "non" and "verbal" are not associated in these conventional dictionaries. "Nonverbal" does not come up as the antonym of "verbal" like "noncombatant" might for "combatant," for example. The antonym of the word "verbal" is the word "written"! The expression "nonverbal" is conspicuous in its absence.[3]

Nonverbal language is essential at every stage of life. At birth, a doctor who leans over a newborn to observe it is looking for information that is nonverbal. For example, he checks skin color, which turns pink the moment the newborn's lungs fill up with air for the first time; vital signs, which inform him of the newborn's state of health, etc. Later, in school, what do we most often rely on when we say that a child "looks intelligent"? In another vein, how do lovers choose each other, if not for the most part using criteria that are almost totally nonverbal? And, for job interviews, don't men shave and don't women put on make-up? They know that first impressions are nonverbal and that it takes an enormous amount of time to dispel them.

At every stage of life, we use nonverbal information from our environment to adapt in order to communicate more effectively.

Some people are unable to decipher nonverbal language. They are, in fact, incapable of deciphering other people's facial or body expressions in conversation. This difficulty in understanding other people can become a real problem and has a name—Asperger's syndrome.[4] People who have it feel handicapped. They feel their own emotions but are often incapable of recognizing those of the people around them, and their inability to decipher the unspoken greatly reduces their performance in relationships. Put yourself in their place: Imagine that you approach one of your friends and you are laughing because you have just gotten some good news, while he is despondent because he has received some bad news. You risk passing for someone who is inhuman if you persist in joking around instead of appearing affected, because you failed to perceive his state of mind. It is nonverbal language that permits us to not make this mistake and to adapt the way we communicate.

Body language expresses emotions, the unspoken, so well that human beings are generally more skillful at deciphering video footage of lies that have been uttered by individuals if they look at images that have been muted rather than if they listen to what is being said.[5]

One of the things that IQ tests calculate is nonverbal aptitude, but this test is limited to the person's ability to manipulate three-dimensional space. Nowhere is the form of intelligence—which is so precise that it allows, for example, someone to negotiate skillfully or gain the good graces of others by understanding what they feel—taken into account.

Companies that hire new employees do not measure this capacity either, even if they ask them to demonstrate active listening. All occupations in the service sector are techno-commercial today—technical and commercial. Employees must be capable of resolving problems and selling their solutions to internal and external clients. It is in doing this that we must take the capacity to read emotions into consideration.

The Rosenthal Rats and the Pygmalion Effect

The importance of body language is not exploited or just barely so; however, its true impact on everyday communication has been measured scrupulously by Robert Rosenthal, an American researcher whose work we cannot overlook.[6] In concrete terms, he explained to his students that he had selected two populations of rats for the purposes of an experiment: common rats, and others from a line of superior intelligence. In reality, the rats were cerebrally identical. He asked the students to lead the animals through a maze. The inevitable happened. Those that were designated as more intelligent succeeded in crossing the labyrinth faster than the others! Rosenthal, anxious to understand, began more thoroughly observing—not the rats, of course, but the students. He saw that they were more attentive, more empathetic, and more affectionate with the animals that were said to be more intelligent, and, in fact, that the most pampered rats were also the most calm. Guided by the unconscious attention from the experimenters, they did better.

As they were animals, it was not a question of an attitude that had been affected by the students' vocabulary. The entire success of the brighter rats had to be attributed to the impact of nonverbal communication.

Obviously, Rosenthal did not stop there. He pursued his experiment—on humans, this time. At the beginning of the school year, he spoke to some professors about a certain number of students whose tests had supposedly revealed more intelligence. He proposed that they meet again at the end of the year to measure the evolution of their students' work. As you have already guessed, these students were neither more nor less intelligent than the others, but at the end of the school year they had better than average results, some ranking extremely high. Rosenthal spoke, on this occasion, of a Pygmalion effect.[7] (You call someone who knows how to encourage the full potential of another person by projecting success—or, for that matter, failure, which is less often evoked—a pygmalion). The phenomenon that causes this effect is mostly nonverbal.

The Five Dimensions of Nonverbal Language

The expression "nonverbal language," designating everything that is not verbal, needs to be clarified.[8] In fact, the human brain recognizes, when communicating, five different forms of nonverbal information that are handled by different cerebral zones. Body language is one of them. It is important to briefly distinguish them here in order to not have to come back later and to focus on carefully considering the messages of body language.

When you talk with someone, he will hold himself at a certain distance from you; he will speak and send subliminal messages, but also conscious ones, both through specific body language.

That distance is the **periverbal** dimension, the space and time at the heart of communication. It influences how we relate to each other.

You will communicate differently depending on whether you are near or far from the person to whom you are speaking, next to him or across from him, if you are in a hurry or not . . .

The voice has a **paraverbal** dimension. It affects communication beyond words. When leaving the table, you can say, "This was a great meal!" in such a specific tone that everyone understands that it was actually inedible. This dimension is not directly of interest to our discussion of body language.

The subliminal **infraverbal** information also unconsciously transforms communication. These are the smells, the colors, and shapes of clothing, among others.

The distinctive **supraverbal** signs are deciphered consciously: clothing, rings, and watches, for example, are identified in another part of the brain and also contribute to nonverbal communication.

But body language is something else. We must not forget the **preverbal** dimension. Before speaking, in an exchange, one part of the brain unconsciously adopts the body posture of the other person.[9] It is thanks to this mechanism that we naturally experience empathy and adapt ourselves to that person. The discovery of the existence of the cerebral zone responsible for this phenomenon, in the left cortex, dates to less than 15 years ago. It establishes that body language is all-powerful by demonstrating that a human being is armed with a device that permits him to understand another simply by looking at him. To read the body language of another is to decipher his emotions.

- Nonverbal language consists of five dimensions: *periverbal* (the connection between time and space), *paraverbal* (the different modulations of the voice), *infraverbal* (subliminal unconscious realities), *supraverbal* (the conscious signs, clothing, etc.), and preverbal (body language).
- Body language corresponds to the trace left by emotions on the physical frame.
- Body language reveals emotional states.

CHAPTER 2

What Is an Emotion?

Our civilization is at the point of being turned upside down by several discoveries whose repercussions could very well transform even our most everyday thoughts. It was not very long ago that we still believed, for example, that emotions prevented us from keeping a "cool head" and that emotional outbursts prevented human beings from taking reasonable action. We now know that emotions are not the animal spirits that were spoken of long ago.

Since Charles Darwin's time, specialists have all agreed that fear, anger, joy, and sadness are universal emotions,[1] but that was about the only real agreement between all the schools of thought until the 1990s, at least with regard to emotions. A new and recent interest has arisen as a result of major discoveries that fall under the term "emotional intelligence."[2] First, Joseph LeDoux identified an area in the brain that stores emotional experiences and can sometimes react before even having understood a danger: the amygdala.[3] This was a bombshell, the first breach of the theories of reason that excluded emotions. We also discovered that the neocortex, the conscious brain that appeared relatively recently in the history of our species, is not always necessary for making intelligent decisions.[4]

At about the same time, Antonio Damasio, assisted by his research team at the University of Iowa, made another discovery.[5] He showed that people in whom certain emotional areas are destroyed are incapable of making sound decisions simply because they are no longer able to sense what is really important.

These two researchers gave emotions their rightful place. They showed that emotions are responsible for accurately making the most complicated decisions. Emotions allow us, in good conscience, to distinguish between what is important and what is less so. Without them, it is even impossible to be reasonable! Emotion was inducted into the palace of reason, of which she became the queen. We are at the dawn of a revolution whose themes are still being debated in the insiders' circle, but which is preparing to overturn the twenty-first century—of that we can be certain.

Emotion Selects Important Information

Emotional intelligence[6] allows us to synthesize different data, information, events, and facts, and, above all, to prioritize their importance. It makes us intelligent. Let's take a specific example. Imagine that your spouse leaves this message on your voicemail: "Dear, I am calling because I was supposed to pick up the children after school, but I've run into a hitch, and you are going to have to take care of them. They'll be waiting on the sidewalk outside . . . And also, by the way, did you see the refrigerator this morning? It was empty. It would be nice if you could buy two or three things to eat this evening . . ." *Beep-beep-beep* . . . Your love has hung up.

You find yourself with two missions on your hands: to get the children and to find something to eat. Where will you start? The children on the sidewalk or grocery shopping for the evening?

When this question is presented to a group of people, everybody responds in a single voice: "The children on the sidewalk!" Nobody asks: "Can you tell us which one is more practical?", "Which order will be more convenient?", "Which order will be fastest?", "How old are the children?", or "Are the stores going to close?" They all systematically gave, without consulting each other, the same answer, as if it were self-evident. The emotional charge of the words *the children on the sidewalk* makes everyone respond quickly and at the same time: "The children!" That is emotional intelligence! To feel what is important without having to analyze it, to have confidence in the brain and the body that transmit appropriate information to us. Faced with whatever problem, they establish a balance of costs and advantages for each solution based first on emotional criteria. All good decisions are made based on this principle!

Emotions draw a demarcation between what will be remembered and what will be forgotten, and body language plays a considerable role in this process.[7]

Fact, Information, and Body Language

Information filters through our mental space all day long. Most of it is excluded from our consciousness. Messages that are preserved are of a different kind. A trained eye can find traces of emotion. Why do certain messages touch us more than others, and what is the role of body language in this process?

Information that leaves us cold is forgotten as soon as it is heard. Information touches us because, in one way or another, it moves us. The news in the past ten years that remains, still today, the most vivid in the memories of the Western world, is, without a doubt, the destruction, on September 11, 2001, of the World Trade Center in New York. This is also the information that triggered the greatest emotion. It is forever recorded in every brain that witnessed images of it. The event was so distressing that nobody will ever forget it.

If the destruction of the Twin Towers had been just a simple event, it would have been erased from memory like all the other facts from the news that day—you have forgotten them, haven't you? Simple facts do not interest us. They are classified in databases and later cut out of our collective memory. On the other hand, when information is transmitted,[8] its vehicle and its fuel are emotion. A fact that is emotionally charged constitutes information that lingers, as long as it provokes emotion. Do we remember exactly all the earthquakes that have occurred over the past ten years?

Some of them were far more deadly than the events of September 11, yet we have forgotten them. They were natural catastrophes, unlike attacks that were caused by a human hand whose emotional contagion was maximal. The amygdala system of all human beings reacted so strongly in the face of the images of the collapsed buildings that we will never forget them.[9] The fact shocked us, then revolted us; we transmitted what we received at great speed, turning the fact into information. You ask, how is this related to nonverbal communication? It is metaphorical and yet, at the same time, direct.

A discussion between two people is, at first, an exchange of raw facts, but it is the emotional impact of a body and a face that will give them force and color. One day, our children, our unborn grandchildren, will hear about September 11, and they will read the dramatic reality of that information on our faces. They will transmit it to their friends simply because they will have been touched by the body language of the person who spoke to them about it. Information that does not touch us, on the contrary, will not be transmitted. This is true for all information, and it is true for everybody.

Numbers, for example, are raw information. However, when we look at mathematicians' brains using an MRI, we see that—unlike with mere mortals—certain emotional areas are stimulated when numbers are projected onto a screen! Ask them to talk to you about it and they will tell you that a beautiful equation is a harmony of form. They will use words typically relegated to the emotional universe to describe mathematics.

The brain is receptive to emotional information sent by the environment. An infant interacts much less with its mother when she is depressed than when she is happy. The brain is thus programmed to recognize emotions embedded in our most basic nonverbal expressions.[10]

An anecdote told by the mother of a small, two-year-old boy illustrates this point. He once said, thoughtfully, pointing to a logo on the refrigerator: "Mommy, the refrigerator is sad!" There were two marks:

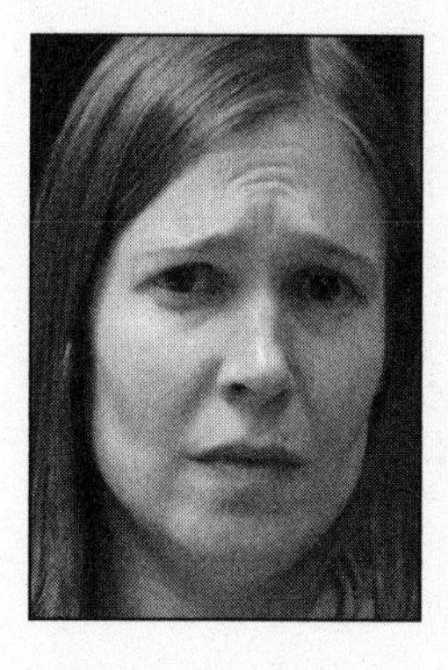

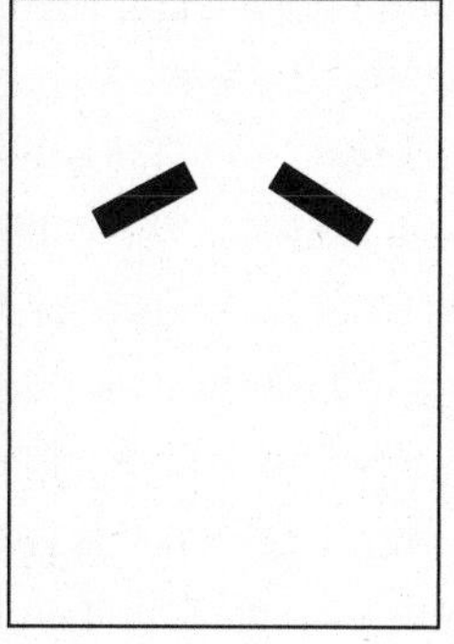

The two small marks resemble the configuration . . . that our eyebrows make when we are sad.

Our brains are programmed to recognize primary information about other people. Experience will then strengthen this innate material throughout our lives. Without knowing it, when we look at a person, the recognition of their features is supported by a cerebral module that processes emotions.[11] It is in this way, through these bodily messages, that we are able to understand what someone is feeling without having to ask.[12]

Empathy, or The Bodily Transmission of Emotional Information

For a very long time, empathy—the capacity to understand what someone else is feeling—had been considered an indispensable condition for social relationships.[13] Then, it became an ethical reference.[14] We know today that the brain itself "fabricates" empathy by "naturally" deciphering the micro-movements of another person's face and body. The other person's thoughts are deduced through their emotional expressions and the emotions read in their bodily micro-movements. Of course, in this context, the role of body language is essential.

Empathy Through Evidence

Babies mimic the facial expressions of people in their environment, thereby understanding them even before being able to speak.[15] The mother who feeds her baby holds him very close to herself (*periverbal* language); she accompanies her movements with an enthusiastic "Yum . . . that's good!" (*paraverbal* language); his eyes are wide open, staring at her eyebrows, her dilated pupils, and her slightly parted lips while she puts a spoon into his mouth, nodding along with the movement (*preverbal language*). The baby smiles, feeling good (*infraverbal* language), the mother is proud of him (*supraverbal* language), and she is happy. The child not only eats the food, but he also shares in the relationship and gets a "taste" of the outside world. By reproducing and mimicking his mother's attitudes, he forms his own emotional tones and discovers, without knowing it, what an emotion is. These mechanisms are mostly nonverbal. It is this grasping of consciousness that prepares the baby to feel his own emotions and to communicate them more elaborately in these same terms.

The mother, through her body language, deciphers the world for her baby. But he is now only armed to read facial expressions, not to interpret the whole world.[16] She translates exterior messages for him using emotional signals. We find the same phenomenon in animals: For a long time, researchers had thought that small monkeys had an innate fear of snakes, but they realized that that was not the case among those raised in laboratories. If you show a snake to a baby monkey in the absence of its mother, it does not become anxious. Instead, baby monkeys learn to fear snakes by seeing their mothers be scared.[17] Mother monkeys demonstrate, through their body language, what is important for their little ones to know. They translate the world for them.

Innate motor mimicry allows a baby to reproduce the movements of an adult. This is not pure reflex, since a child will not do this with a robot.[18] Babies imitate human movement very intentionally and selectively.[19]

A child's face is extremely lively compared to the coarse motor skills of his body: He communicates face to face from birth[20] even though he is incapable of sitting up on his own before the age of four months! The discrepancy between the maturity of the face and the motor weakness of the body's central axis is incredible. Only a mechanism attributable to evolution, with the simple goal of permitting him to communicate with an adult, can explain it.

Thanks to this empathetic phenomenon, a child is unconsciously clued in to the role of inclining one's head from birth.[21] He inclines his own at certain key relational moments, notably at the age when he might start attending kindergarten.[22]

Doesn't one of these women seem nicer than the other?

In the photo on the right, the woman seems warmer, more human, more focused on the relationship, because she is tilting her head to the side. The stiffness of the more upright head is gone. Do you think it is her general facial expression, rather than the tilt of the woman's head, that produces this softness? Let's look at another example. Which one of these dogs seems friendlier?

People who observe these images agree that the dog with the inclined head seems friendlier than the first one. We are programmed to think that. Adults, when listening attentively, will gently incline their heads slightly. Our faces and bodies have the tendency, in empathetic situations, to pick up other people's facial expressions and body language. The same resources are thus working in both people's brains, sharing attention and emotions.[23]

The cerebral basis of a collective unconscious gesture that permits us to recognize each other beyond cultural origins seems out there, but the cerebral basis of morality needs to be redefined. Until recently, we thought that human beings were moral because it was in their personal interest to be: "Do unto others what you would have them do unto you."[24] But now we know that we perceive physical pain in another person because the same cerebral zones are active in us. Therefore the human capacity to behave in a moral fashion does not rest upon reason but on the capacity to experience the same emotions as another person and thus sympathize with him or her. The message of tolerance is emotional; the reason, an emotional reason.[25]

Our unconscious capacity to focus on someone else's face[26] and carry out the same cerebral tasks permits us to acquire an astonishing aptitude for deciphering his or her emotions and thoughts. Nevertheless, empathy is not the same as sympathy. Understanding another person does not oblige us to experience the same thoughts at all costs. The connotation may be different. Certain people, for example, upon the death of a loved one, are so overcome with grief that they would like to die themselves. We can understand their feelings without wanting to die ourselves. This is empathy without emotional contagion. Other ingredients are necessary for the latter.

What If Body Language Completely Modified Communication?

Words—in which we place so much confidence—do not represent more than 7 percent of communication, but body language can alter, in many cases, 100 percent of the nature of an interaction! Imagine a friend approaches you in a corridor. You are thinking of telling her that you are happy because of an unexpected personal event. You extend your hand to her. She gives you hers. Your eyes meet. Her face looks like this:

Do you still feel like sharing your well-being? No. Her look has transformed the course of your thoughts . . . and instead you say to her, "You look pensive this morning . . . tired?"

Only a single exchange of looks was sufficient to change the whole trajectory of your communication. Body language transformed 100 percent of your interaction.

The topic of conversation changed because unconsciously you understand that the other person's preoccupations have made your thoughts obsolete or have displaced them. This happens every day. Other people change us without saying a thing, and we, unknowingly, in turn transform them as well.

Body language not only affects the tempo of dialogue, but even more so, it modifies its contents. No one ever welcomes someone sad by laughing. Their sadness first modifies the other person's expression of happiness, and then the happiness itself as well.

Why, in your opinion, are there certain people that everyone seems to confide in, while there are others that you never see being confided in. Simply because certain faces, certain bodies, give an impression of trustworthiness and a feeling of openness. It is a question of shared resonance. Without knowing it, some people, by their posture, their movements, their micro-movements when they communicate with others, give off sensitive body signals that encourage others to open themselves up to them. Tangible evidence of translated emotions[27] . . .

- **Information is prioritized based on emotional criteria that let us understand what is important.**
- **Emotions transmitted consciously or unconsciously can transform up to 100 percent of the content of verbal communication.**

CHAPTER 3

How Do You Build an Emotion?

Studies on emotions come up against a difficulty that is tied to their very nature. Everyone thinks that they know how to pinpoint emotions naturally without understanding that while our unconscious abilities to decipher them are enormous, our conscious resources are much more limited.[1]

Deciphering emotions forces us to get rid of the belief that observation leads to understanding. In fact, **one must understand in order to observe.** In order to see, we must already know what we are looking for!

Learning to observe an emotion will be easier once we know how it is constructed.

Terms as different as "affect," "mood," "feeling," "impulse," "mental state," "humor," or even "behavioral program" and "emotion" are not distinguishable, yet they are obviously not synonymous. But the theoretical issue surrounding the systematic labeling of emotional states is not the best way, in our opinion, to obtain an understanding of emotions. Fear, for example, can be an emotion as well as a feeling![2] A snake crossing our path provokes a strong emotion that translates into a pounding heart, while for some people, the solitude of a walk in the woods gives rise to an incomprehensible and unfounded fear: a feeling.[3] It will therefore not always be easy to know if the person facing us is feeling fear or terror, but on the other hand, it will be of the utmost importance to understand that if he is telling us that he is calm, then there is an incongruity between what he is saying and what he is showing. This incongruity is what we will learn to identify first and foremost.

Regardless of whether a human being is fearful, afraid, or terrified, some general constants always emerge. Emotions are defined by their nonverbal constants, grouped into emotional categories. These observable constants will permit us to speak in the same language when we refer to emotions.[4]

What Does an Emotion Look Like? Like a Movement!

The word "emotion" comes from the Latin *emovere* which means "to move."[5] An emotion changes something in the configuration of our faces and bodies. The etymology itself provides precise information about how to decipher emotions: We must first observe movement, because emotions are movements.

Emotions can be read thanks to movements. Spoken language regularly establishes this correlation between body movements and mental states. Take, for example, phrases like: "He is sad; he has not stopped crying," or "He is very proud; you saw how he puffed out his chest," or "He is pouting; I don't think he agrees," or "Now he's dragging behind; he must be exhausted," or "He is so rigid, it looks like he swallowed a broomstick." Body movements, thoughts, and emotions are interrelated in our brains, and they have a real impact on each other. Sports allow us to better understand this reality. Walking, swimming, or bicycling, for example, are not just a sum of movements, but they trigger well-being and often give birth to a flow, just after the exercise, of thoughts and emotions different from those preceding the action. These movements somehow transform us.

Behind an emotion, there is always a movement. It even precedes the emotion and is the prerequisite for experiencing it! William James, in the nineteenth century, illustrated the process thanks to an example that has become classic today: If on a walk you come across a bear, do you first think about running away and only later realize that you were afraid, or do you become conscious of your fear and then run away?[6]

In this debate, the thinkers of the twentieth century said he was wrong. They believed, in fact, that it is the fear that sets off the flight instinct, which was indeed quite logical.[7] But recent research shows that the flight precedes the fear and that it is only while running that we even become conscious of the fear![8] This mechanism is at the heart of survival.

When driving, we step on the brakes before analyzing the nature of the danger. If we had waited until our "conscious brain," the neocortex, intervened, it would have been too late. The emotional components did the work much more quickly. Starting with facial and body movements in order to describe emotions seems to make sense.

How Does an Emotion Form? In Three Ways!

Human emotions get all of their substance in three stages, found using nonverbal criteria. In terms of their integration, all of the indispensable "ingredients" needed to feel the most elaborate emotions are present.

The Tonic Stage

Emotion does not exist in a newborn baby in the same way it exists in adults. At the same time, all adults have been babies at one time or another. We must consider the baby and the child still living in us in order to decipher the emotions we have as adults.

In the days and the hours following birth, a baby tenses or relaxes to the rhythm of his autonomic nervous system. Two categories—his brain cannot understand more than that—alternate in and around him: the hard and the soft.[9]

Cold is hard, and warm is soft. These states are punctuated on the one hand by a breast or nipple, warm milk, his mother's soft body, prior to the state of abandonment; and, on the other hand, by the absence and the resulting lack of contraction, the hard and the cold experienced in tears, in the dark.

If the baby relaxes, his face and his body are hypotonic; if he tenses or convulses, they are hypertonic. This is the tonic stage. The body tenses up or relaxes, moving in a continuum that goes from positive hypotonicity to negative hypertonicity.

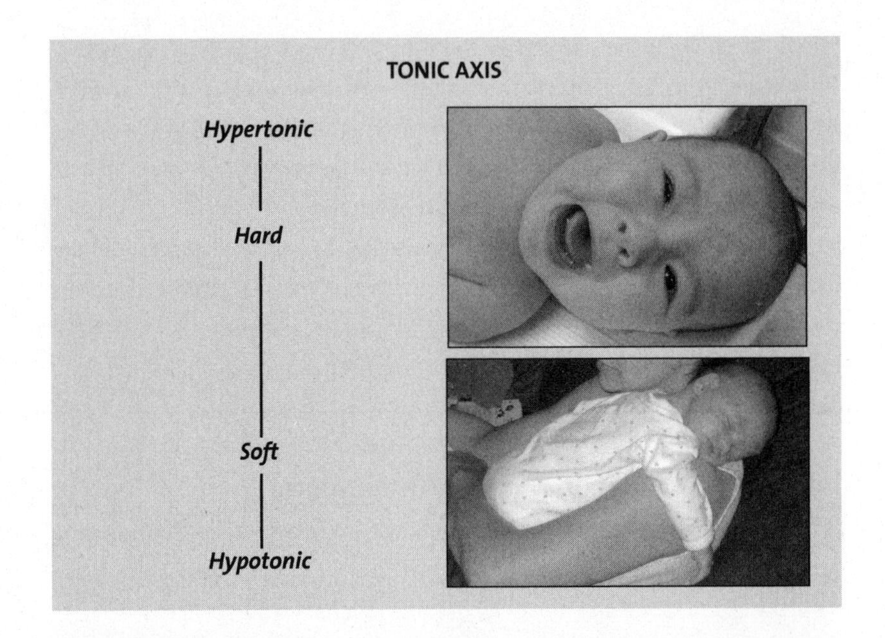

The continuum between hypertonicity and hypotonicity of the face and body begins at birth. The emotions of an adult depend on this stage of development.

The face and body are tense or relaxed depending on the state experienced.

The Sensitive-Emotional Stage

Quite rapidly, this tonic stage, which is essentially binary, becomes more complex, leading to a second "sensitive-emotional" stage. Growth of the brain allows the baby to perceive categories of pleasure and displeasure.[10] The experienced states are no longer just hypotonic or hypertonic but rather agreeable and disagreeable.[11] Gradually, during this stage, what is sensitive becomes emotional, from which we get the descriptor "sensitive-emotional." The child likes something or doesn't like it. We go from pure sensation to the meaning this sensation has for him.

Hypertonicity is no longer only associated with what is cold, harsh, and negative. Besides expressing anger and negativity, being hypertonic can also now include expressing joy and positivity. A baby can "burst" with joy. He was not capable of it until then. Regarding hypotonia, besides its beneficial relaxation, it can also express sadness and other similar states.

During the sensitive-emotional stage, the child makes a huge leap in nonverbal competence, distinguishing himself forever from the other large primates. He points his finger at objects, making it possible to interact with adults, and, most importantly, he does so without seeking an immediate benefit, simply for the sole pleasure of sharing, of communicating,[12] while an ape only points its finger in order to obtain something.[13]

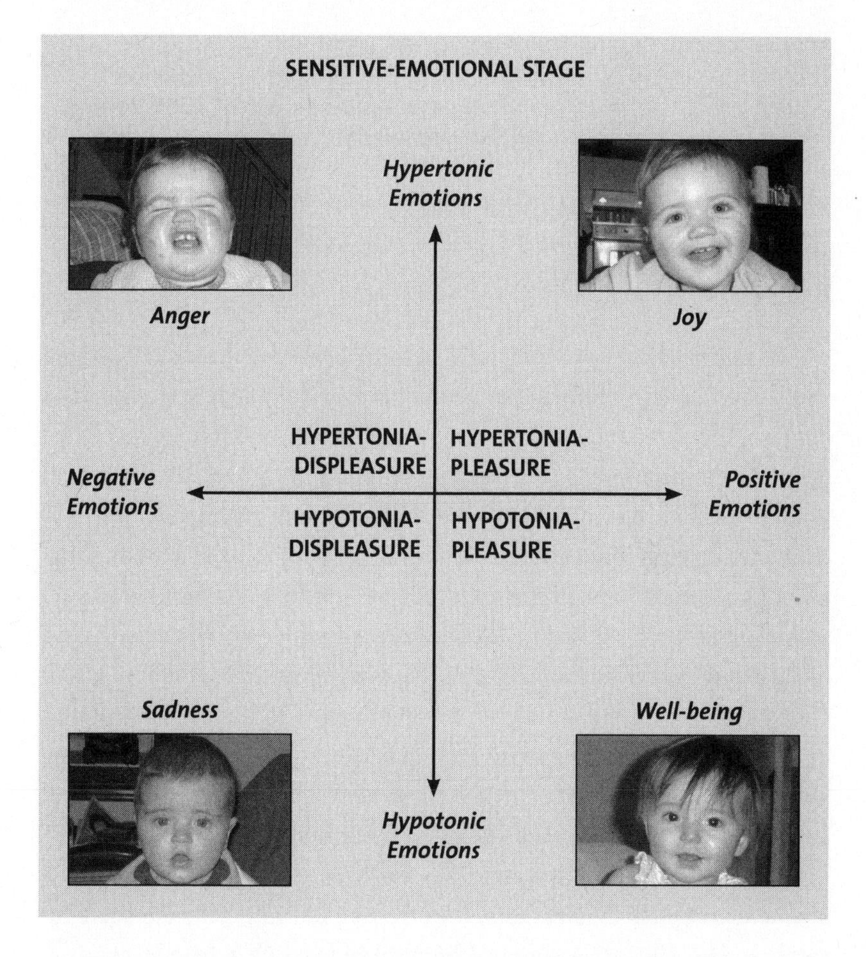

During the sensitive-emotional stage, which lasts until about the age of four, the emotional categories will constantly change. The sensitive-emotional stage lasts until the child makes a new cerebral discovery. . . .

The reflective stage

Up until the age of three or four, the child does not make a distinction between himself and others. When his mother hurts herself, he cries. He speaks about himself indistinctly, in the first and third person without perceiving the difference.[14]

When he plays hide-and-seek, the child who is younger than four years old puts his hands over his eyes and believes that others cannot see him.

He still has to make a cerebral discovery in order to maintain the same connection to his emotions that adults have: understanding that he does not have the same thoughts as everyone else.[15] Around four years old, he acquires the awareness that his thoughts are his alone, different from those of his mother or father, and that his body belongs to him. He understands then that certain emotions are meant to be shared and that others should be kept to himself; that he can hide his foolishness by making others believe that he feels different emotions from those that he really experiences; that when his mother glances at the half-empty box of chocolates with a menacing air, if he manages to appear sufficiently detached, she might not realize that he is responsible. His first attempts are not very conclusive, but little by little he will become more adept and begin to lie more effectively by disguising his emotions.[16]

The child discovers that emotions are strategic and that certain ones are more acceptable than others. The little boy will say, "Girls are scaredy-cats!" and he will understand that being afraid results in being picked on. The little girl says to herself, "But what does he take me for? I am not afraid!" They have both come to realize that fear is not acceptable and one must keep it to oneself—that it is preferable not to reveal it to others.

What is true for the child will be even more so for the adult that he will become. In a general sense, negative emotions and states are not socially acceptable, but certain ones are less so than others. Fear is socially prohibited. Depression suffers the same banishment. No one, in the professional world, would risk saying, "I feel depressed," fearing being sidelined by his colleagues or superiors or even by his friends. On the other hand, some negative emotions can be conveyed without fear. This is the case with sadness, which is accepted and even sometimes socially valued. It is natural to be saddened by a difficult event. It even appears suspicious not to be . . .

Positive emotions, more socially favored than negative emotions, will experience the same divide between states "to be kept to yourself" and "to be shared with others." Only the most acceptable positive emotions are shared. It is socially more correct to say, "I am happy this morning!" than "I feel proud this morning!" We will be happy for the person who is joyful; that emotion can be turned toward another (exocentric), but of the proud person we risk thinking, "Who does she think she is?" It is a good idea to keep this emotion to yourself. Similarly, someone declaring, "I am a calm person!" will make the people around him cautious. They will doubt the serenity announced as if on a banner. This he should keep to himself. Kindness, conversely, is transmitted. Imagine someone taking this line of reasoning: "I'm pretty nice, but I make sure not to show it!" What would be the purpose of kindness that doesn't have a concrete translation and that is not addressed to another?

Here are the three criteria to consider when deciphering emotions:

- The body is tonic or atonic.
- Experienced states are positive or negative.
- Emotional states are directed toward another or kept to oneself.

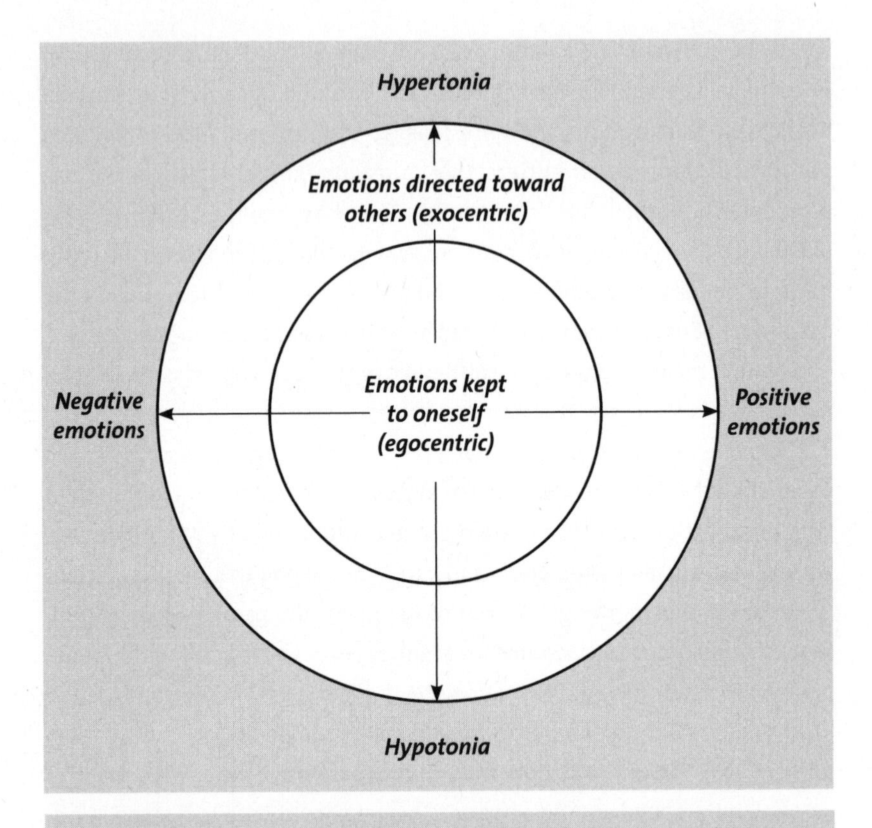

The range of emotional states that we will see over the course of our lifetime can be divided into eight categories.

Before even seeing which body items distinguish these eight emotional groups, the emotions can be concretely positioned on a table of eight quadrants.

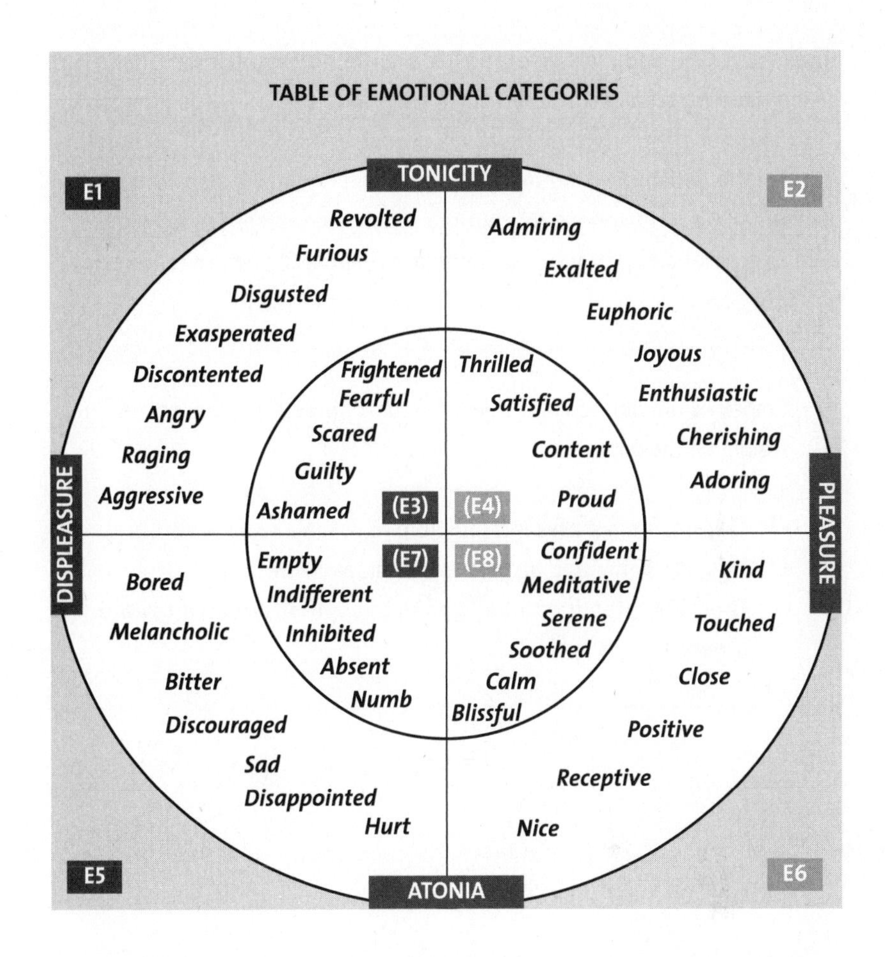

Several states have been organized in this chart of emotional categories. This list is far from exhaustive, but it can be useful if you decide to fill it out. That is not, however, our objective. This chart was not created to make body language specialists champions of emotional semantics. It is merely a tool that allows us to determine if someone is truly in the state he claims to be in, because evidently each one of these eight emotional groups has bodily characteristics.

The interpretation of this chart leads to another point: People can have a different understanding of the same state, affect, or emotion. It is not a question of harping on definitions of this or that emotion. This table is designed to be flexible. Let's take an example: anger. This emotion is always hypertonic (the body is tense), and it is always a negative emotion (it is fueled more by displeasure than pleasure), and, normally, it is directed toward another (e.g., "I am going to tell you what's wrong!"). It is therefore found in the upper left quadrant (E1), but sometimes we keep our anger to ourselves (e.g., "He annoys me, but this is not the moment to tell him so!") (E3). The emotion is the same in both cases—only the desire to transmit it has changed.

Emotions are defined by three universal characteristics that are visible on the body:

- **They result in states ranging from hypotonia to hypertonia.**
- **They are generated by pleasure or displeasure.**
- **They are intended to be kept to oneself or directed toward others.**

CHAPTER 4

How Do You Read an Emotion?

As a specialist in deciphering the nonverbal, I frequently find myself in front of this type of statement that is difficult to qualify, at the innocent intersection between ethnocentrism and well-intended common sense: "It is very difficult to perceive the emotions of the Chinese!" And I invariably answer: "Which Chinese?"

Whether we are Asian, Western, African, or Assyrian, if we experience an emotion, it will be visible on our faces. Only its intensity will be different depending on one of four principal reasons:

- Certain cultures value expression of emotions more than others.
- Some people are more outgoing than others.
- Some people are more sensitive than others, and events will affect them more.
- Some people have a great deal of difficulty hiding their emotions because they feel like they are cheating.

Each one of us has a gestural heritage of our own that differs from one individual to another. Culture is not sufficient to explain these differences,[1] but let us never forget one thing: Whoever the human being is that we are speaking to, if he feels an emotion, we will find it and identify it.

The Concrete Traces of an Emotion on a Face

Two different states make their mark on the face and on the body: states that are lastingly imprinted on our physiology by the passage of time and temporary states that are necessary to convey emotions, meant to be recognized and understood by others.

If these states are present in the brain, they will also be visible on the body; it cannot be otherwise. A condition exists, or it doesn't. If it exists, it can be seen.

Permanent Emotions, Also Known as Background Emotions, and Transitory Emotions

Life has a cadence, seen on our faces, in our features, and in our most precious legacy of life—wrinkles.[2] Wrinkles are permanent features, imprinted states, but these marks of time are not the only punctuations on the face. Each emotion expresses itself there and transforms our faces momentarily.[3]

Two types of wrinkles are present on the face: permanent wrinkles and transient wrinkles. A permanent wrinkle indicates a fundamental component of personality; a transient wrinkle, an ephemeral emotion. It is important not to mistake one for the other.

But first, what lets us say that a permanent wrinkle translates into a personality trait? Common sense would lead us to think that if this wrinkle is permanent, it is more likely physiological—beware of using too much common sense.

When an emotion is expressed, two different types of muscles are activated: smooth muscles and striated muscles.[4] Striated muscles are the ones that move our bodies. The brain, consciously or not, gives orders, and their response is immediate, in our faces as well as throughout our bodies. If we are afraid, for example, the blood drains from our face and moves toward our arms and especially our legs, preparing them for fight or flight. What we often forget is that in order to make this action possible, it took another category of muscles to act: the smooth muscles. These small muscles surround our veins, venules, arteries, and arterioles. They ensure the vasodilation or vasoconstriction of the muscle groups required for action. When blood empties from nearby vessels, these smooth muscles cannot react at the same rate the striated muscles do. The smooth muscles take—depending on the extent of this effect—40 to 400 times longer to react.[5] Is it abnormal, in these conditions, that an emotion experienced many times ends up becoming a lasting imprint on the face and body? Someone who feels tension, for example, will have a tight face for a certain amount of time, even after the source of tension has disappeared.

I still remember the face of a man who was beaten as a child until, around the age of 15, he left his parents' home, never to return. The fear of his father, that this man had developed in spite of himself, lasted his entire childhood and had molded his adult musculature. His shoulders were so clenched that he seemed to not have a neck. This was the work of his smooth muscles, not a result of his physiology. His negative, hypertonic emotions for the time that they lasted, made his shoulders tense up. A sustained fear alters our morphology, which is much more affected by the trials of life than we might think.

The shoulders never contract without the general physiognomy also transforming. When anger arises, a wrinkle emerges in the area of the glabella, cutting across the space above the nose horizontally. This phenomenon is very visible, and it is temporary, but it, like the contracted shoulders, can become permanent.

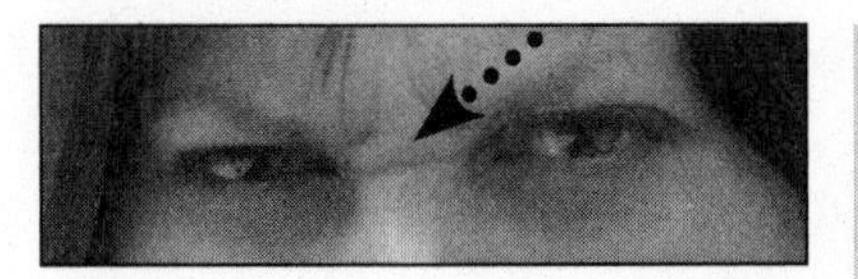

When the forehead area and that of the nose contract toward each other, a horizontal line over the nose that marks the bottom edge of the lower forehead appears on the glabella.

Look at the difference between a passing anxiety state that is already visible on a baby, a passing irritable state experienced by an adult, and when this state becomes permanent.

Transient anger ends up imprinting itself permanently on the face.

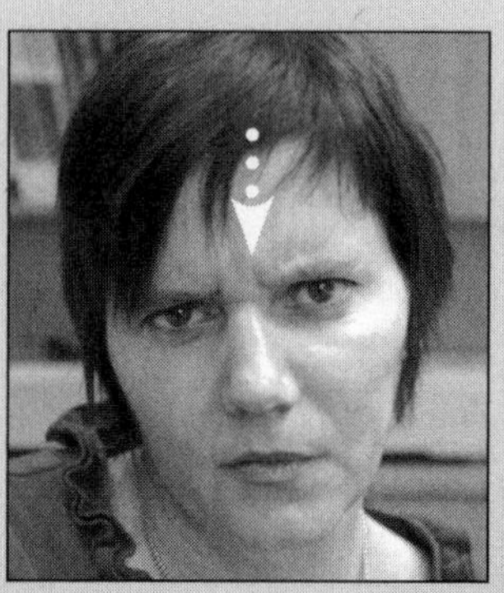

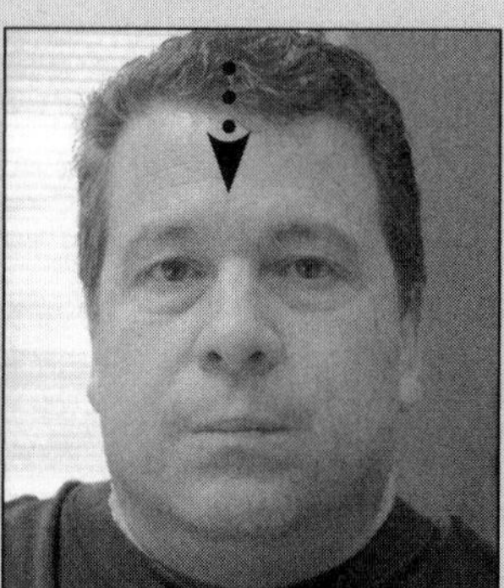

When the face contracts as a result of anxiety, it closes up and a wrinkle cutting across the space above the nose appears. If this emotion is frequent, the face eventually stops relaxing, and this wrinkle, known as "the glabella," finds itself permanently imprinted. This is the case in the image on the right.

The frequency of an experienced emotion ends up transforming our physiognomy in a characteristic way. Wrinkles of anger appear on an angry person's face for as long as the emotion lasts. But if the anger becomes a personality trait, the face transforms to integrate the expression. Lasting, permanent anger randomly settles in several wrinkles, including that of the glabella.[6]

Today, neurobiological processes are better known. Specialists speak of background emotion to mark the difference between passing emotions and lasting ones.

Wrinkles take a lifetime to settle in and their natural movements change, fade, and transform at random every day, in a happy or unhappy way. **The same emotions leave their mark as similar physical traits on all individuals.** This is a universal reality. That being established, let's look at concrete examples of how to decipher the eight emotional groups.

The Eight Emotional Groups in Three Looks

Facial movements are guarantors of emotion. Three questions suffice to spot any type of emotion:

- Is the person in a state of hypertonia or hypotonia?
- Is the person experiencing a positive or negative emotion?
- Is the person looking to share an emotion or to keep it to herself?

Is the Person in a Hypertonic or Hypotonic State?

Tonicity reflects the degree of involvement in an interaction. People who are alert and willing to participate in conversation always have tonic bodies. This has been true since time immemorial. Imagine one of our great ancestors in a jungle or savannah, on the lookout for the slightest noise. Is it possible that his mind is focused on what is happening around him while his body remains completely lifeless? No.

The jungles and savannahs of those times are the job interviews of today, or the meetings where contracts are signed, or even personal encounters. Our ancestors were preoccupied with hunting prey to bring home for their survival. It is still necessary today to ensure our means of subsistence. The risk in both cases is to return empty-handed, from a corporate meeting or from the jungle. The environments are different but the same adrenaline flows through our veins. The strange noises of the jungle are replaced with annoying questions during business meetings today. The same dopamine raises our level of vigilance. The same signs of hypertonicity are visible on our faces and bodies. When hypertonic, our bodies are ready to react.

Hypertonicity is especially visible on a central item that is like a red thread you don't want to lose sight of: the position of the shoulders. A person in a hypertonic state has the tendency to raise his shoulders while a person in a hypotonic state lowers them. This is easy to visualize. On the other hand, the original position of the shoulders is not the same for everybody, so this can be difficult to decipher. We must therefore imagine a situation in which the body will be naturally hypotonic and ask this question: "Would this person in front of me be able to hold that position if she were alone and relaxed in her living room?" If you think this is possible, the person facing you is without a doubt in a hypotonic condition. Here are a few examples:

Positive hypertonic emotion

Positive hypotonic emotion

POSITIVE SITUATIONS

In the girl, the shoulders lifting up toward her neck indicate hypertonicity.

In the man, the lowered shoulders indicate hypotonicity.

Hyper- and hypotonicity are characterized here in the context of positive emotions. The same characteristics are found when the experienced emotions are negative.

Negative hypertonic emotion

Negative hypotonic emotion

NEGATIVE SITUATIONS

In the woman on the left, the raised shoulders indicate hypertonicity.

In the woman on the right, the lowered shoulders indicate hypotonicity.

Sitting in her living room, melancholy, the woman on the right could be watching television alone. It is difficult to believe, on the other hand, that the woman on the left is seated in a state of tranquility.

Among other signs, the position of the shoulders has been chosen because we cannot conceal it. It is impossible to be vigilant and attentive, and have relaxed shoulders. In a position of relaxation, alertness inevitably falls with the shoulders. This reality is built into our genetic makeup.[7]

Hypertonicity can measure the degree of another person's presence. The more hypertonic his shoulders are, the more vigilant or desirous of participating in the interaction he is. It is now a matter of qualifying this presence.

Positive Emotions and Negative Emotions

In the same way, the positivity (or not) of an emotion can be gleaned from a single sign.

Positive emotions at every age in life, in every culture, and for all social groups have the same configuration that is easily found on the face. These photos symbolizing a positive hypertonic emotion have a common point. Can you guess what it is?

EXPRESSION OF POSITIVE EMOTION

Neither of these faces shows vertical wrinkles. That is one of the characteristics of positive hypertonic emotions.

Things are very different when we observe negative hypertonic emotions at work.

EXPRESSION OF NEGATIVE EMOTION

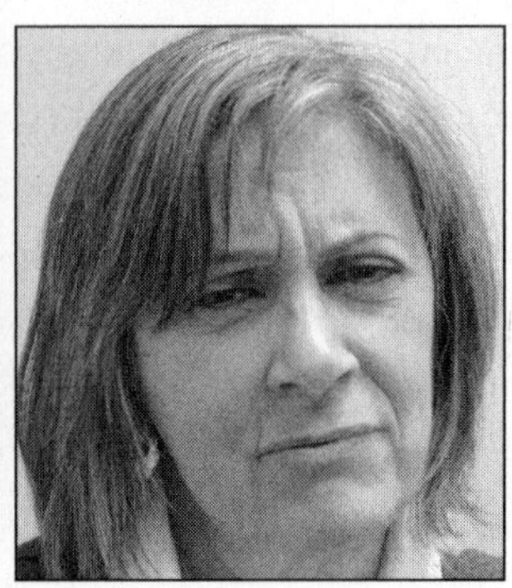

Both these faces show negative wrinkles. The vertical wrinkles that are very visible are not specific to a physical age but to a shared emotion.[8] They are always more apparent when the emotions experienced are negative, and they are even visible on children!

The vertical direction of the wrinkles is visible in three places. The presence of two of these three constants suffices to confirm the negative character of the emotion experienced by a person in silence.

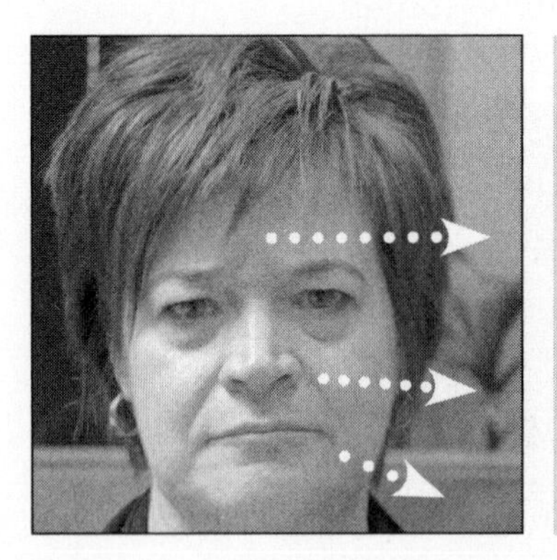

The three types of wrinkles that guarantee a negative emotion:

- ***vertical between the eyebrows;***
- ***vertical next to the nose;***
- ***vertical at the corners of the mouth.***

There is no need to shout for the negative character of an emotion to become known "beyond a reasonable doubt." It suffices that our features take the form of vertical wrinkles.[9] While this woman does not scream, her interior tension is nonetheless palpable.

Any positive emotion crossing the face wipes away vertical wrinkles, for its duration, even if these wrinkles are permanent.

Emotions That One Keeps to Oneself and Those That One Entrusts to Others

Are emotions destined to be kept to oneself or transmitted to others? This question is relatively easy to settle from a nonverbal perspective.

How does someone who does not want to transmit his emotions feel? Exactly like someone who does not want to speak. Whether it is expressed with words or with facial expressions, the emotional state is the same. *A man lowers his head slightly,* thereby showing, consciously or unconsciously, (the movement will always be very nuanced), that he doesn't want to speak. These situations are not always easy to distinguish because a person may lower his head without breaking eye contact with the other person.

Let us compare two positive emotions.

The young woman's head is lowered, and the emotion is kept to herself (egocentric).

On the right, the woman's head is raised. The emotion is addressed toward another (exocentric).

In the case of the young woman, the emotion is positive, but for her own reasons, she tucks it away, maybe because she simply doesn't want to show off her happiness in front of others. For the woman on the right, on the other hand, the emotion is clearly addressed to someone else. She raises her head pointedly.

The act of closing or opening one's mouth is not an indicator of a desire to communicate or not, but rather of an introverted or extroverted character.[10]

Egocentric emotions (kept to oneself), and exocentric (addressed to another) also occur when people find themselves in negative situations. Here are two examples:

With the woman on the left, her head is lowered, and the emotion is "egocentric."

With the woman on the right, her head is raised, and the emotion is "exocentric."

Here, the position of the chin is clear enough, but the reality behind it is less evident; it is preferable to trust in a general impression rather than focusing on one point, like the chin, for example.[11]

Putting bodily signs aside, we will always be able to pinpoint the eight emotional groups when necessary. We can thus distinguish:

- a positive hypertonic emotion directed toward another;
- a positive hypertonic emotion kept to oneself;
- a positive hypotonic emotion directed toward another;
- a positive hypotonic emotion kept to oneself;
- a negative hypertonic directed toward another;
- a negative hypertonic emotion kept to oneself;
- a negative hypotonic emotion directed toward another;
- a negative hypotonic emotion kept to oneself.

THE EIGHT DISTINGUISHABLE EMOTIONAL CATEGORIES

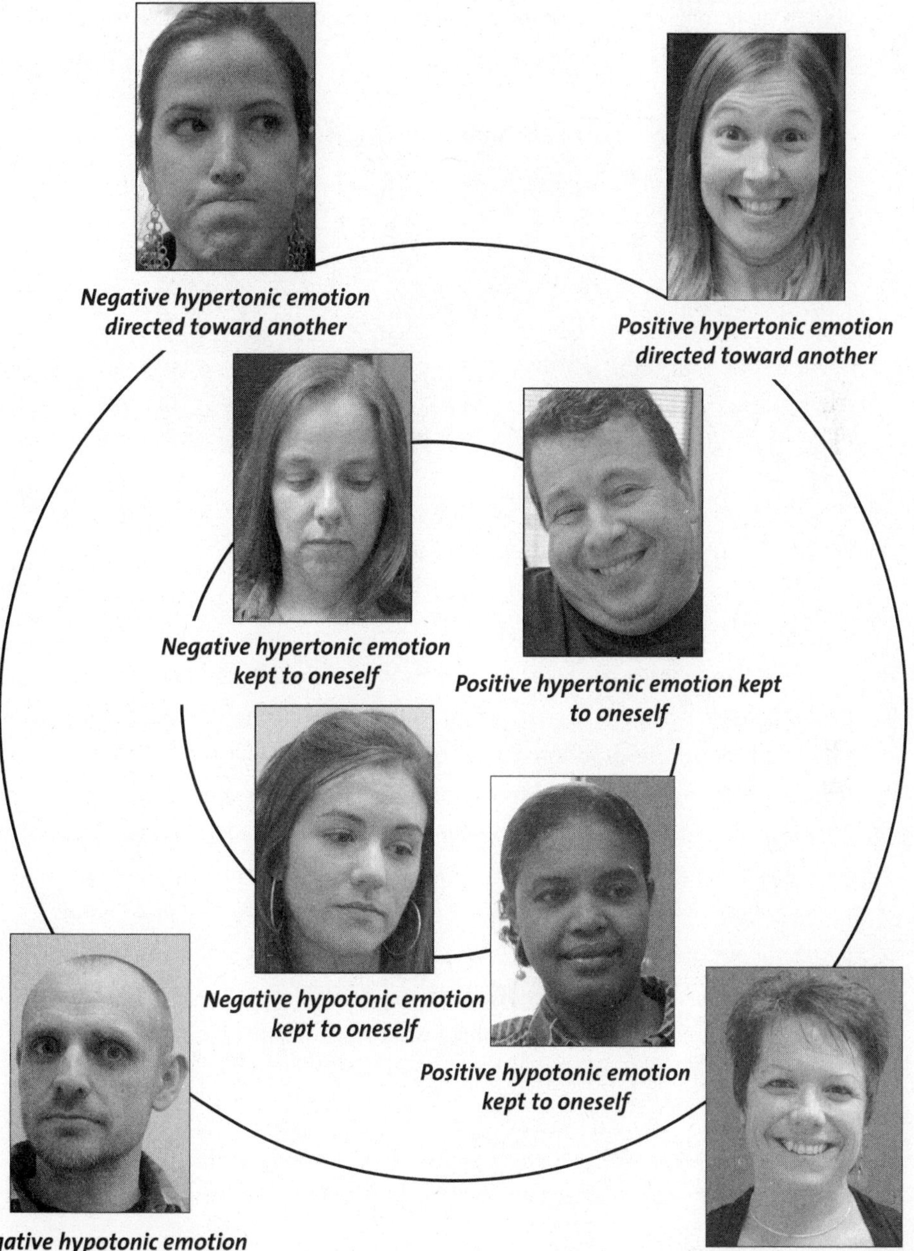

The Eight Emotional Categories: Application of Rules to a Practical Case

Some key nonverbal information permits us, with a single glance, or rather with three glances, to understand what emotional state another person is in. Which state are these two people in?

1. Their shoulders are relaxed: hypotonic.
2. They have no vertical wrinkles: a positive emotion.
3. Their heads are slightly lowered: an emotion kept to themselves.

These are photos of people experiencing a positive *hypotonic emotion kept to oneself*. It belongs to group E8 in the table of emotional categories (see page 41); a serene emotional environment—calm, peaceful, tranquil, level-headed—rules here. These people do not feel exactly the same emotion, but they are in the same general emotional state. It is possible to go looking for other items or signs in order to come as close as possible to the exact strain of their emotion, but let's not forget our initial objective: to understand if someone is in agreement with what he is saying: "He is telling me something, but does his body tell me the same thing?"[12] "In this case, is body language giving me other indications about what he is saying to me, and above all, does his body manage to hide its messages?"

An emotion that is not observable does not exist.

CHAPTER 5

From Visible Emotions to Those That Are Hidden

Trying to always be transparent and knowing how to remain discreet with one's emotions are two rules of social life that seem to apply to everybody. They are also proof that good rules can also be antagonistic. We cannot speak and be silent at the same time, desire to be transparent but keep our emotions to ourselves. If this contradiction exists, it will be translated to the body, which always shows what the brain is thinking. To deny it would be to deny the very rules of human biology. When the brain tries to hide what it is thinking, a part of the body hides what another part has already shown!

When someone is not being transparent, it is most often upon the implicit demand of another! We hide the truth because we feel that the other person does not want to know it, and this happens with big existential lies as well as with small, unspoken, everyday lies.

Here is an example of an existential lie: If you listen to parents talking, they often say they have taught their children the importance of always telling the truth. Yet at the same time, certain parents do not hesitate to affirm, when talking about homosexuality: "If my kid turns out to be gay, I would prefer not to know!" Their homosexual teens—in the company of their parents, at least—sometimes risk behaving like liars . . . at the implicit request of their parents. These lies, because they are at the heart of their identity,[1] risk leading to more lies in order to preserve a secret that the people around them do not want to know.[2] That is the problem with all conscious, existential lies, but also with many small lies as well.

The implicit request for positive information also introduces the necessity to lie in order to not disappoint. For example, a manager asks his colleague about the development of a meeting that he was not able to attend. Will this colleague feel like precisely describing all of the stages that led to the rejection of some project or another? Without a doubt, no, or not always, or not about everything, or not completely. Is this colleague a liar? Is he weak because he shows signs of empathy?

Before calling this person who left some things unsaid a horrible individual, it is a good idea to ask ourselves what message was first sent to him such that the interaction ultimately led him to lie.

Emotions Are Paradoxical: They Let Us Hide Emotions!

That takes the cake! In fact, to use a metaphor, it acts on occasion in the same way that certain performance-enhancing drugs do in sports: What does one do to avoid getting caught taking illegal drugs? One hides it with the help of another drug! How can we hide an emotion? It is simply a matter of dumping another emotion on top of it!

Hiding One's Emotions in Order to Protect Oneself

The unspoken can be small or large, but it is always governed by the rule that it wants to be said, on the one hand, and that it wants to be felt, on the other. Each time **the underlying emotion** is of the same nature as **the overlying emotion,** the one we express out loud, we are being truly authentic. On the other hand, if the underlying emotion is different from the overlying emotion, there is a noticeable discrepancy . . .

The True Emotion Is Always Visible at One Time or Another

The human being who lies does not do so with a cheerfulness in his heart but only because it seems necessary to him, and the larger the lie, the more frightened he will be of being discovered.[3] His autonomic nervous system reacts against the wrongness of the lie, and unfortunately for him, he cannot voluntarily change this. He cannot ask his heart to beat less quickly, his viscera to not send messages to their destinations in the brain, his circulating blood volume to stop sending information to his somatosensory cortex, or his brain neurotransmitters to interrupt their discharges and their release of serotonin, or any of these other beneficial effects that might permit him to calm down. During moments of negative stress, our neocortex has no control over what happens on a more basic level. It is a bit like if we tried to ask our stomachs or spleens to stop working![4]

Signs of fear are spotted through bodily characteristics that are very visible. Faced with the fear of having his lie discovered (hypertonic negative emotion that is kept to oneself), the person who lies has only one solution: to dump—in massive doses—serenity, sadness, or some other emotion onto the fear, in short, something that will allow it to hide . . . There is only one problem: The discrepancy between the truth and the lie never hides itself completely.

The Woman Who Would Have Actually Preferred to Be Sad

The discrepancy between the underlying emotion, that we are looking to substantiate, and the overlying emotion, that we see, is visible on the face. An observation of a woman who got rid of her children and is looking to place the blame on others, allows us to understand this.

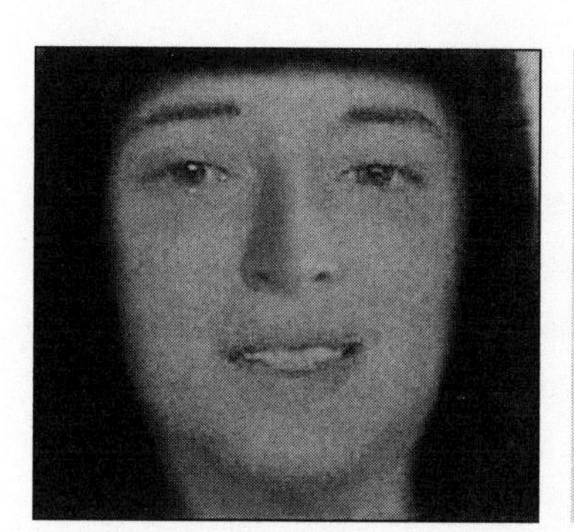

This woman, at the time of a press conference, makes a request to the "abductors" of her children; she seems sad and presents this face to the crowd. The moment she says, "Give me back my children!", a tear is even visible in her right eye.

Now, if the right half of the face is compared to the left (see the following page), we notice that one is crying while the other seems to be smiling.

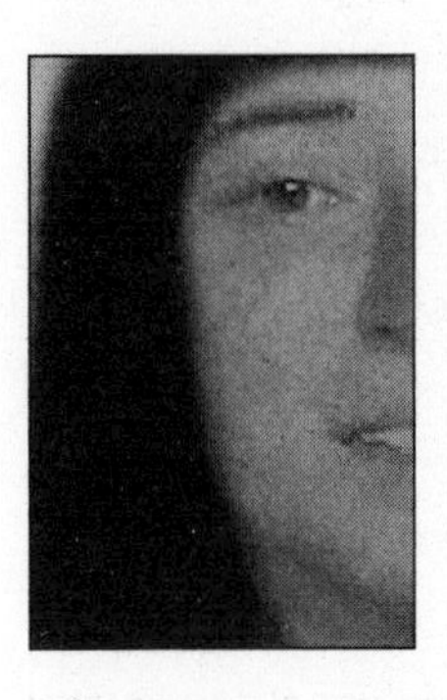

The right side of her face transmits a message of sadness.

The left side of her face does not transmit a message of sadness. The upper left half of her mouth is raised.

When we are not totally honest, certain parts of our brain cannot be controlled. Our brain refuses to lie.[5]

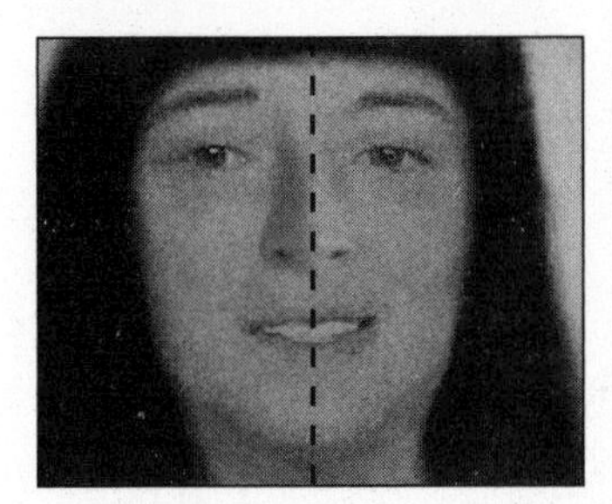

Behind the emotion we see, another is visible. The wallpaper that is stuck to the wall reveals the wall joints.

"Give me back my children!"

These examples are radical and, happily, the key to the mystery behind this emotional discrepancy is not murder. But these emotional discrepancies are easily found each time that an emotion expressed through verbal language is not the one that is really felt.

For a psychopath, emotions are lifeless and appear absent. We must not therefore wait for his heart to get carried away. On the other hand, he knows that he is lying and this is lucky for the person observing him! He cannot allow his body to relax completely because he would no longer be able to control his speech and would risk transmitting important information in spite of himself.[6]

The way in which emotions are disguised in order to avoid being perceived always follows the same process: one emotion patched on top of another. However, evidence of intentional control will always be visible on the face and body while a person who has nothing to hide will not show this. That is the entire difference between a guilty person and an innocent one. Both of them might be uncomfortable in front of police authorities—who are always a little intimidating—but an innocent person does not try to control his speech because unlike the guilty one, he has nothing to hide and thus nothing to control, and that is very easy to perceive: Signs of control are a different kind of discomfort.

We know that the face holds visible traces of contradictory emotions. We will now see that the manner in which people direct their gaze indicates the nature of their emotions.

The Man Who Looked With Eyes That Couldn't See

The purpose of an interaction is primarily to share information but also and especially to maintain a relationship. It is not possible to be both kind and watchful at the same time. It is necessary to choose, and we do so unconsciously, an attitude for which information is conveyed to the appropriate cerebral structures. This choice is visible, decipherable. Do you think this woman is looking at you with both her eyes?

If you get the impression that this woman is looking at you with both of her eyes, you are mistaken and for a simple reason: You are looking at her eyes!

Now, instead of looking at her eyes, look at the position of her ears(!); you won't make the same mistake . . . It is with the left eye, the left ear being more visible, that she is looking at you.

By looking with one eye rather than the other, we decide to let information into one hemisphere over the other!

If information enters principally through the left ear, the left eye, the skin on the left, we direct it toward the right hemisphere. If it comes in through the right eye, the right ear, the right nostril, the right skin, it is interpreted by the left hemisphere. Quite obviously, it is then and almost simultaneously that the information is processed by the other hemisphere, but this is an unconscious choice that leads to the tensing of one eye and one ear over the other.[7]

When someone looks at you principally with one eye, it is not that he is looking at you but rather that one of his brain's hemispheres is taking you in.

Your image, captured by his retina and transformed into electric and biochemical signals, penetrates the control centers of his brain. But that's nothing. It will then be cut into small pieces by multiple neurotransmitters that want your image to cross their portion of the cerebral cavity, to take you here rather than there. If your image enters the right hemisphere, it is because the doorman, the left eye, has received an order. It is important to observe this phenomenon well. There will be time later to ask ourselves why information goes to one hemisphere rather than the other.

Let's look at what frequently happens in a surreptitious and, in fact, unconscious way. In the following three images, a man is speaking in confidence. Observe the winking of his left eye.

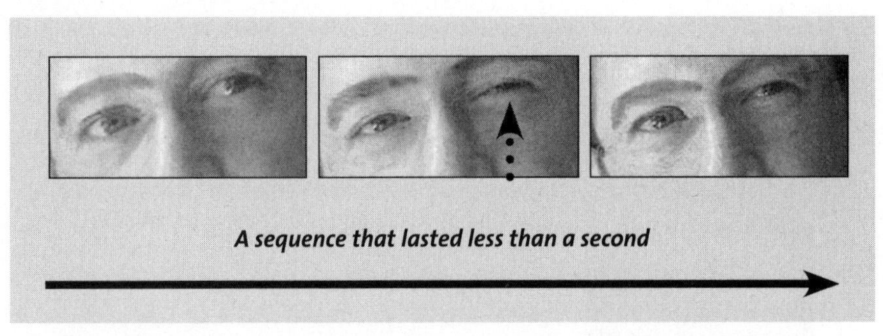

The man winks unconsciously[8] with his left eye. But here, beyond the banality of the gesture, something more unusual has taken place: The man shown in the image is blind in his left eye! As it happens, that is what he is in the middle of telling us here. Take note of what we just said: A man who is blind in his left eye (and only using his right eye to look at us) is in the middle of blinking the eye that can't see!

A facility of language tells us that the man blinks with his left eye. In reality, he blinks with his right hemisphere. It is active because this man is in a good mood, and it is a facial nerve that executes this movement.

There are three possible ways to "guide" a look: Either both eyes are coordinated in order to measure the contrast or relief (e.g., in order to drive a car, cross a sidewalk on foot, grasp a small object, put a key in a lock, etc.) or the leading eye is predominant. This happens in cases when a task is carried out that requires conscious visual precision (e.g., shooting a gun, threading a needle, etc.). But in **about 98 percent of other situations, information is looked at with the hemisphere appropriate for dealing with the emotional interest of the moment.**

While we're on the subject, let me mention an ambiguity that can be the cause of misunderstandings. A long time ago, popular psychology promoted the idea that left-handed people have inverted hemispheres compared to right-handed people, that is they function "inversely." Since the beginning of the 1980s, specialists have known this to be incorrect.[9] What is true is that 30 percent of left-handed people—about one person out of 30 in the general population (10 percent of people are left-handed)—perform certain functions not in an inverse manner, but with both hemispheres.

Don't bother trying to figure out which eye you use to look at the person talking to you because this would turn it into a conscious action, and *it is impossible to consciously activate our unconscious reflexes.* On the other hand, you can definitely observe how the other person is looking at you! He will not be using his more functional eye nor his leading eye, but rather his more interested hemisphere. It is by looking at his eyes that you will know if he is really listening to you!

The example of *the man who looked with the eye that couldn't see*[10] and the one of *the woman who would have actually preferred to be sad* show that:

- Human beings treat information primarily according to their desires.
- Behind a hidden emotion, real desires are visible to those who know how to look for them.

In the two cases, the asymmetries of the face are indispensable marks for deciphering unusual emotions. They are not misleading, but rather they take the form of the impulses of the heart.

- **In order to hide an emotion, there is nothing to do but patch another emotion on top of it.**
- **Unconscious treatment of information uses different channels from conscious treatment.**
- **The cerebral treatment of information is determined by emotional choices and is observable thanks to certain visual marks.**

CHAPTER 6

How Do You Decipher a Hidden Emotion?

Faces should always be symmetrical. A human being, when moving is not . . . half move. There is therefore no reason why a face should be half open or closed—especially since the brain possesses a single command center.[1] But it turns out that 70 percent of neurons primarily have an inhibitory function. Their role is to say stop, to compel muscles not to intervene. When a person takes a piece of paper, for example, she does it generally with one hand. An unconscious but very substantive order is given to the other hand not to move. In the case of certain emotions, exactly the same phenomenon is produced. A part of the face can be more subdued, as if it were saying, "Keep what you are feeling to yourself!" Divided between two states, a person rarely verbalizes this, but this reality is seen by whoever learns to look for it.

Let us observe the brain in order to understand how its activity can be visible on the face and body.

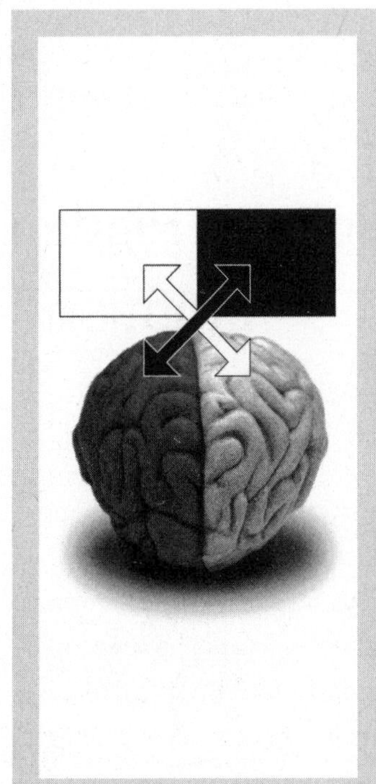

Information is transmitted from one hemisphere to another via the corpus callosum.

In regard to principally emotional information, the right hemisphere sends information that allows it to manage the left part of the body, and the left hemisphere the right.

The dividing line between the two hemispheres is quite visible at the center of the brain. Information provided by one side of the face is sent to the opposite hemisphere.

Hippocrates, close to 400 years before Jesus Christ, had already noticed that a wound on the left side of the head would cause convulsions on the right side of the body. On the other hand, some information does not cross the body. If you tap the left knee with a hammer, it is not the right leg that goes up.[2] But with regard to emotions the crossing occurs. If the right hemisphere is more active, a change in the left half of the face will occur, and vice versa.

The Right Hemisphere and the Left Half of the Face

A consensus has largely been established about an issue that interests us: Emotions are seen more on the left half of the face than on the right.[3]

The Gaze of the Left Eye and the Search for a Connection

The two halves of a face do not express the same realities; neither do the two halves of a body.[4] The nature of the physical connection between a mother and her baby is particular and uniquely characterized. When she takes the baby in her arms, no matter where she is from, no matter her culture or ethnicity, she will have a greater tendency to carry the baby with her left arm than with her right.[5] A father will act the same way when trying to soothe the baby.[6]

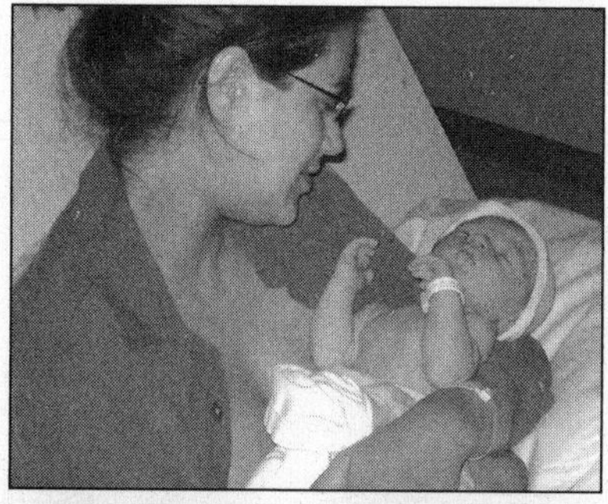

Mothers hold their babies more with their left arms than their right, whether they are right-handed or left-handed. They also look at their babies more with their left eyes.

Fathers place their babies on their left arms when they want to help them fall asleep or simply when they want to create a gentle environment.

The baby, for his part, looks more at the left side of his mother's face. Therefore, they communicate more with the left halves of their faces. This rule is so universal that human beings even share it with the great apes![7]

This rule of carrying babies and emotional sharing has a character so absolute that one can say that it is ontogenetic—integral to the human species.

English scientists have asked themselves if a mother carries her baby on the left in order to hold it closer to her heart, but they came to the conclusion that there is no direct connection. In fact, in an epidemiological study observing young mothers whose hearts happened to be on their right sides—as is the case for one in 1,000 people—they realized that there wasn't a difference. These mothers still carried their babies on the left, just like the other mothers did.[8]

Lovers' kisses are another illustration of hemisphere transference properties in our behavior.

Two-thirds of kisses look like the one in the first image. The left sides of these two people's faces lean toward each other.

Mark this well: Lovers kiss in many ways and the most inventive couples are not the least loving, but the kiss of abandon—relaxed and heated—is done in this way rather than the other. Recent observations made by Americans and Germans confirm those that we made previously.

Relaxed lovers kiss each other left eye to left eye. The left sides of their faces are in contact more so than the right. In fact, without their knowing it, it is their two right hemispheres that are kissing.[9]

A child learns, unconsciously, to decipher the more emotional side of the face: the left. An adult, one who would like to create a connection, also shows this side to the person with whom he is speaking[10] and looks even more at the left half of the other person's face, thereby helping information enter the other person's right hemisphere.

When affective positively, we will directly address the left side of our faces toward the person to whom we are speaking.

On occasion, we can see the left side of the face of the person with whom we are speaking literally light up, that is to say become much more visible, more present, "larger." The left eye appears to be more open, the left eyebrow more lifted, the left half of the mouth higher than the right. In short, not only is the left side of the appearance more lively, but at the same time it is enlarged. Whoever does not pay attention to this phenomenon will not see it, but for those who are interested in this kind of thing, it is easy to spot. These asymmetries are observable among all human beings struggling with the same emotions, these emotional mechanisms being universal.

Observe closely the left half of these people's faces compared to their right.

THE OVER-DEVELOPED LEFT HALF OF THE FACE

These asymmetries are common when a person experiences a positive emotion but cannot or does not want to express it. These asymmetries are very visible among politicians the evening of election victories, while they are among their supporters. A part of them is very relaxed and happy to have won while the other part finds itself facing new responsibilities to assume, decisions that need to be made quickly, and so on. This phenomenon is noticeable when three circumstances are brought together:

- the experienced emotions are relatively intense;
- the experienced emotions are positive; and
- the emotions are controlled so as not to let them be too transparent.

Only three conditions are necessary, and they are often fulfilled.

During intense emotions,[11] "emotional commotion" is triggered by the right hemisphere. It becomes overactive and the left half of the face becomes flushed with blood while the right finds itself under the tight control of the left hemisphere. Metaphorically, one can say that the left hemisphere produces "seriousness" so that the growing emotion does not become too visible. Unfortunately, in spite of these efforts, it does not manage to constrain the side of the face that is managed by the right hemisphere, which remains enlarged.

If an emotion is negative, or if a person is depressed, the opposite phenomenon will be observed. The left side of the face will then be more restrained than the right. Less than 3 percent of people in a positive situation will show the left half of their faces more lowered than their right. This phenomenon is impossible to see when a person is experiencing a positive emotion.

People who have the left half of their faces more restrained are emotionally tired, and this is true at every age.

When the emotions that are felt are positive, the left half of the face has a tendency to grow, and when the emotions become negative, it shrinks.

- Someone who is personally interested will look with his or her left eye.
- In a situation of positive emotional intensity, the left half of the face is more open than the right.

When a person looks at you with his left eye and the left half of his face is bigger, he is open and interested.

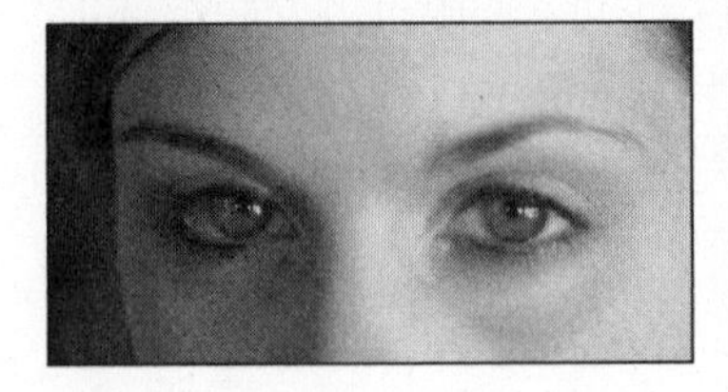

This woman is looking at us with her left eye. She is personally very interested in what is happening, but the left half of her face is not open. Nothing indicates that she is in a positive situation.

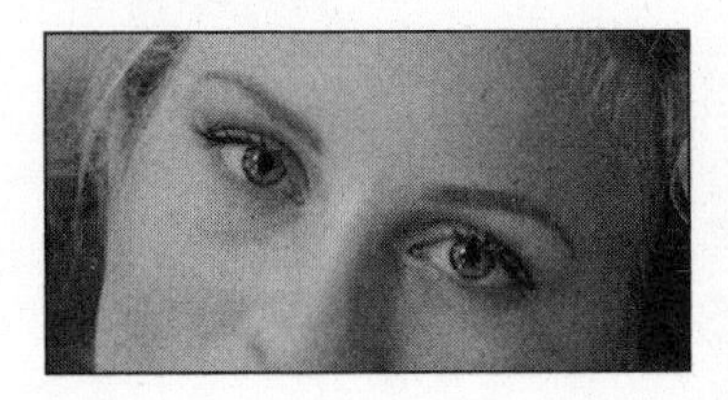

The left half of this woman's face is enlarged; she is in an intense emotional situation but it is not certain if she is looking at us with her left eye. Therefore nothing indicates that she is trying to create a relationship with anyone else (this phenomenon is common at sporting events, musical performances, and the theater, etc.).

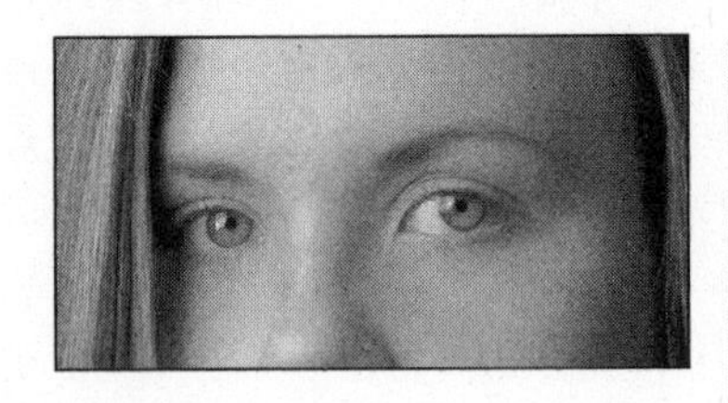

The left half of this woman's face is enlarged. She is experiencing an intense emotional situation and she is looking using her left eye. She is therefore personally interested in the exchange. These elements are often seen together. The human connection she is making is therefore of a very good quality.

From the left half of one person's face to that of another, from right eye to right eye, emotions of a different tenor are transmitted. . . .

The Right Half of the Face and the Foray Into the Exterior World of Our Universe

With the brain's left hemisphere, a human being discovers the logic of "keeping his distance," also of vigilance. The right eye is witness to this.[12]

Up until around six months, a baby is tied to his internal world. Specialists speak of a fusion stage. He still cannot conceive of an outside world. He does not really perceive a contrast between himself and others. But quickly, at around five or six months, the baby will surprise his family by taking and throwing objects in order to hear them echo at a distance, which makes him burst out laughing. He suddenly becomes aware of depth, distance, and space. Now that he can hold up his own head,[13] he will look at his environment, his milieu, differently. The development of the left hemisphere has just caught up with the right hemisphere.

The outside world first makes its foray into the child's life through his ears. He perceives his father's voice more clearly, whose wavelength is better discriminated by the left hemisphere.[14] Then with his eyes he begins to conceive that his father is his father.[15] Before this age, when his mother and another woman were speaking to each other, the child looked at his mother more, while if his father and another man were speaking, he did not look more at his father, but from the age of six months on, he will look more at his father. The psychiatrist Boris Cyrulnik does not mince his words when he talks about the importance of the father at this age: The father does not have to be available to the child except for during a sensitive period at sixteen to eighteen months. If an accident ruins this biological moment, the father will not be recognized as such.[16]

In the right hemisphere, information is welcome and often remains in an informal state. It is here that feelings blend with information. In the left hemisphere, on the other hand, information is processed, classified, arranged. Attention to detail is established. When the exterior world is not conceivable, classifying it is not either. An imaginary exchange between a parent and a child helps us understand what this means:

The parent: "Have you gotten dressed?

The child: "Yes, I put my socks on my feet, my sweater on my body, and my pants on my legs."

Getting dressed is no-nonsense. To get dressed is to organize and therefore take a step back from oneself. This is the work of the left hemisphere.[17] Therefore, for example, fans of music and professional musicians listening to the same piece of classical music will not use the same hemisphere. Fans will let themselves be lulled by the music, and their right hemisphere will work harder, while professional musicians will try to classify the auditory information in order to compare it, thereby stimulating their left hemisphere more.[18]

The left hemisphere deciphers.[19] Therefore a person looks at the right half of the face when addressing another.

For those activities that demand a great deal of attention, the right half of the face will be very present and a person will look with her right eye (her right ear will be more visible). The left cortex will go to work and the cerebral energy that circulates in the left hemisphere will make it so that the right side of the face opens up. Dopamine that is involved in precise control and in integrative superior functions will be more present in the left hemisphere.[20] This side will react more quickly to control the parameters of a situation. The omnipresence of the right half of the face and the more open right eye are characteristic, for example, of the features of chess players in a tournament.

Calculation and vigilance are the order of the day in the functioning of the left hemisphere. It is often a question of restricting, but not always. For that, we need two additional signs.

The Calculation of Keeping a Distance and of Rejection

The right half of the face calculates. A person does not let himself go during an exchange.[22] His vigilance is born from the necessity to protect himself and from becoming aware that there are situations in which the best defense is a good offense.

The emotional graduation from skepticism toward an attitude of contradiction, and finally of altercation, is easily spotted visually as the head leans to the right and the chin lifts.

If a person talks to us while looking at us more with her right eye and if her head leans to the right, this is the sign that she has crossed into a feeling of rigidity or discomfort in front of us.

Rigidity increases in intensity and takes on a different tone as the chin lifts.

This man looks with his right eye, his chin is raised, and his head leans to the right.

Skepticism, which can keep him at a distance, transforms his attitude into a more aggressive one as his chin goes up.

Analyzing, frame by frame, dozens of thousands of archived videos allows us to be more definite. If a person looks at us with his right eye, his head leans to the right, and his chin is raised, he will always and systematically be in a situation of contradiction, conflict, altercation, or have an objection with us.[23]

People we talk to look at us, and by observing the way in which they do this, we can understand how they are greeting us and how they feel at that moment. Unlike with a material object that is possible to conceal, we can't really hide our emotions, because whatever we do, they exist inside of us, in us, on us, are a part of us, and permit us to access our humanity! Without them, we cease to think.[24]

When, in order to "look good," an artificial emotion is plastered onto our faces, the real emotions come out through visible asymmetries. Some, more telling, express more emotional content . . .

- **The dominant hemisphere at the moment of observation permits us to understand what general emotional state a person is in.**
- **The side of the face that is more present lets us read the emotional difference between openness or keeping a distance.**
- **The configuration of certain facial features offers an observation and an exact reading of the emotion felt.**

CHAPTER 7

Do Hidden Emotions Have Their Own Language?

No human being can be replaced by another. Humanity can be read on the faces and bodies of men and women through their flaws. To be "flesh and blood" is to accept some flaws, some asymmetries, some imperfections to work on. Face to face, we can see doubts, the cracks, the renunciations, but also the strength and conviction of the person speaking to us. His face does not betray him; he conveys all of these things. His subtle expressions allow him to be better understood. These irregularities represent the humanity of an honest man. If he ventured to speak, he would ask for one thing: that we look him straight in the eye, recognize his flaws, help him to understand them, and frankly give him the means with which to resolve his personal enigmas.

What if, instead of talking about a visible assymetry of the face—*"Ah ah ah . . .* this person is hiding something from me!"—we asked ourselves, "What message am I sending him such that he does not want to tell me more?"

A good number of everyday things that are left unsaid are born of our own attitudes.

Asymmetry of The Eyebrows

There are many asymmetries but some are more meaningful than others and reflect more of that which is unsaid. An asymmetry of the eyebrows are one of these.

Eyebrow movements are easily spotted from more than thirty feet away. They are involved in every emotional tonality and are the first to greet those that are nearby, with a slight raise. Human beings communicate with their eyebrows even before speaking. This phenomenon is universal. It can be seen in every "jungle" that is observed,[1] beginning with the Western jungle.

We raise our eyebrows more rarely when we don't think about both of them at the same time. The right hemisphere is the neurobiological seat of self-awareness.[2] This reality is closely corroborated by the left eyebrow. When it "climbs" up higher than the other, it shows that its owner does not like talking to this other person and this reticence is translated into this movement. The person does not move; only the raised left eyebrow shows this resistance.

Just as we've noted in this turn that our discussion has taken, in the second image, the left eyebrow alone is clearly raised. Each time that this micro-movement appears, it means that the person is retreating into herself, and this situation is making her uncomfortable.

It is often modesty that causes this kind of movement. The eyebrow will come back down as soon as the emotion passes.

The left eyebrow becomes asymmetrical when you freeze in spite of yourself. If, during a group activity, you ask, " Would someone like to participate?", observe the people around you well. The person whose left eyebrow is raised is telling you of his desire to not be involved in the activity or, in any case, not to get any more personally involved. Reserve[3] and modesty are often the personality traits motivating this movement.

People who keep us at a distance raise their right eyebrows. They do not want to show their emotions [the other features do not move], but their right eyebrows display their skepticism on their face.

People who make this movement do not react warmly. It is by creating distance that they are most naturally comfortable. The left hemisphere managing the right side of the face is already distancing itself from the other person in the conversation. This is reinforced again by the activity of the right eyebrow.

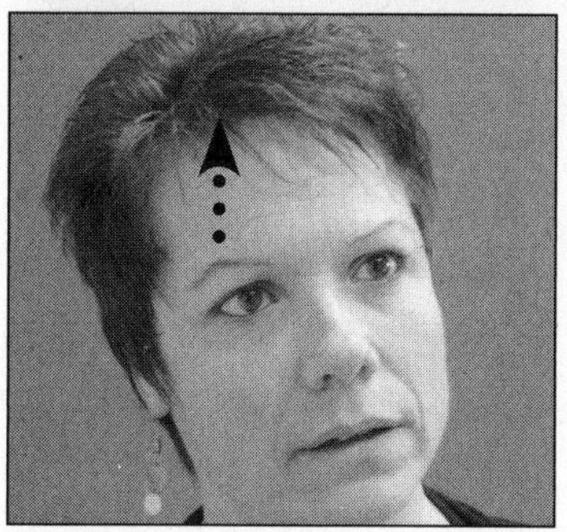

The other person is kept at a distance.

The hypotonia of the body points toward incredulity or skepticism rather than rejection.

If someone raises her right eyebrow while listening to an anecdote that you are telling her, it is because she finds it weird, idiotic, out of place, or objectionable. Only other signs that are present on the face and body will allow you to determine the exact nature of her thoughts and to make the distinction between rejection, skepticism, or simple suspicion, for example.

We can draw parallel conclusions thanks to an analysis of video footage in which people look at each other and speak loudly to each other, which creates a verbal tendency to put the other person at a distance, that shows that 85 percent of them have right eyebrows that are higher than their left.[4]

A higher left eyebrow indicates that we are taking a step back from ourselves; a higher right eyebrow, that we are taking a step back from someone else. If there is an altercation, the person with the perched left eyebrow will seem to be saying, "What have I done wrong?" and thus make himself seem more responsible for what happened. A higher right eyebrow has a tendency instead to indicate that the problem is located in the opposing party, generating thoughts such as, "What is he thinking?"

The Upper and Lower Eyelids

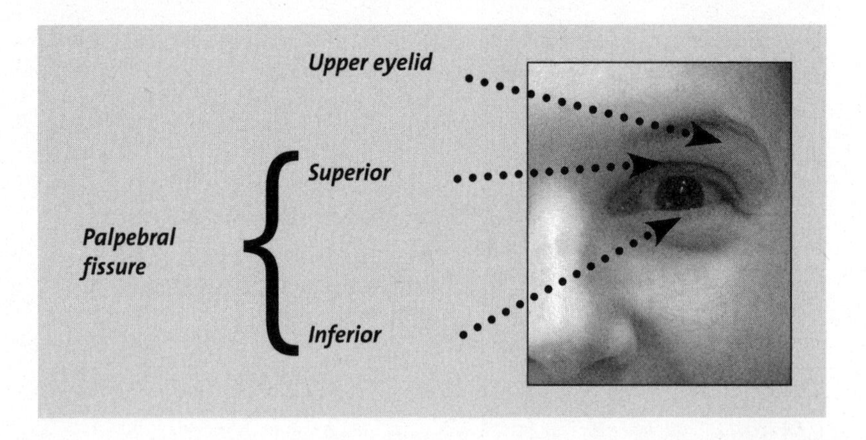

The upper eyelids are hardly present during childhood. They swell up when we cry and it is then that they are most visible. They become more important with time and end up becoming one of the trademarks of maturity.

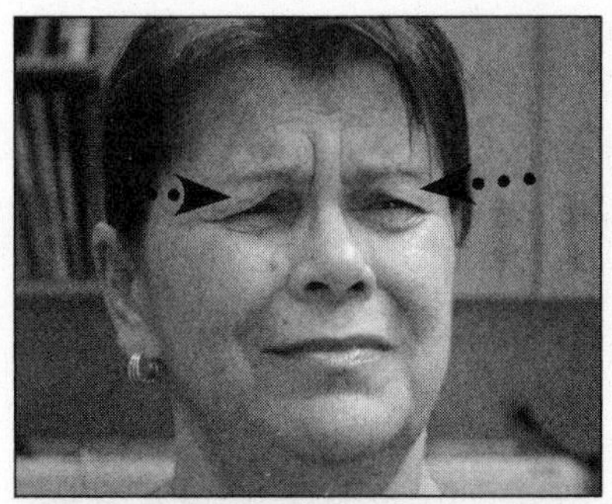

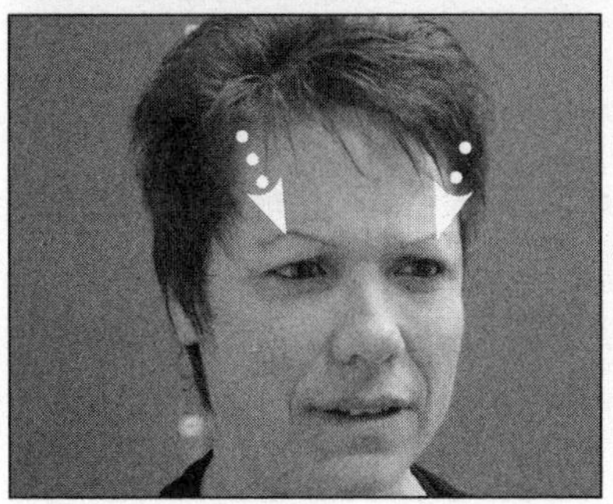

Tear fluid swells the upper eyelids. Adults who have had difficult childhoods end up having superciliary arches that seem to "cut with a knife" they are so prominent.

The upper eyelids are almost always involved in negative hypotonic emotions: The face closes up and the upper eyelids droop down the outside of the eyes.

Do not speak of the harshness of life to people who have swollen eyelids; they already know. A raised upper eyelid can be prominent, but there is no genetic reason for it to be swollen.

The upper eyelids are very good markers of emotion, via right-left asymmetries. When a negative emotion surfaces, the left side of the face has a tendency to close up and the left upper eyelid to fall over the eye. This is the case in these images. Let's take a look.

THE LEFT OUTER UPPER EYELID DROOPS

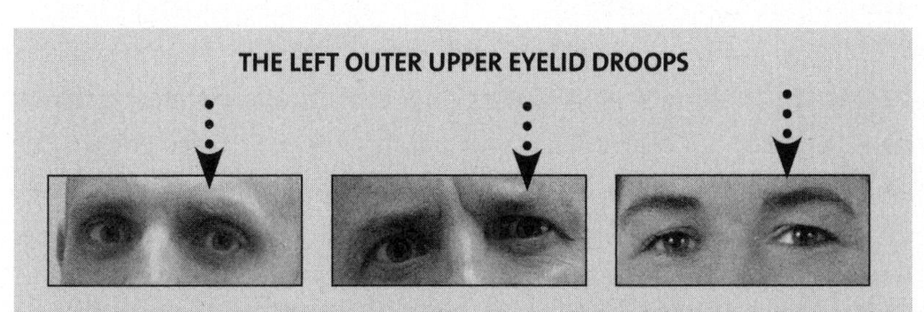

The left eyebrow gently droops, pulling the upper eyelid toward the outside of the eye. This movement that is exerted on the left communicates a sadness passing over the face.

The left upper eyelid is lower than the right on the faces of nearly 80 percent of older people. This phenomenon is easy to observe when fixed in the image,[5] but it is important to see if it has registered permanently or if it has just recently appeared on a person's face. In the latter case, it is the nature of the communication that will have triggered it.

The right upper eyelid can also be lower than the left but this is a less frequent expression.

Stress is the reason the right eyelid falls down over the eye. This eyelid seems tighter, more closed; this person will use her right arm more when speaking. She is not relaxed during this exchange.

Here, her head does not completely incline in the direction of the person to whom she is speaking.

In fact, the exterior fissure of the right eyelid informs us of a person's feelings with a great deal of accuracy. When the body is tense, the right side—more tonic—is more so.[6] We can observe this state among people who are cold, for example. But when this becomes constant, it is because stress has been permanently registered on the body.[7]

The Palpebral Fissures

Our eyes open more or less depending on the emotions that cross them. There are more than thirty ways of opening our eyelids, and therefore different gazes are distinguishable.[8] The palpebral fissures are particularly reliable when deciphering emotions because it is impossible to modify them through an effort of will. Because of this fact, they are an extremely precise barometer of the tone of an interaction.

The top of the face moves up when it is experiencing tension. The whites above the pupils only appear in negative situations (except, in certain rare cases, when a person is surprised).

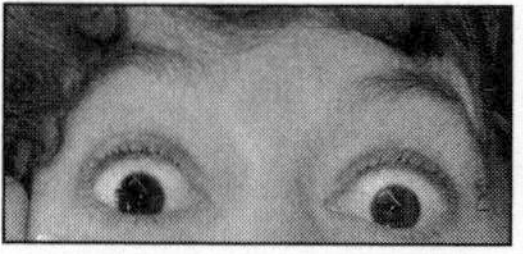
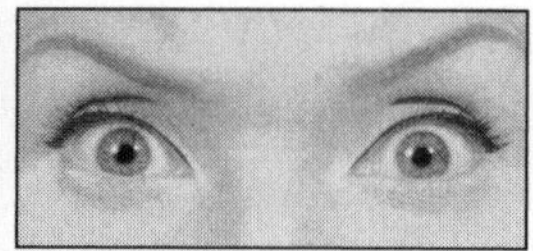
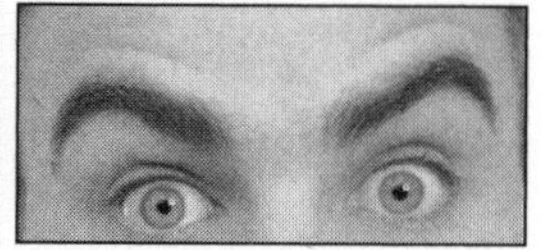

The Japanese call this phenomenon *sampaku eye*,[9] which means "three points in the white of the eye." At the top of the eye, the whites of the eye are characteristic of tension generated by fear. The top of the forehead therefore has a tendency to go up on its own.

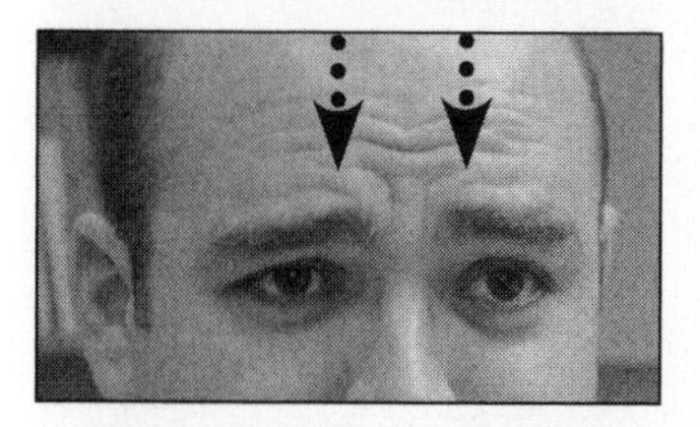

FEAR

Across these three images, a gradation of fear is presented, since uncontrollable fear is shown by the fact that the whites of the eyes are visible in the upper area of the eye (negative hypertonic emotion kept to oneself).

When fear is hidden, some muscles, situated in the eyebrows, unfortunately cannot be controlled, and the interior of the eyebrows go up.

When someone is afraid, waves are visible on the forehead, but when the fear is hidden, they do not last longer than two seconds.

These signs, when they are read independently from each other, indicate a feeling of anxiety.

To know how to observe fear on a face is one of the skills of those specialists who decipher nonverbal language. Fear is an emotion that you keep to yourself, when it is not an uncontrollable fear, because it is not socially acceptable; "only cowards are afraid," that is well known! If a person is tired, the two upper palpebral fissures droop; but if they are emotionally tired, the upper left palpebral fissure does not go up completely. We must be attentive in order to observe this phenomenon because emotional fatigue is not detectable without visual confirmation.

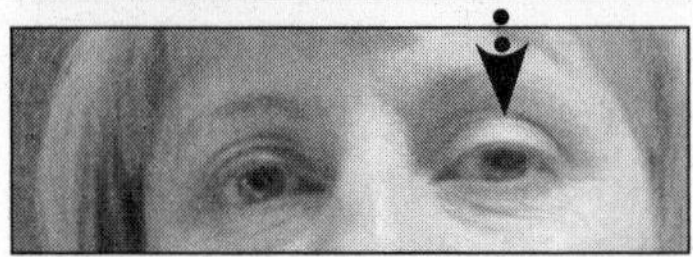

EMOTIONAL FATIGUE

Fatigue is observed when the upper eyelids, normally well raised, have a tendency to droop.

When the upper left eyelid is lower than the right, the person, even if she is smiling at the one she is speaking to (overlying emotion), is feeling emotionally tired (underlying emotion).

Look at these other examples of emotional fatigue.

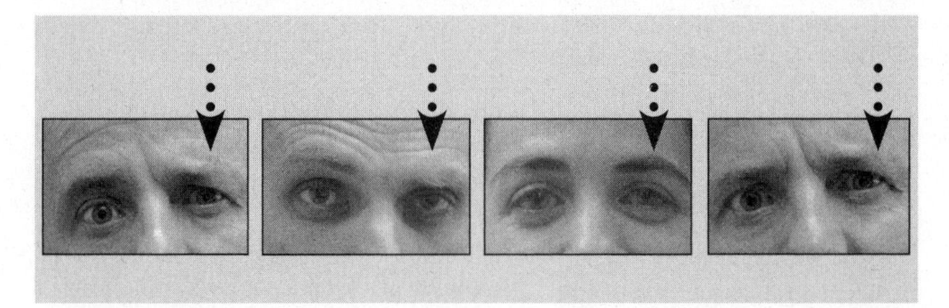

Understand that emotional tiredness is not the same as sadness. We can think that we are joyful and find ourselves in denial, incapable of identifying our tiredness. This situation doesn't normally last. This condition is therefore not permanent.[10]

The same small muscle that is present above the eye goes up or goes down under the lower eyelid also. The opening of the eye changes due to certain negative emotions.

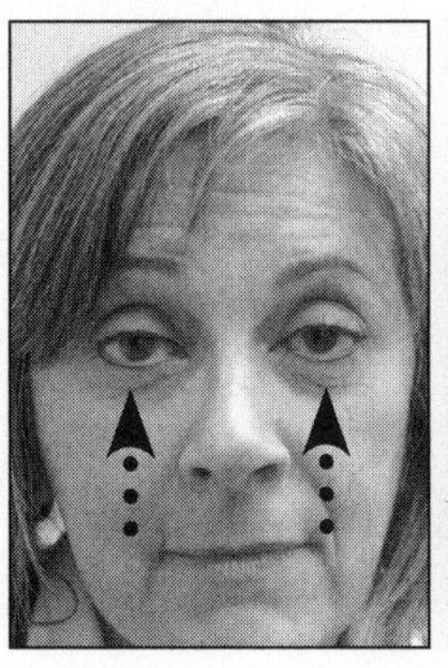

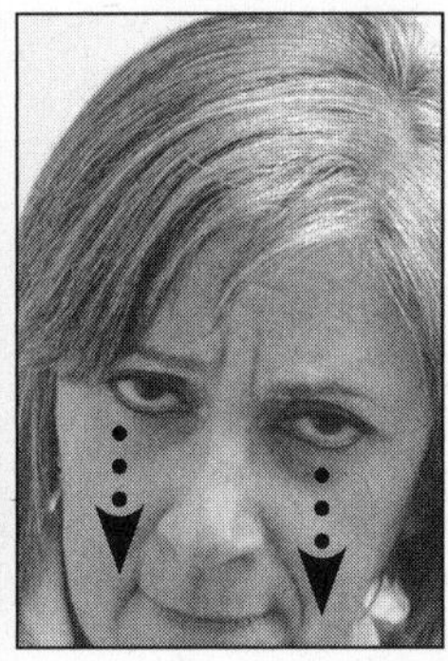

When an emotion takes on a negative tonality, we can see the whites appear under the iris.

Here, the drooping movement toward the corners of the lips is another element that lets us see this.

Palpebral fissures that droop symmetrically convey the passing of negative emotions over our emotional landscape. We cannot change the position of our lower eyelids voluntarily, unless we are stimulated positively!

The lower palpebral fissures are a good barometer of the transition from a positive emotion to a negative emotion.

Let's now compare these positive emotions with negative emotions under which a base of anxiety is present.

   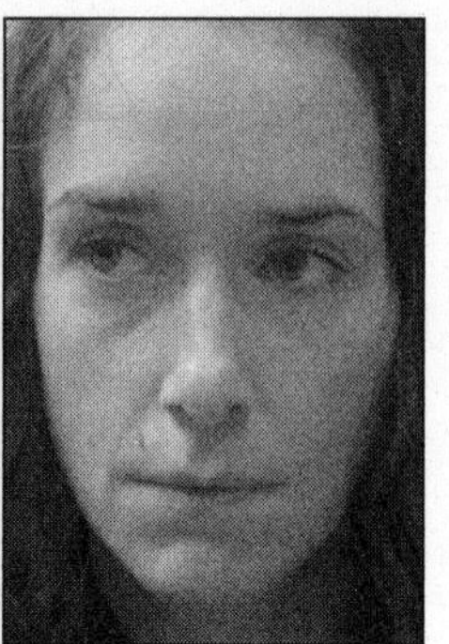

Here, the whites are visible under the iris. What we call lower *sampaku* eye. The lower eyelid loses its tonicity in all negative hypotonic situations.

Genetics and life conditions contribute to the differing aspects of eyelids in each person, but the universality of these phenomena remains. The lower eyelids droop from the blow of negative emotions and are pulled upward by positive emotions. Here is the way to tell the difference between a sincere smile and a diplomatic smile![11]

The first smile is sincere; the palpebral fissures are closed.

The second one is conditional. The eyes remain very open.

And why not? A smile can also be simply diplomatic and polite. That is certainly how you would smile if someone gave you a compliment that you didn't think you deserved, for example. If you are reserved, you will remain sincere by not smiling "from the bottom of your heart." Your eyelids will not crease.

The Asymmetry of the Lower Palpebral Fissures

As an emotion occurs, the palpebral fissure lets us see more of the white in one eye than the other. We quickly understand through this how much esteem the person with whom we are speaking has for us.

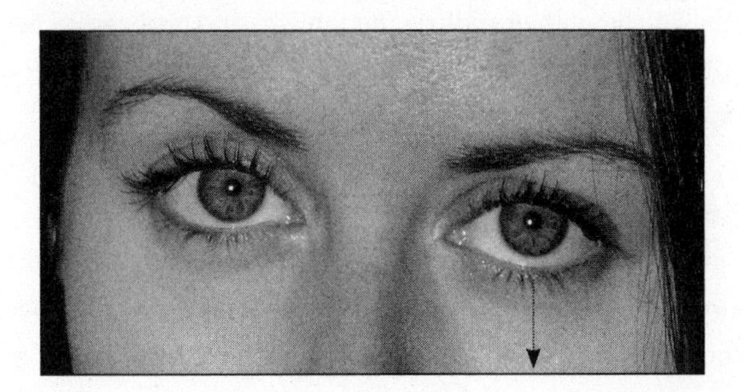

When the lower left eyelid loses its tonicity, we express, with our faces, a deficient self-esteem[12] and it is very possible that this is due to the somewhat proud, insolent, haughty, or contemptuous way the person to whom we are speaking looks at us, which triggered this mechanism. It is good that this line of questioning is our first reflex before anything else.

The inverse situation can also occur. This is by far the most common situation.

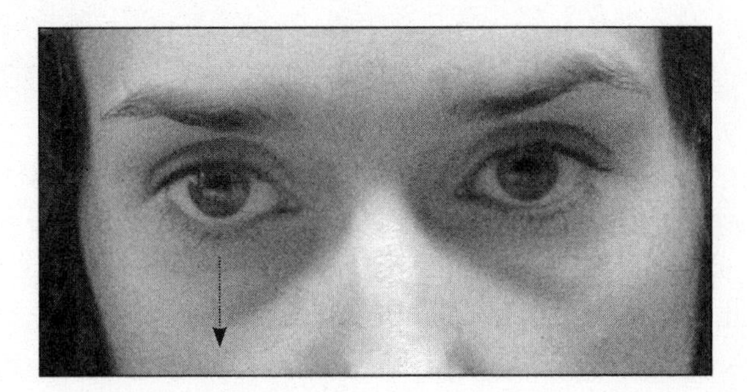

When the lower palpebral fissure lets us see more of the white in the right eye, it reveals a person's negative opinion, tied most often to the nature of the conversation. It is the right half of her face that is more visible, eight or nine times out of ten.[13]

When the white is permanently present under the right iris, it indicates a structural overworking—a permanent one. It is suitable then to ask ourselves about the rhythm of life that this person has imposed upon himself.

It would be a shame and certainly false to think that the messages conveyed by the palpebral fissures are always negative. When someone's lower eyelids go up, this reveals her dynamism and pleasure of being in our company. Once again, the face and the body do not betray us, but rather they allow us to communicate in any language.

The Nose and Its Wrinkles

The nose is not as animated as the eyes or the mouth. Its messages are more discreet than those of the other parts of the face. It is a good idea just the same to note that the nose is often involved in the expression of anger, and on this occasion it takes a characteristic appearance.

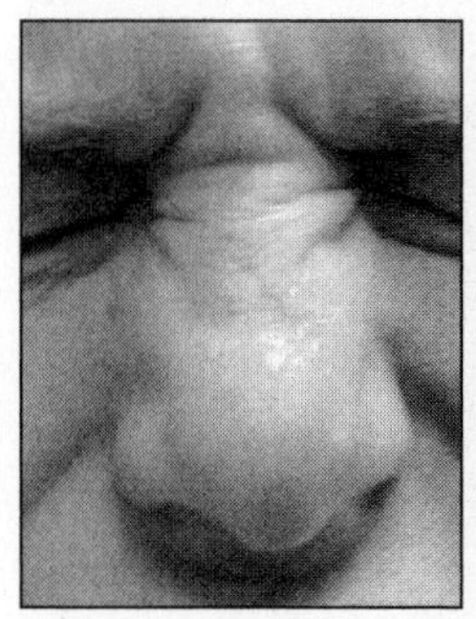
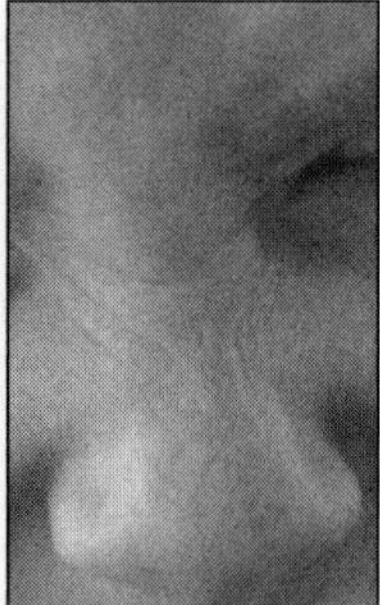
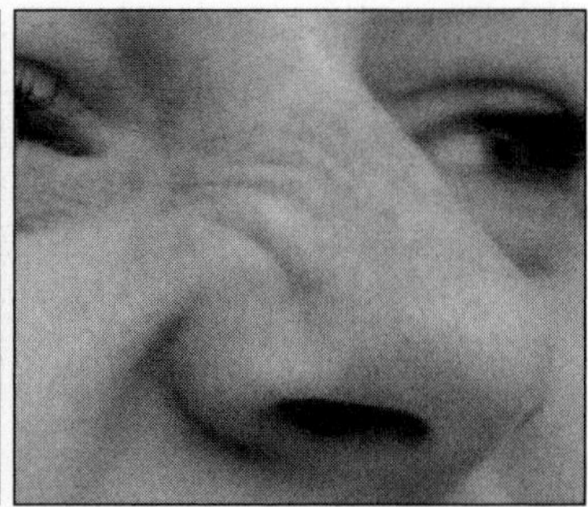

The nose has a tendency to curl up, creating an appearance of folds between the eyes when a person feels angry. In everyday life, the nose does not always tense excessively, but fine lines appear surreptitiously at random due to annoyances. These lines preclude fear and anger, which are, however, two negative hypertonic emotions. The nose becomes totally smooth in fearful situations.

The Lips

The messages of the mouth are extremely numerous. Contrary to the eyebrows, whose motor control is unique, the mouth is activated by two different motor commands. People have a great deal of difficulty voluntarily moving their eyebrows independently from one another, while the corners of the mouth can be moved consciously and separately, very easily. Try that with your eyebrows! Few people can do it. Now do the same thing with your mouth, and you will find that it is easier . . .

In the interest of efficiency, we will only consider the clearest messages. A happy person expresses his joy with upward movements of the corners of his mouth. There is not a happy person whose mouth corners do not go up. The configuration of the lips is an infallible sign in differentiating between positive and negative emotions.

NEGATIVE EMOTION

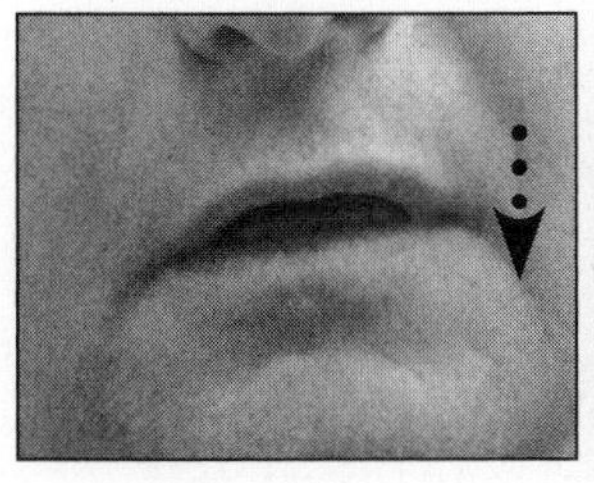

POSITIVE EMOTION

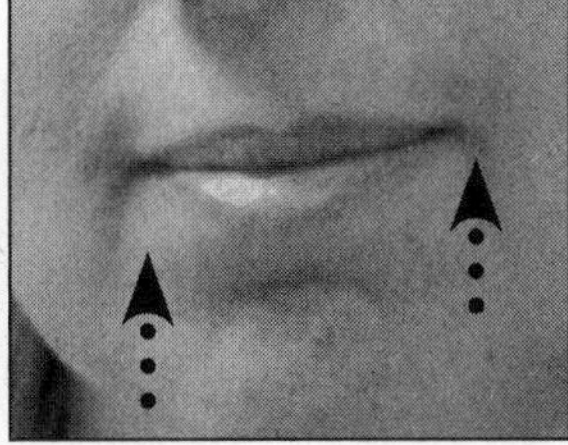

It is impossible that the person in the photo on the left is happy. Even if the joy is internal, the corners of the lips have a tendency to lift.

When a smile is real, the mouth is more rounded and the lips are redder. An introvert can smile sincerely with a closed mouth. One of the characteristics of a fake smile is that it lasts just a little too long,[14] while the one that is spontaneous is more fleeting.

Negative emotions generate a drooping movement in the lips that can become permanent, an expression of bitterness that only fades during a transition to a positive emotion in a person's psychic landscape. Only one negative emotion—and it is considerable—is an exception to this rule: anger.

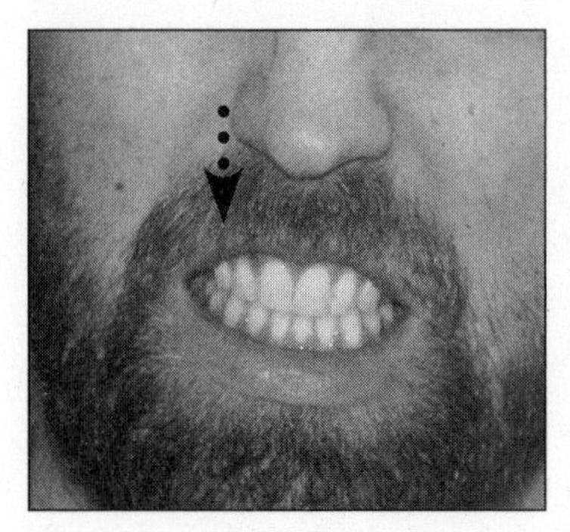

In the specific case of anger, only the upper lip lifts, the lips tense, taking on a white color, and the person shows his upper jaw.

An angry person's upper jaw greatly resembles that of an angry dog.[15] The corners of the lips go up but we can see the central incisors at the top of the mouth. These are the asymmetries of the mouth that give a more precise indication of the expression of anger. When this is directed at another—which is most often the case—the right side of the mouth seems higher than the left. This asymmetry can be visible in aggressive smiles.

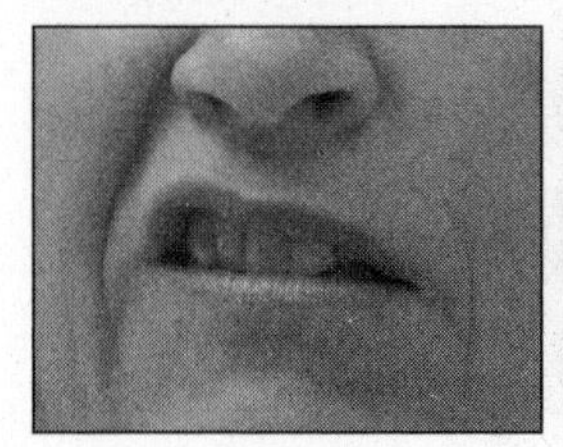
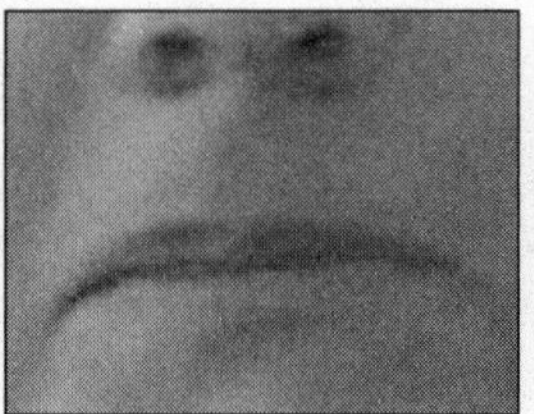
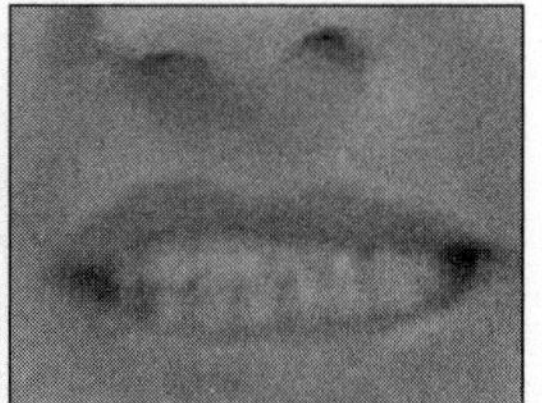

This expression can engrave itself on the face as we age. Then it also becomes visible when we speak.

The left half of the face lifts to expose the canines when a person is vexed by a situation that affects them.

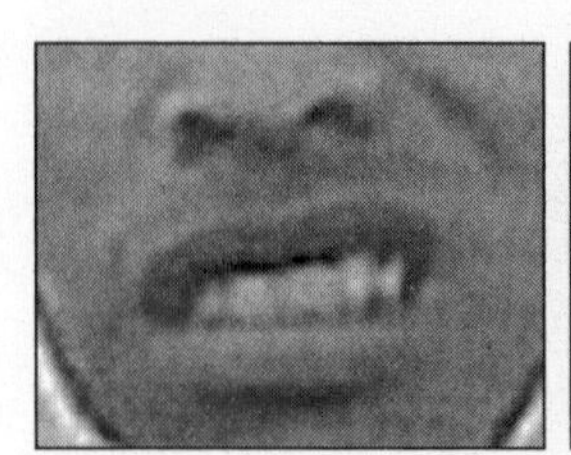
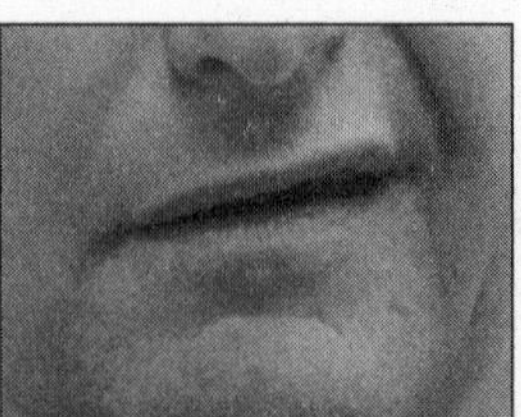
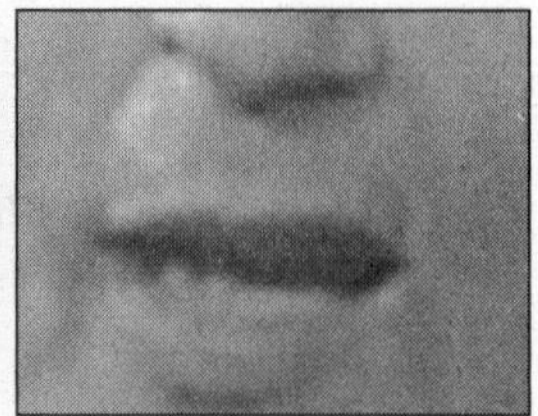

The first of these on the previous page shows the mouth of an Indonesian filmed in front of the location of his house after the gigantic tsunami that engulfed a part of the region of Bali. His house disappeared and he found himself alone. He has an expression of vexation. His despair is profound, he retreats into himself, and he is aware of his solitude.

The movements of the mouth are numerous, but these few signs are so often present that they will always capture a person's emotional landscape.

More About What the Gaze Says

Who has not said to himself at one time or another, "It's all in the eyes!" Well, not everything is in the eyes; each part of the face and body speaks as well! An attitude, an impromptu gesture, is always likely to surprise, and no one can really predict in advance on which part of the face an asymmetry will appear. Nevertheless, even if not everything is in the eyes, everything most often begins there, and it is because of this that we attribute to it all virtues and that there exist so many expressions, like "keep a watchful eye," "giving the evil eye," or "having a keen eye." So let's try to "keep our eyes open"!

Do Not Confuse "To See" with "To Look"

Thoughts need comfort zones. They cannot reinvent the wheel with each reflection, but they are also the source of prejudice. One of them, significantly, concerns the eyes: We believe what we see!

Indeed, the eyes allow us to see.[16] Besides, what other purpose could they serve? But they don't look each time they land on an object, a thing, or a person. Besides the conscious, intentional gaze, there exists another type, unconscious this time, that does not see!

The gaze is more driven by a moment's interest than by the dominant eye. The left eye becomes dominant in a situation of bonding and the right eye when caution is appropriate, but most of the time our eyes wander, and it is this gaze that is often the most interesting.

The direction of the gaze reflects a person's thoughts. The gaze that wanders off is never alone. It takes with it the person behind it, and it expresses the direction of his thoughts.

Two major rules justify movements of the gaze and allow us to decipher many situations:

- Eyes look to the past or project into the future.
- Our eyes show if information is loaded with emotion or if it is cold and cognitive.

The Past and the Future

If, for example, a person is facing you and, over the course of the conversation, eye contact between the two of you is not sustained, observe the direction of his eyes; it will be full of information.

If he needs to access information from his past, his eyes will have a tendency to go toward the left.

If he needs to elaborate, to construct something new, to make something up, they will go toward the right.

Communication theoreticians thought for a long time that eye movement depended on how the brain functions.[17] However, this reality had only been tested in the West.[18] Looking at visual evidence from other parts of the world, notably, from the Near and Middle East, has allowed us to see this differently, even though our brains are the same.

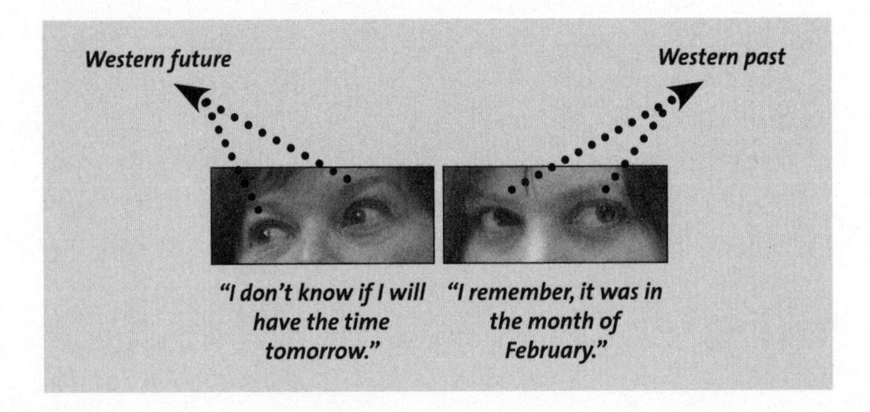

Westerners evoke the past with their eyes directed toward their left, while for people from Aramaic cultures (Arabs and Israelis, notably) the eyes go toward the right!

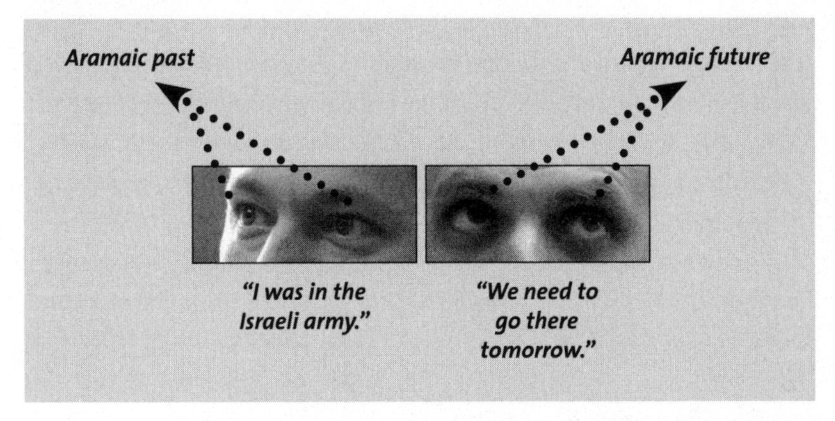

We were on the trail of this discovery that shows that the logic of our eye movements are transformed by our early education and, of this, the most socializing of all skills: writing. Our eye movements take on the direction of writing![19]

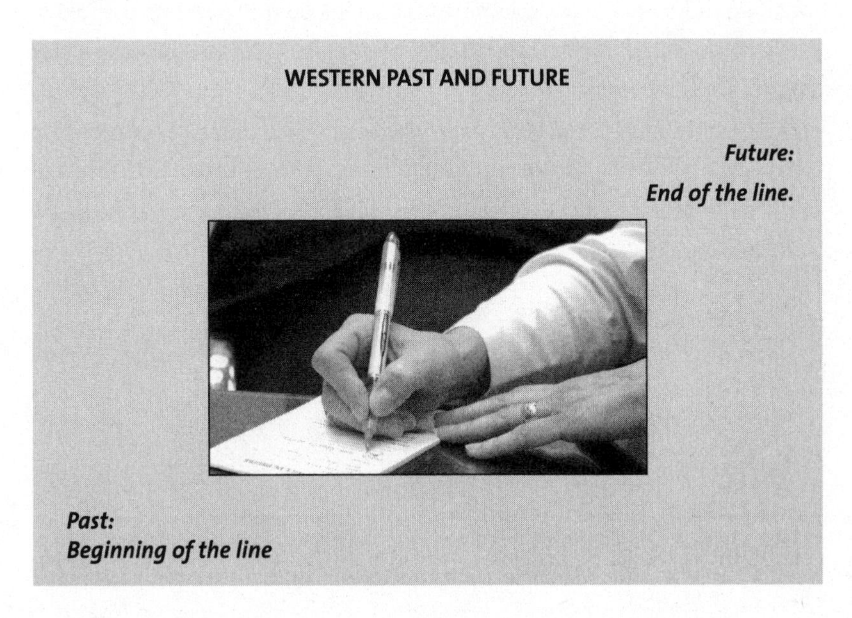

A Western child writes from left to right. He learns that the beginning of the page is on the left and by deducing that the beginning is always on the left, it is there that he will search for the beginning of all things. Publicists play with this reality in order to create their advertisements and psychologists when analyzing patient drawings. For them, the beginning of the page corresponds to the security experienced at the beginning of life.[20] On the other hand, if the writing style is reversed, the unconscious direction that the eyes will go is also. This is what happens among Syrians, Israelis, or Arabs, who look for the past on the right.

Early education has an important role in the lateral movement of our eyes. On the other hand, it doesn't explain why the gaze turns toward the sky or to the toes of our shoes . . .

Emotion and Information

The eyes go from left to right with thoughts of the past or the future, but they don't always do it at the same height. The presence of our bodies explains this difference. When human beings think of complicated information or even pure facts, they direct their eyes above their bodies, thereby escaping the environment around them. On the contrary, emotions lead the gaze into the fold of the body cavity, below. The direction of the gaze is therefore said to be either emotional or cognitive.

Here, this young Western woman was asked to describe her relationship with a member of her family. At the moment that this question was asked of her, she needed to come up with pure information. Her expression looks away.

SEARCH FOR INFORMATION (COGNITIVE)

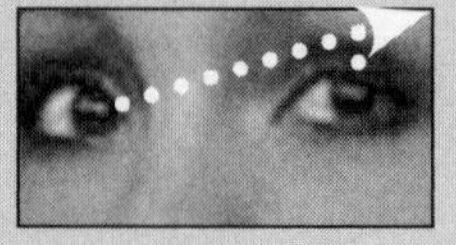

"When my father would approach . . . "

EMOTIONAL RECALL (EMOTIONAL)

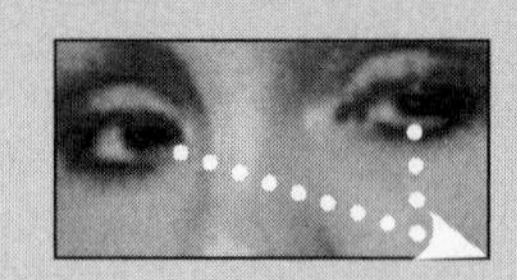

". . . he would beat me."

These two images are spaced out over one second.

The recovered information is of a very emotional nature. It triggers a wave of emotions, so her expression turns inward, into her body, her own inner world.[21]

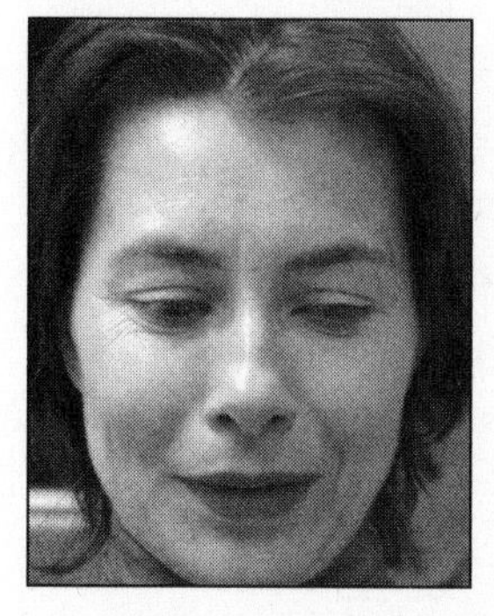

This woman retreats inward, to look inside herself. We get the feeling that her eyes are looking at the insides of their sockets.

The marriage of the past and of the future with the cognitive and the emotional dimensions allows us to identify the four quadrants of an expression.

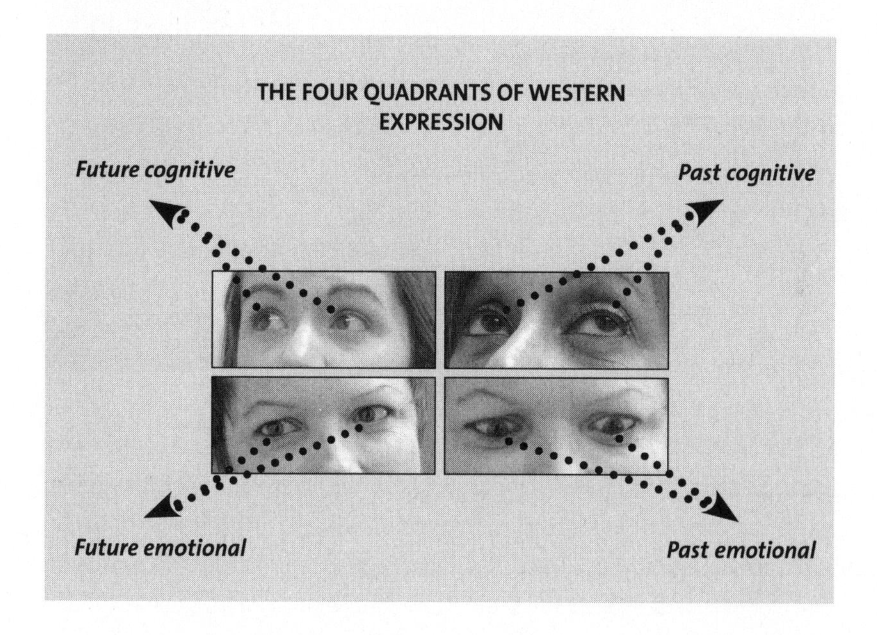

Obviously, eyes can look in every possible and imaginable direction, but these four well-identified major directional quadrants help us define the nature of the thoughts that are being dealt with more rigorously.

The Gaze of Small, Everyday Fabrications

The gaze goes to the right when something imaginary is thought up. It also goes to the right when we make up or embellish reality and sometimes when we misrepresent it.

Some experts—detectives, among others—must consider the distortion of reality every day. The "clients" that they question talk about a past that they sometimes have the temptation to make up or restructure into an ideal past in which the actions for which they are being blamed no longer exist.

Here, a suspect in a theft investigation is being asked where he met up with certain people.

His eyes are looking to the future even though the event he is relating would normally be referred to in the past. In reality, he is making up this information.

An interrogation specialist can precisely measure the coherence of a person's statement by the sometimes astonishing eye movements and by exploring other means of inquiry. A person who lacks authenticity rarely fabricates a lie from A to Z. Everything that he says is probably true, except for one element. Here it is appropriate to delve deeper into information related to the Lafayette train station. The suspect really was in the subway, but not at that station. That was the weak link in his statement.

Someone who tells made-up facts on several occasions ends up looking for them in his past, in order to make them seem real. We must then ask the suspect to clarify his statement, and try to find some new detail that he has not yet made up to see if he will look toward the future or the past for the information. Only when speaking the truth will he find true, actually experienced details in the past.

A recording has allowed the transcription of this scene between an investigator and a suspect:

> Investigator: Where were you at noon on the eighth?
>
> The suspect: At the café . . . Chez Jeannette! [The answer is given while looking the investigator in the eye.]
>
> Investigator: What did you order?
>
> Suspect: A beer! [The answer is given while looking the investigator in the eye.]
>
> Investigator: Beer in a can or draft?
>
> Suspect: Uh . . . draft beer . . . [The answer is given while looking the investigator in the eye, but the suspect blinks three times.]
>
> Investigator: What was the glass like?
>
> Suspect: A stein . . . [His eyes look in the direction of the future cognitive.]

The suspect has prepared an outline of his lie and knows that he is going to say that he drank a glass of beer, but he did not foresee being questioned about the shape of this glass. He must make up what he does not know and look toward the future. When he says, "A stein," he cannot go searching for this information in the past because it never happened in the past. He evaluates the consistency of his story.[22] It is at that moment that his eyes go toward the future cognitive.

When a person has Alzheimer's disease, their eyes do not look toward the past either. People who suffer from Alzheimer's cut themselves off from their past little by little and end up losing self-awareness and can no longer recognize themselves, even in a mirror. When asked about their past, their eyes will not go searching for their memories to the left. They will go to the right, as if they are trying to find their memories in the future, whether or not they are recent or very old.[23] In this specific case, eye movement is an active witness to one's own forgotten history.

In the present state of our knowledge, a whole book could be devoted to eye movements, but it is unclear that reading it would make their interpretation more concrete. Expression is malleable; it can choose to adapt as it sees fit. Thus, the human being who is uncomfortable will look for points of escape. These are dependent on the immediate environment, which is different every time.[24] Suffice it to say that Western observations have every chance of being realistic if people are placed in front of each other, if they grew up in the Western world.

"I talk with my body, and this without even knowing it. Therefore I always say more than I know."

—Jacques Lacan

PART TWO

The Hand Says Out Loud What the Body Thinks to Itself

The body speaks whenever we feel emotions. Emotions change its position, creating asymmetries on the face, particularly with eye movements. Faced with their internal tidal waves, moved from side to side by what they feel, people who are anxious about not wanting to be read openly do not stand with their arms relaxed and dangling. They control themselves, masking and hiding as much as they can. Their bodies are their accomplices, accomplices that help and hinder at the same time, that show their emotions in spite of themselves and then hide them, again in spite of themselves! In order to decipher hidden emotions, bodies therefore are a sure ally, because, to put it succinctly, they always end up telling the truth.

CHAPTER 8

Body Symbolism Is Universal

We experience those emotions that we want to conceal. If we remained serene faced with them, no one would see those emotions, but it is by trying to hide them that we make them visible!

Look at the hands. Following all of the movements across the face and the body seems to be the best way to decipher someone's emotions and therefore their thoughts. The body never expends energy pointlessly—this is the basic principle of homeostasis, the foundation of human and animal biology. The hand never moves without a reason. If it moves, it is because it has "an idea in mind," which leads it to this part of the body rather than another . . .

Body Symbolism

Body symbolism is the same for everyone for a basic reason: All human beings have the same body! Each one of its parts fulfills the same physical and symbolic function everywhere.[1] The mouth is always in the middle of the face, no matter the culture that is being considered, and it is through the mouth that food is ingested and words come out. People look at each other with their eyes, grab things with their hands, take those whom they love in their arms, and run away with their legs. The universal functions of the body often even exceed the human condition since certain unconscious behaviors link us undeniably to apes! But why do our hands choose our faces more often over our bodies to settle on, to stroke, or to scratch?

The Face: To Look Good

The face is a sponge, the sum of tactile sensors. It is stimulated by our hands that activate the skin around our sensors—the eyes, the ears, and the mouth—but our hands are also what obstruct the senses in order not to "see" or not to "hear" . . . Because of its structure, the face is of no assistance when we need to act in concrete terms. We will never say, "Bring your face; I need some help!" but rather, "I need a hand!" However, we also say: "If you want to watch me do it, you can stay where you are!" Our hands will not wander to our faces when we roll up our sleeves, move forward, and act.

The hands go to the face when a person withdraws within themselves to reflect. The side of the face that is chosen testifies to the mental climate of the interaction. When the person is less nervous, her hand moves to the left half of her face. Additionally, when she is sad or relaxed, the hand goes to the left three times more often than to the right.

Alternatively, the hands are placed on the right half of the face when situations are tenser and energy is turned more outwardly.

The Body Speaks: "I Say, I Show, I Am, I Have"

"I have a body." The expression is incongruous because as soon as you think it, you must say instead: "I *am* a body." Without a body, there is no longer a Self.[2] The messages that it sends us—in a visceral form, humoral and venous—are very clear and full of common sense and makes us who we are. They are a real, concrete, palpable part of ourselves and our brain cannot do without them. If you doubt that, put on a sweater inside out. Just the sensations of the garment's seams touching your skin in unusual places will be sufficient to make your brain understand its error.

The sternum indicates the ego: "I." This reality goes beyond East and West and is logically found among preliterate people. It is even observable in children's drawings.

Drawings done by children from seven to nine years of age, who were asked to faithfully depict themselves, led to the realization that those who had suffered mistreatment drew themselves with a smaller sternal area, going from the chin to the base of the rib cage, than the other children did.

This measured area proved to be more than 50 percent smaller compared to the same area drawn by other children of the same age. Such is the case here in the second drawing.

Because the sternum represents the ego, it is not surprising, when the self is injured, that its graphical representation has a tendency to be reduced.[3]

The stomach sometimes takes an important dimension, and not only in an abstract way, but also in an interaction. The meaning of this part of the body appears when the baby is about five months old. He begins to touch it then, to invest in it, to understand that it belongs to him, that it is his.

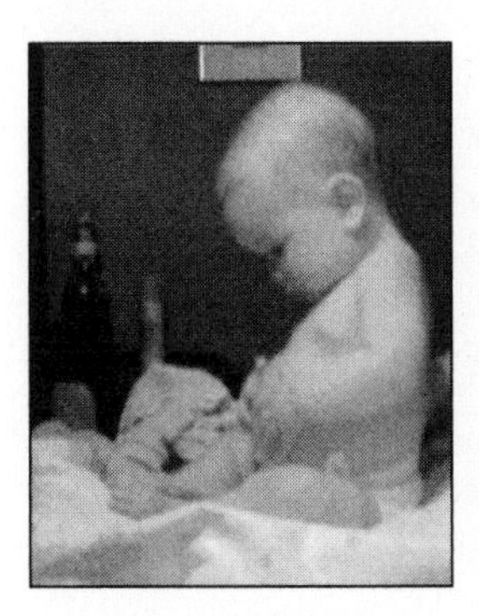

The baby looks at his stomach; he gets in touch with the fact that it is his. Without the progressive discovery of his stomach, he would never be able to differentiate between "being" and "having."

The discovery of the stomach must be integrated by the brain and it becomes reinforced symbolically in the aging process.[4] The adult strokes his stomach while talking about “possession,” “assets,” and of “having.”

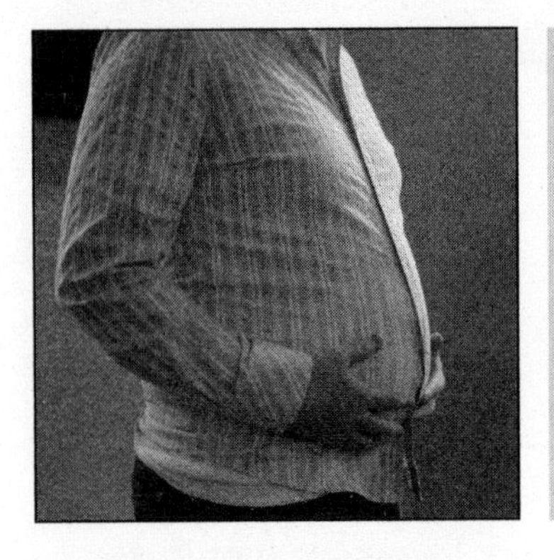

“You have a beautiful home.”

“Yes, it’s not bad . . . but, you know, we worked hard!” says this man while holding his stomach in his hands.

By touching his stomach and stroking it, he can reassure himself of his own possessions, be proud of them or wonder about them, and be jealous of other people’s possessions.

The stomach represents having. Consciousness of the “stomach” (material) allows one “to have” (symbolic). The identification of the original links connecting the body and relational space—in this case, the stomach and materiality—is thus for each body part, the indispensable prerequisite for accessing the keys to body language.[5]

The trunk is “sawed up,” in our representation, into several symbolic parts.

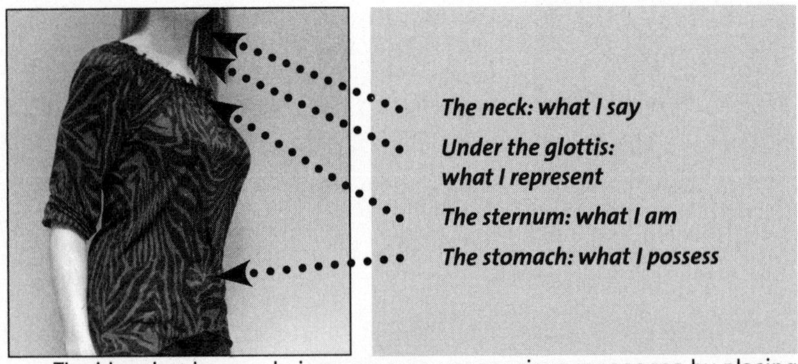

The idea that human beings express unconscious messages by placing their hands on their bodies is becoming more and more accepted. These movements are decipherable; they connect the body to something other than the physical body. Physical space is also a relational space.

The Arms and Relational Space

The arms are links. They allow for relationships. Just think of expressions like: "Let's shake hands!," "Let me take you in my arms!," "His is a shoulder I can lean on," etc. But arms are also the weapons of conflict: On occasion, they become *the military arm* of someone who teases *the right-hand man* or who fights *tooth and nail*. The worst insult is *the finger*.

The arm consists of several parts and each one of these segments is associated with a specific symbol. Popular speech glorifies *the helpful shoulder*, allowing us to understand that the shoulder . . . supports.

Joints give the body its suppleness and its flexibility.[6] A brilliant speech is said to be "very articulate." Bent wrists are even considered to be a mark of refinement. This affectedness can be compared to the stiffness of a person who *swallowed a broomstick*, caricatured by an erect body, straight trunk, and rigid neck.

Observe the arm movement when gifts are given.

The forearms of the adult are partly bent when the gift is being given, while the young boy offers his gift with his arms outstretched. At his age, physiologically, he would, however, be capable of presenting it with his arms half bent. But why doesn't he do so? Simply because the gesture of bending the arms to offer a present unconsciously says, "I" give to "you." An adult folding his arms at the elbow joint signifies that the relationship is mutual. It is necessary that "I" meet "you" halfway. In a child's mind, this is less clear. This idea exists as a single block, spontaneous and without nuances, without polish. "I" give you a gift. Period. The double emotional[7] and relational positioning of one adult in front of another has not yet been acquired.

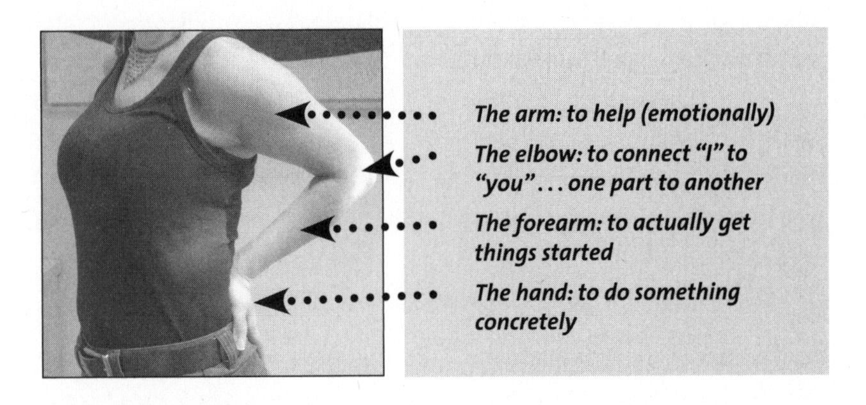

The legs are like the arms, a spatial link. They come closer or move away—people stand closer to people that they appreciate than to those whom they "put at a distance"—but legs are less intrusive than arms, preferring, in the imagination, to escape the relationship. Expressions that are related to legs refer to this connotation in every language: "Take to his heels" or "Run as far as your legs can carry you."[8] Legs are used to run away while arms are used to attack. This reality goes further than the human species. No animal has ever trapped its prey by simply running next to it. With humans, the more the hand moves down toward the extremities, the more concrete is the need for action, the more urgent.

The knee joint separates the tibia from the thigh. Psychologists who are less miserly with their metaphors speak of the knee as what attaches the "I" to the "we": "I . . . we." Thanks to it, the body that gets up unfolds, stretches out, and lengthens. We must recognize that when people who are sitting down massage their knees, they are wondering if they will rise to the occasion.

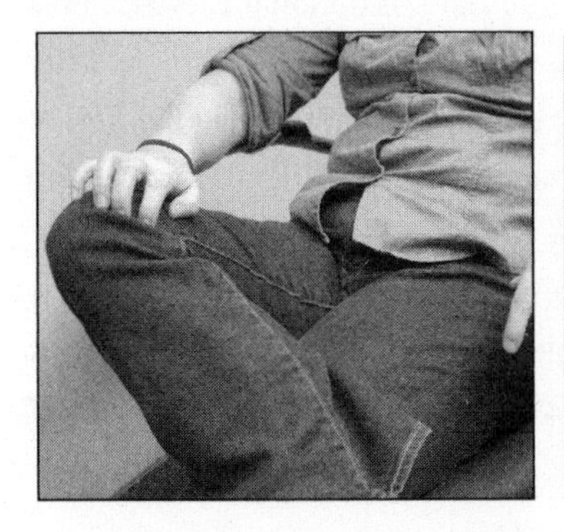

Here, the person hesitates to make a request. To do so would be to create different kind of rapport. Asking for more . . . for something bigger. He scratches his knee.

Human movements are not made simply for pleasure; they have a social and even emotional meaning. *Transportation* transports.

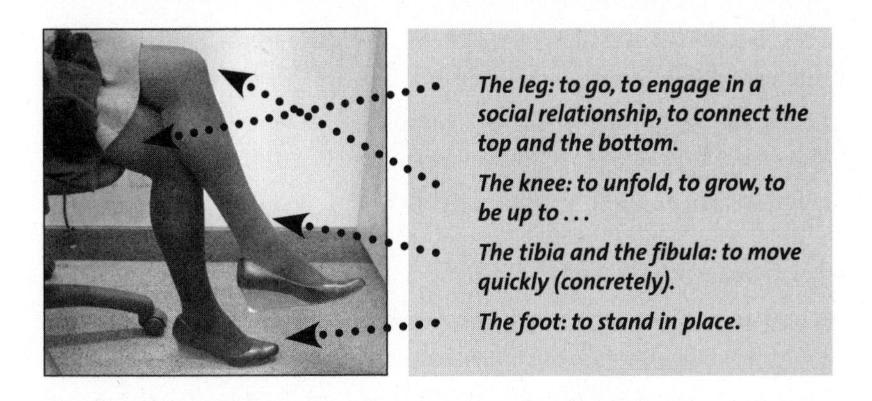

The body lives and expresses itself in three dimensions; it has four sides.

The Four Sides of the Human Body

The face and the body are symmetrical, to such a point that one often forgets how to distinguish the right from the left. We say that a person has lung or breast cancer without specifying which lung or which breast is in question.[9] In reality, the body is not really that symmetrical. If that were the case, lung, breast, or any type of cancer would be triggered on both sides at the same time. This only happens in very rare cases. The hand touches one point on the body at a time, just as we scratch ourselves, for example, at one place at a time. Only one point itches at a time.

On the left half of the body and on the right, emotional expression is different. It is also not the same if a conversation takes place toward the front or the back of the body. The body has four sides. Thus, there are four different ways to act according to each decision that is made. Whether it is a question of going to a meeting, going shopping, or filling out an application, you can: 1. do it spontaneously; 2. do it out of obligation; 3. decide to bypass the action, by finding an excuse, for example; or 4. do nothing. There are four sides to a functional body corresponding to the four possible strategies of interaction.[10]

The Left and the Right

On the left side of the body, driven by the right hemisphere's unconscious decisions, the micro-movements that are observed are more sensual.[11] Certain gestures, to which we will return, are less abrupt. These people are therefore participating in a relationship.

On the right side, it is the left hemisphere that does the work. The decisions seem to be more solitary, opinionated, sectioned off, and the actions are voluntary.

The Front and the Back

A human being touches the front of his body when he wants to move forward, when he wants to go toward something or someone. The general message is one of reconciliation. On the other hand, he scratches the back side of his body when he wants to flee from a situation.

The Front Right Side

Each time that it is a matter of moving forward in a structured way and when there is something logical at stake, the hands go to the front right side of the body; it is there that it will "tickle." A spatial position toward the front combined with activity in the left hemisphere are the explanations that are the most plausible and operative, consistent with our state of theoretical knowledge.

The Front Left Side

The hand is placed on the front left side when a person is in a dynamic of reconciliation. This willingness to reconcile is associated with the right hemisphere, the one of connection, which is on the left side of the body. Spontaneous desire and the desire to act are felt.

The Back Right Side

The hand is placed on the back right side when a person wants to escape. The interpretation is generally facilitated by a clear context in which flight seems to be the most honorable alternative.

The Back Left Side

The hand is placed on the back left side of the body when we want to move forward, in the relationship, (left) and move away (back) at the same time. It makes more sense than it sounds. Take, for example, waiting in line at the airport and seeing someone else who is possibly trying to sneak in without paying. Her left hand goes to her left side a few seconds before she secretly passes in front of several passengers. She wants to move ahead more quickly but only with a strategy of bypassing others can she succeed. The back left part of the body addresses all of these moments during which an objective cannot be attained except by indirect means, the direct way not being feasible.

The Hand on the Body

We can understand emotional states through hand movements on a part of the face or body:

- If the hand scratches, the person feels an *itch*.
- If it strokes it, this is a *micro-caress*.
- If it rests on a spot, this is a *micro-fixation*.

These represent three different states of mind.

Itching

The sensation of itching is born in the insular cortex[12] of repressed emotion. "That itches," so we scratch! In this type of itch, there isn't a pimple causing the sensation, and the plant environment (pollen, dust, etc.) is not the cause either. Itches always appear on the opposite hand in embarrassing situations that provoke interior contradictions, when we do not approve of what we are feeling, when we censor our words or our attitudes . . . when we are uncomfortable![13] There is also now evidence that the simple act of scratching calms one's mood.[14]

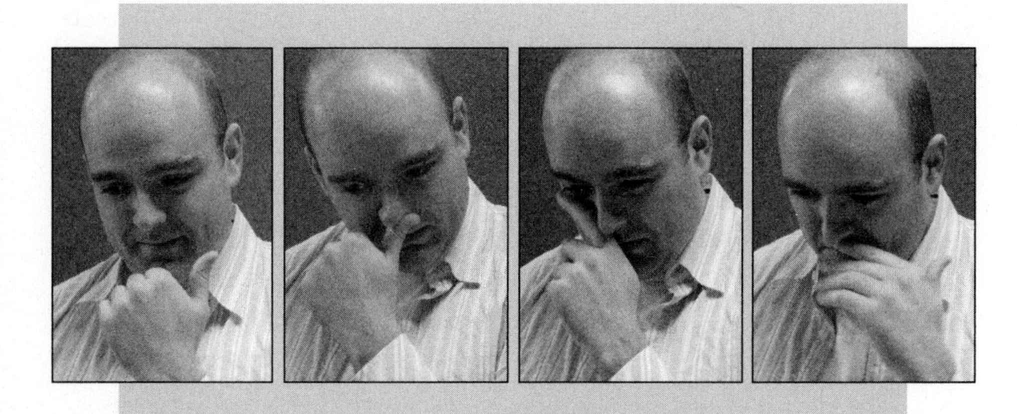

This sequence lasts one and a half seconds.

Itches in general last less than a second and sometimes no apparent cause can explain them. People who have had a limb amputated may even feel a tingling sensation in this "phantom limb," as itching is activated by the brain.[15] The limb may no longer exist but the problem that caused the itch is still present.

Surprisingly, the great apes, in situations where they find themselves facing the same contradictions as human beings might, feel the same itch.

These are also very short and should not be confused with those caused by insect bites, for example.[17]

Too many similarities exist between human itching and those of the large primates for this to be a coincidence.

Micro-fixations

The hand sometimes strays to the face and stops there. Micro-fixations[18] allow us to hide or to retreat into ourselves.

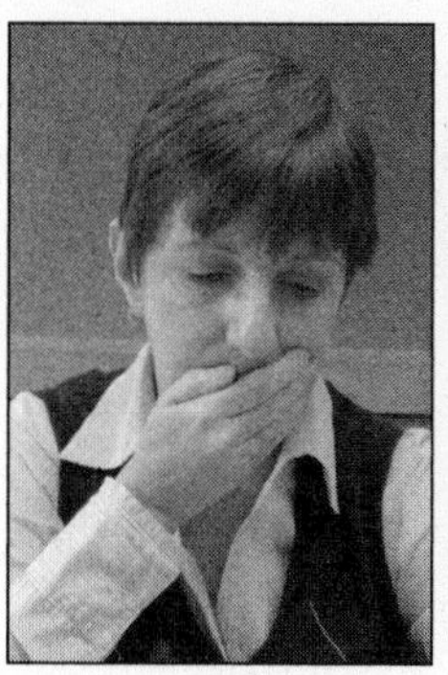

Micro-caresses

The hand moves to the face and strokes it. This sensual movement is often made when the atmosphere is bathed in amiability or gentleness. Observe in these images that were taken that the micro-caresses and the micro-fixations are not easy to differentiate; only a slight movement distinguishes them.

MICRO-CARESS

The middle finger strokes the mouth very gently, directing our gaze to this sensual area of the face.

MICRO-FIXATION

The finger does not budge; this woman is skeptical.

Micro-caresses are sensual; they allow us to be noticed, to direct the gaze of another to ourselves, to hide our desires while showing them!

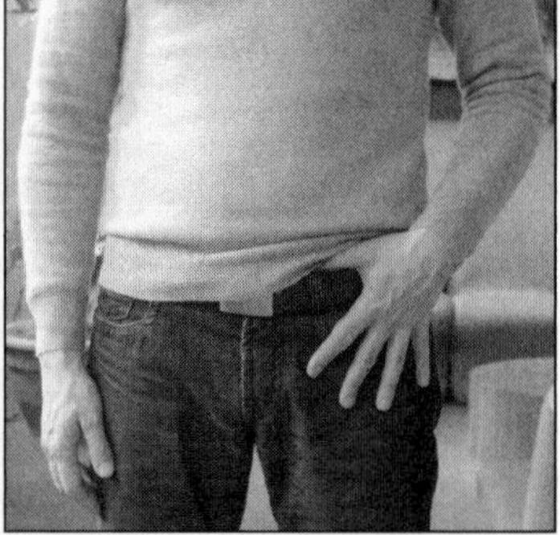

The hand leads the gaze of another to where it settles. It reminds human beings that we are first and foremost a being of flesh. Micro-caresses are unconscious and usually last less than five seconds. It is completely appropriate to wonder if they are a vestigial gesture passed on through evolution. In fact, the great apes, when they want to be deloused by one of their fellow creatures, show the spot where they want to be touched with their hands.

Which Hand?

Surprisingly, the hand that acts on the body is not the one that is moving. If that were the case, the right hand would land on the face in 90 percent (the proportion of right-handed people in the population) of cases.[19] It is not which hand but where it is going to settle that is important! When the left side of the face "itches, it is logically the left hand that intervenes, and inversely so with the right hand on the right side, but hands can on occasion cross the face or body, thereby permitting the person to hide or to protect herself.

It would have been more logical and ergonomic for the left hand to go to the left ear . . . but then that arm would not be able, as she uses it here, to protect her whole body.

It would have been more logical and ergonomic to use the left hand since it is the left side that itches . . . but his hand does more than scratch his ear; the movement allows his whole body to twist.

It would have been more logical and ergonomic to use the right hand since it is the right side that itches . . . but then the person would have been much more exposed.

In these last three situations, if the other arm had been used, these people would have saved energy, and everyone knows how economical the brain is. But here it decided to give a more complex order. Their hands cross their faces or their bodies, protecting them.

The opposite phenomenon also occurs. The hand that is least ergonomic to use is placed on the face or the body, but this time in order to expose it, show it off, uncover it . . . The person desires therefore to get closer to the other, but she cannot say so openly, yet she experiences the feeling and conveys it through the position of her body.

The woman above, by behaving this way, exposes her body in a look of complicity. She opens herself. The hand used is not the most ergonomic, and the gesture is not necessarily useful, but the motivations are something else entirely. In everyday life, when an arm leads to some contortion of the body, it is always appropriate to ask ourselves what the other person is trying to say: Is she trying to connect with the person to whom she is speaking or get away?

All elements of response seem to imply that the hand and the body are joined. The part of the face that is touched (left or right) expresses involvement in the exchange. The place that is touched (face, arms, legs, etc.) show the nature of the need to engage. The movement of the hand (itching, micro-caresses, micro-fixations) show emotional contradictions, if there are any. The chosen hand allows us to measure the person's spontaneity or desire for protection.

Body symbolism is universal because each part of the body fulfills the same functions for all human beings.

Each body part is specialized in the expression of a specific emotion.

The body is managed by the two cerebral hemispheres and has a front and a back side. Depending on the area that is touched, the need or the desire to communicate is different.

Itching allows us to manage emotions that are held back. The place where it appears determines the nature of the emotion.

The unconscious choice of hand that moves on the body is not random.

CHAPTER 9

Hide-and-Seek on the Face

The human being who tries to hide his emotions often places his hands on his face rather than saying what he feels, but this reveals in detail what he believes is kept silent. That is without a doubt one of the reasons why, without knowing exactly why, certain communication experts advise us not to put our hands on our faces. However, good communicators and debaters do it, primarily because they are not puppets, and also because they know that a human being is not just a collection of gestures and that with these gestures the unconscious rises to the surface. Perhaps they feel unconsciously that gestures cannot serve them, and in fact, some expressions shown on the face are very positive.

Someone who says, "It's a bit complicated; it's giving me a headache!" places his hand on his forehead. Not on the eyes, the cheeks, or the chin. The hand does not perch itself so high by chance. The top of the head symbolizes reflection or thinking the popular parlance of body language. "Egghead," "big-headed," or "bone head" are all verbal testimonies of that reality. When someone puts a hand on his forehead, it is because he must "dig" in order to "elevate" the level of his "thought."

People who are demoralized place their hands on their faces. In 80 percent of cases, the left hand goes to the left side of the face and the body is most often bent toward the left.[1]

MICRO-ITCH

He scratches his forehead.

"I am looking for a solution to these personal problems."

MICRO-CARESS

The forehead is stimulated.

"I would like to recover some information of a personal nature."

MICRO-FIXATION

The hand does not move. We will need to look for other signs to determine if she is feeling despondent or just tired.

The hand is only a tool for the body part that itches. When it is on the left side of the head, difficulties are of a more intimate and emotional nature: someone who does not know how to manage complicated situations or who fears hurting someone close, for example. She isolates herself to think.

The spot that itches is on the right when someone is having difficulty understanding something. Their body is therefore more tonic.

ITCH

"I have to figure it out but it's difficult . . . I have to think."

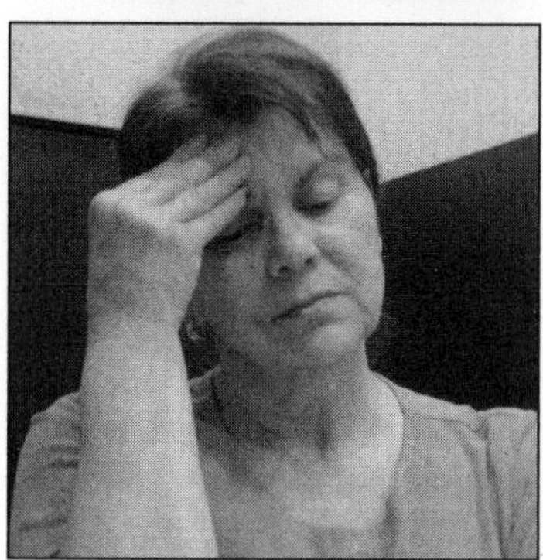

MICRO-CARESS

The body is put to use in searching.

"I have to figure it out . . ."

"I am concentrating; I am searching."

A person whose right hand is placed on the right side of his face is involved in a process of active reflection.[2] This movement conveys the energetic search for solutions.[3]

The women above have their bodies pushed forward in a combative stance to find their solutions, but if these are out of reach, the hand moves to the top of the head. Children doing their homework frequently adopt this position.

"Things are complicated: I will not find a solution."

"Things are complicated: I am going to have to work around the problem."

Faced with the difficulties of children, specifically in schoolwork, parents are always preoccupied about when they should intervene. Should I help my little girl or let her work things out alone, and if I should help her, when should I do so? Where on her body the child makes a gesture is a deciding factor. If her hand is placed on the back left side of her head, it is because she is trying to bypass the problem in order to reach a solution. We can let her make her own way for a while. On the other hand, if it is placed on the back right side of the head, it is often because the solution is out of reach. The parent, in the role of educator, is then welcome.

In a negotiation or an ordinary conversation, if the person opposite you scratches the back right side of her head it is because she is at an impasse with you and you with her, but you know it . . .

The more the hands move to the nape of the neck, the more the itches take on an emotionally aggressive tonality. Difficulty increases and, along with it, impulsiveness.

The Hand in the Hair

Hair softens the shape of our faces. Touching it is soothing to the person who strokes it calmly. In these relaxing moments, messages sent to the other person are often quite nice. However, make no mistake: All hand movements in the hair are not synonymous with relaxation, sensuality, or liking—far from it, in fact.

People who touch their hair with their left hands smile seven times more often[4] than those who use their right hands, and the former leave their hands there twice as long![5] Their facial features, analyzed carefully, show more relaxation and even gentleness: They preen their feathers in a cozy atmosphere. A lock of hair, unconsciously outstretched toward another person, brings him closer to us. Our happiness from talking to him is palpable.

This woman's head moves back but her hand goes toward the other person. This gesture, seemingly illogical, conveys a desire to reconcile.

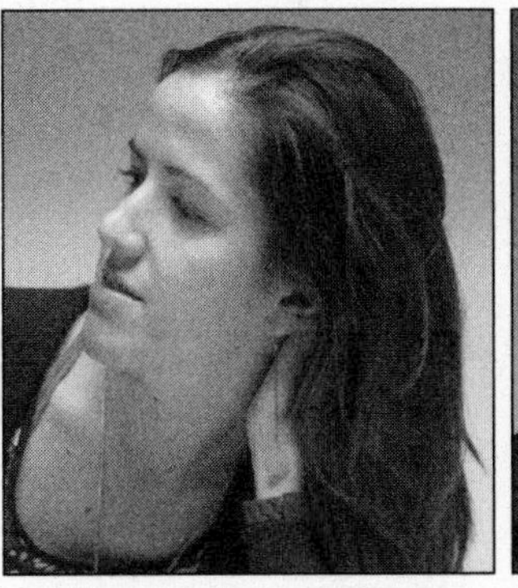

This woman presents the palm of her left hand to another person. This is a sign of openness.

This woman's head leans toward the same side as her hand, which is very relaxed and turned toward the other person.

No person, seated quietly at a table in a restaurant, for example, moves their hand freely toward another person's face without holding their own hair in that hand.[6] This then becomes a concrete connection—a true vehicle of approach. The person, on the other hand, who is disturbed or shocked by another person, will not extend his hand toward her to come closer.

When a strand of hair is held tightly in the right hand, the movement is faster. The facial expressions are also different.

This woman pulls her hair back in order to not let go. She re-centers herself; she takes control of herself.

This woman is thinking about something else: Her hand is not in line with the axis of communication.

When a hand disappears in hair, it is very often closed in a fist and the person is irritated. This is the opposite during reconciliation or when she wants to get closer.

These three situations convey a negative hypertonic emotion kept to oneself. Obviously, the left hand can also be used when clamming up but this is more unusual (about one case in five). The direction of the hand clarifies necessary details. The hand moves back in negative situations. This is more frequent when the right hand is running through the hair.

In 10 percent of cases, the hands cross the face to look for hair on the other side of the head, most likely expressing the desire to protect oneself.

SITUATIONS OF PROTECTING ONESELF

The hand shields the person.

In these images, the fingers are tense, and the face is lowered in the image on the left. The whites of the eyes, very visible under the iris, convey negative emotions. The image on the right, which is more ambiguous, expresses the discrepancy between two emotions. The person, with her chin raised, shows her desire to relate, but her face is asymmetrical and the left half of her mouth droops down slightly. The hand that barricades the face also expresses a need for protection. The gesture at first seems like an invitation to get closer but do not be deceived! As always, it is the combination of several signs that suggests a solid perspective.

People also use both hands, and similar gestures often have very different meanings.

GESTURE TO PUT AT A DISTANCE

By pulling back her hair, this woman reframes herself, refocuses herself. Her unconscious intention is to not let herself be carried away by a spontaneous impulse.

GESTURE OF OPENING UP

This woman, by giving some volume to her hair, gives some of it to her body at the same time. She "offers herself" to the other person. This is a gesture of seduction that is generally unconscious.

A man's hands put up barriers of communication when behind his ears. This gesture is probably a part of our bodily heritage,[7] a legacy from a time when hair was longer. It reveals a willingness to show more honesty and seriousness. On the other hand, a woman's hands call to the person she is talking to. This movement goes from the back to the front. Expansive, it also helps to free up the upper body.

Hands in the hair call for two remarks. Firstly, men pass their hands through their hair as much as women do when it is long.[8] Secondly, it is always possible that a person needs to clear her face of annoying hair! Let's not forget the context of the gesture if we want to be sure of identifying its meaning.

The Eyebrows and the Hand

The eyebrows are located halfway between the forehead and the eyes, between thought (the area of the forehead) and visual images (which take shape in the eyes). When the hand lands on the eyebrow it is because the issues at hand are concrete, brought up to date. The person *imagines*.

In observing gestures of the eyebrow, we must ask two questions. First is the choice of the eyebrow, then the direction of the hand unconsciously chosen to move.

Someone who feels an itch on the left eyebrow is personally affected by events; if these events are distant and anecdotal, the hand moves toward the right eyebrow.

The direction of the hand allows us to distinguish between events that are agreeable to imagine (the hand seems to pass to the outside of the face, as if opening it up) from those that are not (the hand then returns to the interior of the face).

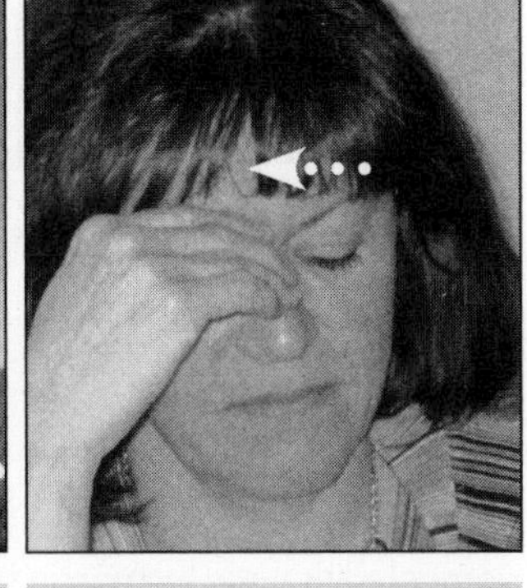

"I am trying to imagine something . . . I am personally invested."

"I don't want to think about it."

The woman in the photo on the left is listening to a friend tell a funny anecdote. The atmosphere is amiable, and she is trying to imagine what he is going to say. Her hand opens her face up. The one in the photo on the right is asking herself personal questions that she does not want to and will not answer. Her gaze is turned inward (the bottom left). Her smile is tight; by scratching herself, she is able to hide her face and ignore the question. She cannot even imagine trying to call up an aspect of her personal life.

Scratching is visible on the right side of the face when a message is processed by the left hemisphere. The person decided to place the information outside of themselves. The context is very serious, unless the situation is negative. The hand's direction provides valuable information.

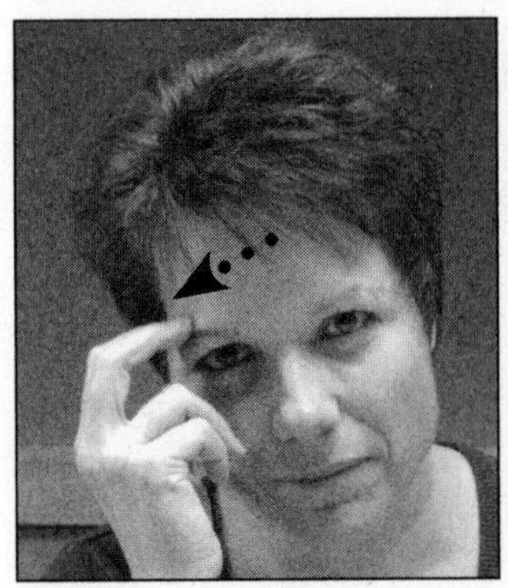

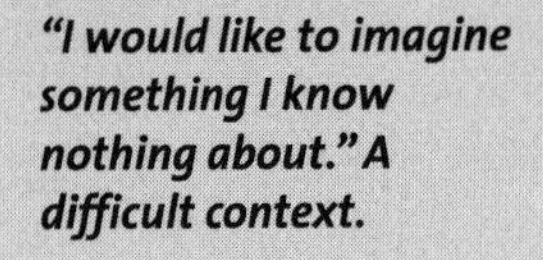

"I would like to imagine something I know nothing about." A difficult context.

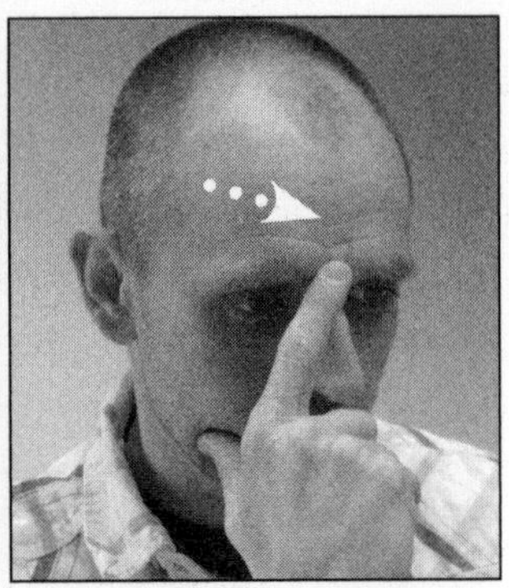

"I do not want to think about that."

We suggested that the woman in the photo on the left go to an exhibit on the Holocaust from World War II. The words "holocaust" and "war" inevitably brought some negative images to her mind, which is why she scratched her right eyebrow. The vigilance that was introduced by these "dark" words stimulated certain areas of the left hemisphere; therefore, the right half of the face showed that she wasn't interested in this proposal. The direction of her hand, toward the outside of her face, in a sign of openness, provides this clarification. She tried to imagine this proposition and decided to give in to it.

On the contrary, scratching closes up the face when we do not want to "imagine." In the photo on the right, we've asked the man about the Holocaust. His face is closed. The movement of his hand closes up his face.

This also happens when the hand goes to the center of the eyebrows.

"I am concentrating so I can remember."

This person is concentrating, trying to remember something. His hand is placed between his eyebrows and his eyes, at the base of his forehead. He closes his eyes to create a void and channel his mental energy.[9] This attitude is frequently seen among athletes before brief exercises demanding great concentration and among those trying to process a great deal of information.

Sometimes people pull on their eyebrows. They are trying then to *see behind what they know;* to imagine further and beyond. This attitude, although not frequent, is still occasionally observed.[10]

The Eyes and the Hand

Eyes are often used metaphorically. From someone who gives the "stink-eye" to someone who has had an "eyeful," or someone who has "eyes in the back of their head," or even when our "eyes are bigger than our stomach," all these expressions have one thing in common, that of giving power to the glance. If your eyes itch and you scratch them, you do it to see better or to not see. The relationship between the hand and the eye is worth discussing.

Unpleasant Visual Information

Common sense has us believe that we look at things, but that is a mistake: The world is remade in the kitchen of the brain. He who sees in black and white and the person who is colorblind, for example, cannot conceive of colors otherwise; this is one of the many pieces of evidence that images of the outside world do not come from the outside but rather from the inside of the brain.

The same common sense suggests that tactile sensors are central to processing information; this is also false. The brain focuses mainly on what happens on the inside. In fact, only 0.02 percent of cortical neurons are used to send information out toward the senses, to the outside. The rest of the 99.98 percent processes internal communication between areas of the brain.[11]

Internal images get mixed up endlessly with external images. When we drive to work via a new route, we compare it endlessly with the one that we normally take, the one that is memorized so we can drive it unconsciously without the help of a map. It even happens sometimes that, having reached our destination, we get the feeling that the car drove there all by itself!

Sometimes we don't agree with the external images that we receive. For example, a woman hopes that she will be offered the beautiful Van Gogh reproduction that she saw in a boutique but instead she is given a Picasso reproduction. While unpacking, she mentally compares her Picasso with the Van Gogh and is disappointed, like the little girl who was promised a red bicycle for her birthday but receives a blue stroller.[12]

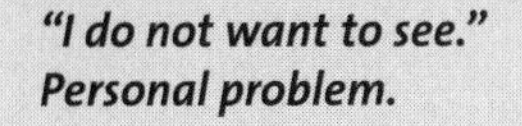

"I do not want to see." Personal problem.

"I do not want to see." External problem.

Our eyes itch when the information that has entered them is not pleasing to us. Children and adults are the same when it comes to this type of itch. It even goes beyond the scope of the human species. Apes, non-human primates, scratch their eyes like humans do.

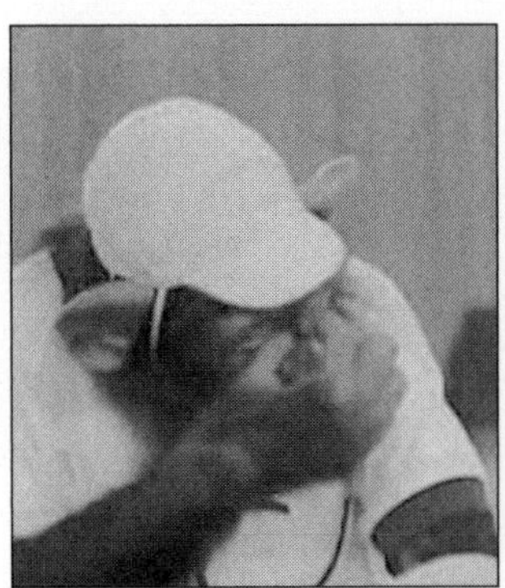

"I don't want to see."

"I don't want to see."

The context is too plainly lined up for it to be a coincidence. Here, the chimpanzee, unable to accomplish certain tasks that other animals can carry out, scratches himself like the human being in the other photo. Helpless before an event, he scratches his eye to make the embarrassing information disappear. This animal's scratching can be interpreted beyond a reasonable doubt.

The man in the image on the right had been summoned for an interrogatory investigation and was ultimately convicted. His body slumps, unstable; he would prefer not to see the situation. His eye itches and his hand tries to erase the images in front of him.

These situations are negative, but the act of scratching one's face does not always express shutting down. Sometimes the skin is pulled in such a way that the eye is more open, and with that, the desire to see better is kindled, a positive interpretation.

. . . as for Pleasant Visual Information

The eye is more open when it is an issue of "seeing" better or better "conceiving" something. While seeing your own medical records on your doctor's desk, it seems human enough to be tempted to catch a glimpse of what is written inside. An area under the left eye tingles and the hand reacts by scratching the skin around the eye, as if we are trying to make it larger.

"I want to see better." Personal information.

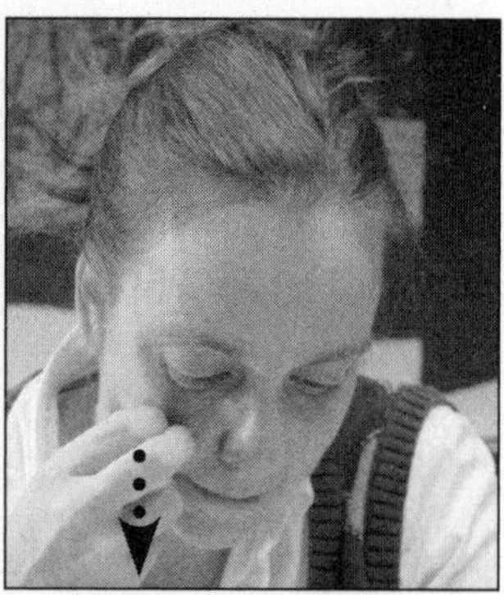

"I want to see better." External information.

Again, the meaning of the images presented from our database can be determined beyond a reasonable doubt. The hand seeks the left eye when we are intimately affected by what we are thinking about. For example, an actor, who is eager to see the results of his work in a sneak preview, scratches the skin under his eye when his image appears on the screen; so does a writer explaining what is written on an advertisement that will introduce one of his works . . .

The right eye is more distant. For example, we observe that an important political and religious dignitary opens one of his eyes wider while scratching it when he is asked about the prospects of the third millennium.[13] His gesture allows us to understand that he is reaching for images within himself while he speaks.

The Nose and the Hand

The nose, for reasons that are both biological and topographical, does not have the same status that the other sensors do. Unlike with the eyes and the ears, its nerve endings are directly connected to the reptilian brain, which is more instinctive. And thus, its motivations are "as plain as the nose on your face." You only have to touch it to hide almost the entire face. This is one of the reasons for the nose's involvement in a lie, for example.

Its position allows it to gather, synthesize, and unify information coming from the other senses. The exact place where the hand lands is of primary importance when we observe the scratching of the nose.

What do all these three people have in common?

"I do not know how to say what I feel."

The index finger, the finger that asserts, is raised.

"I must make a difficult decision and regroup my feelings."

The two index fingers make the shape of a pyramid.

"I must settle this question. This is going to be difficult for someone else."

The configuration of the hands conveys this attitude.

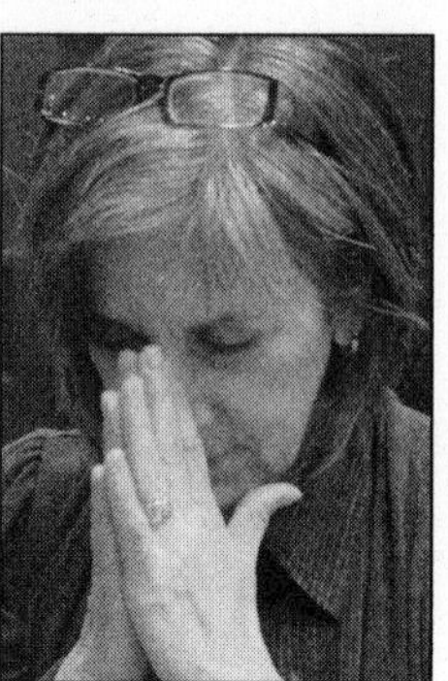

"I am trying to take into consideration all of the parameters."

Visible concentration at the center of the face.

The face is the strategic space par excellence because it is the control tower of the body—a radar that searches, sniffs, feels, senses, and finally ties together all dimensions of information. Our hands have the function of protecting our faces from external forces.

What the four people above have in common is that they are trying to keep information to themselves, at least for a little while.

Human beings are comprised of unique and unified units. The information that we feel, well before it is understood, is synthesized in the depths of the brain rather than on the surface of the nose, but if we scratch the end of our nose it is because evolution has made us do so. The body stimulates and hastens this synthesis of information.

"I am regrouping in order to better understand."

People stimulate the ends of their noses, touch them, and manipulate them when they are curious, when they are looking to connect some information, to "feel" the information better, to learn more.

The hand and the nose show together, at times, more discretion and less transparency. The hand returns to the more secret areas. It is difficult to know if this advantage is inherited through evolution. It is logical, however, to think that at the beginning of humanity, scratching under our noses allowed us to stay hidden by lowering our heads while covering a part of our faces with our hands in order to conceal our emotions even better; and that this advantage entered into our gene pool[14] and our bodily heritage little by little, which means that today, when we keep a number of unspoken thoughts to ourselves, certain areas under our noses itch.

Our hands are guided to different areas if we think the person speaking to us is lying or if we ourselves are not telling the whole truth.

"I do not believe what you are saying."

"I am not saying everything, or at least I'm not saying exactly what I think."

Two points can tingle under the nostrils. An itch under the left nostril indicates something that is unspoken that relates to oneself, a lie. The itch is the same whether this unspoken thing is huge or insignificant: It comes from the right hemisphere, which is always more active when a person relates something—when they are in the middle of speaking.[15] This itch was popularized, in spite of himself, by Bill Clinton, when he admitted to the Lewinsky affair, but it is not specific to this situation. Our database contains hundreds of examples.[16] In fact, the human conscience cannot stand lying. An emotional reaction of rejection provokes this movement.

Something that is unspoken is equally implied when the hand moves under the right nostril, but it is then linked to the other person in the conversation. The right half of the nose is managed, for whoever might need it spelled out, by the left hemisphere.[16] The other person's authenticity, his credibility, is cast in doubt.

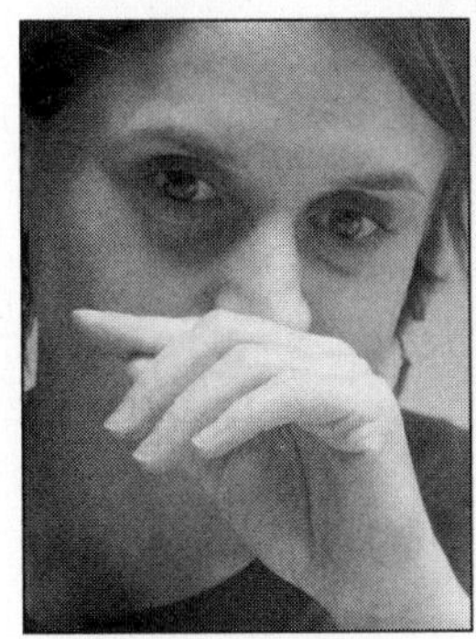

This movement, which shows up in different contexts, is very easy to decipher. It is carried out both by a conference facilitator amused by an expert who claims he is supposedly able to perform human cloning (!), and by a skeptic upon hearing an incredible story, and then again by a politician who sees the empty audience at one of his adversaries' speaking venues.These situations all convey disbelief.

WARNING! Airborne pollen, dust, dust mites, and the like contribute to nasal itching, just as pimples and dirt do. The person who rubs this appendage is not a liar just because she is caught with her index finger under her left nostril. It is the context that allows us to clarify the meaning of this gesture and to determine the nature of the itch. Now, it is true that if you asked someone how a meal that you have cooked for him was and he runs his hand under his nose at the exact moment that he says to you, "I liked it a lot"—actually, come to think of it, maybe it's better to think that there is a bug bite under his nose![17] We also scratch simply in response to a mention of itching, like those who think that they have caught lice because the people around them have it. This demonstration of empathy allows us to feel other people's emotions, and normally it is better to understand them.[18]

Itching on the top of the nose is fueled by curiosity ("feel more") and that on the bottom by what is unspoken ("feel less"). The nostrils represent the external image. Touching them is connected to what human beings show on the outside, that is to say our image . . . and that of the other.

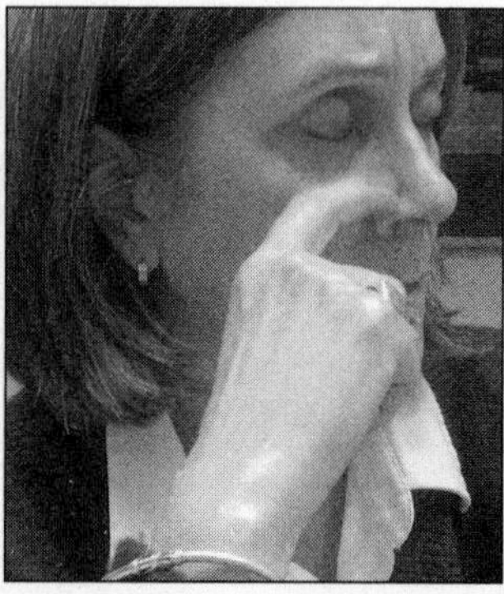

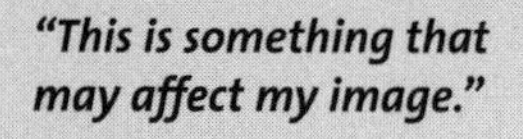

"This is something that may affect my image."

"Something bothers me about what this person is showing me."

The relationship between our own image and the left half of our nose seems well proven. But "image" has multiple meanings. Here are several examples: A man, filmed after a tsunami, scratches his left nostril while relating how he crossed an Indonesian village completely naked; an important French actor makes the same movement while admitting that he comes from a very small provincial town; a man explains his desire to have a boy and make him into an athlete and his disappointment when his wife gave birth to a girl. (He even told the anecdote twice in front of the cameras and made the same movement both times!) *To show himself* strolling around completely naked, *to show* that one was not properly trained for the theater, *to show* that you had a girl when what you really wanted was a boy—these are several different ways of conveying a "tarnished" image. In this context, the image is all that has to do with how we portray ourselves: being ourselves![19]

The right nostril itches when another person's image, that is to say what is not ours, disturbs or bothers us. If the person to whom you are speaking is bothered by you, bored by the part of you that makes a "blemish," by scratching his nose, he "scratches" that blemish. An interesting fact to note: A person who scratches his nostril often has his mouth closed, as if he is holding back some feeling, without a doubt because he is thinking, "This doesn't smell very good."[20]

Some authors make the nose a sexual organ, as if touching it amounts to the same thing as touching one's genitals. Hundreds of scratches that were analyzed in light of their contexts demonstrate, however, that this is not possible. There is hardly a 5 percent chance that scratching around or near the nose could lend itself to a sexual interpretation. The authors were mistaken in good faith since the hand goes naturally toward the nose when taboo subjects, ones that are not easily spoken about in public, are tackled: someone's salary raise, for example, and more generally, his private life and his property. It is certain that in the context of one's private sexual life, with the trail of shame that often tags along, the hand moves quickly to the center of the face, but it is better to read the nose and sexuality separately.

The Upper Lip: A Mouth above the Mouth

The upper lip is like a second mouth above the mouth. It emphasizes authority.

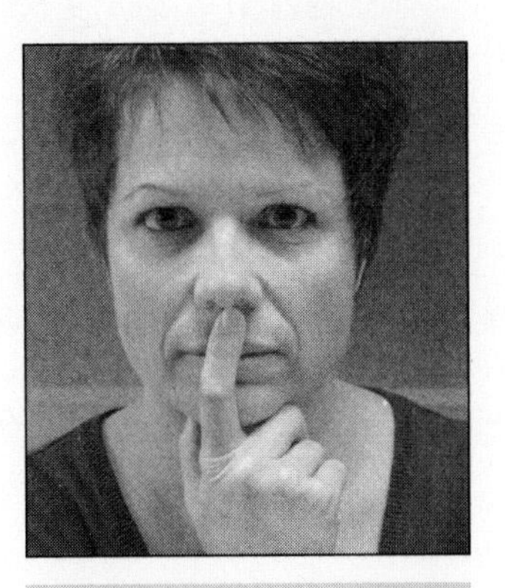

"As an authority on the subject, I know what I'm saying."

The area on the right side of the upper lip rises when the person thinks someone else is abusing their own power or authority. The person has the tendency to start scratching and thinks: *Who does he think he is?* It is rare to see this gesture made by someone who lacks authority in conversation.[21] The hand goes to the left side of the upper lip when a person is rather proud of himself, positive, when he affirms his superiority over another. On the other hand, you scratch the right half of the upper lip when the authority of another, or what they say or do, poses a problem and you must tell them so.

Someone who wants to speak up places his hand naturally and unconsciously on top of his mouth. The atmosphere is then one of taking symbolic power.

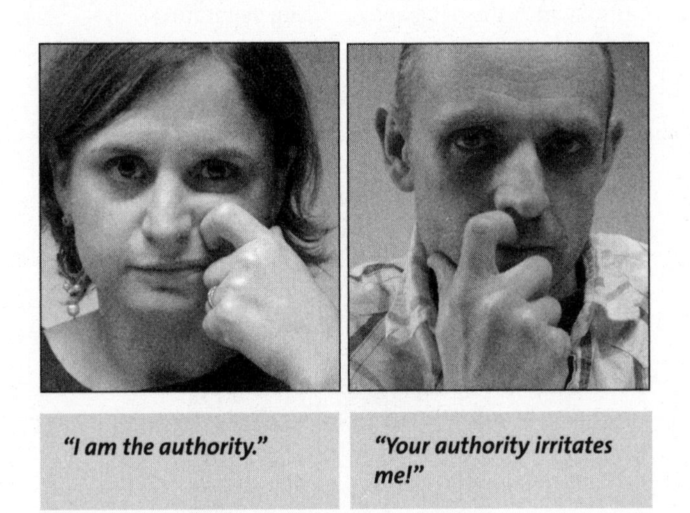

"I am the authority."

"Your authority irritates me!"

When the woman scratches the left side of her upper lip she is asserting that she is the legitimate authority in the situation. She is responsible for setting the rules and that is why she scratches the left rather than the right.

When this gesture is made above the right upper lip, the situation is different. We can see, in the photo on the right, the man has just heard an argument that he finds offensive. His natural authority lets him put the person who made the argument back in his place.

The hands also return to the middle of the upper lip in positive situations. This area, called the peaks of Cupid's bow, tingles when greed is insinuated. Behind power relationships, a wish takes hold; the power of one over another enters the heart of human relationships and transforms them into relationships of seduction.

This itch is clearly more present in hierarchies of power or knowledge (e.g., a doctor-patient relationship, expert-novice, etc.).

The Mouth Obstructs and the Mouth Is Gluttonous

The mouth, from birth, gobbles up the world in the form of food; it is also with our mouths that we engulf the ones we kiss and are swallowed whole by those who kiss us, but it is through shouting, by opening up, that our inner worlds are thrust out. For all these reasons, the mouth needs a chaperone and the hand seems to be, again, an already predetermined natural lookout.

A hand on the face protects the person who takes refuge behind it.

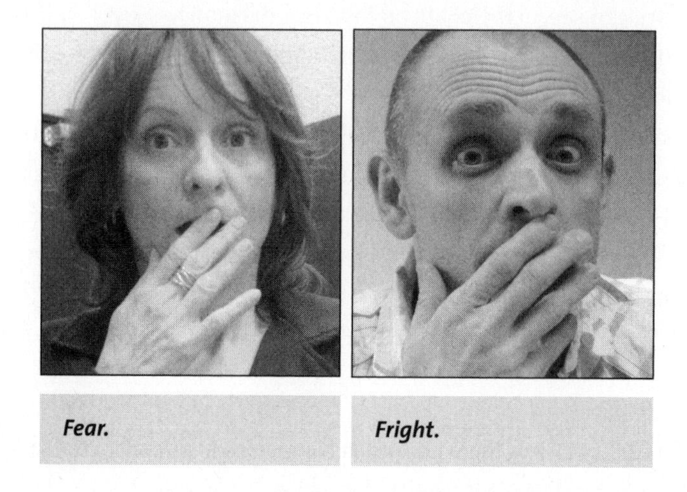

Fear.

Fright.

When fear is very strong, the hand can close the mouth, naturally, so as not to let in the source of fright.

A hand on the mouth also allows us to cut ourselves off from others, so we do not have to speak.

Turning inward.

Negative emotions.

A hand gets placed in front of the mouth and the eyes look away from the other person as soon as the atmosphere becomes heavy. People retreat thus into their inner worlds. They blink fewer times and they lower their eyes. But a hand can also be placed in front of the mouth when the atmosphere is light.

Turning inward.

Positive emotions.

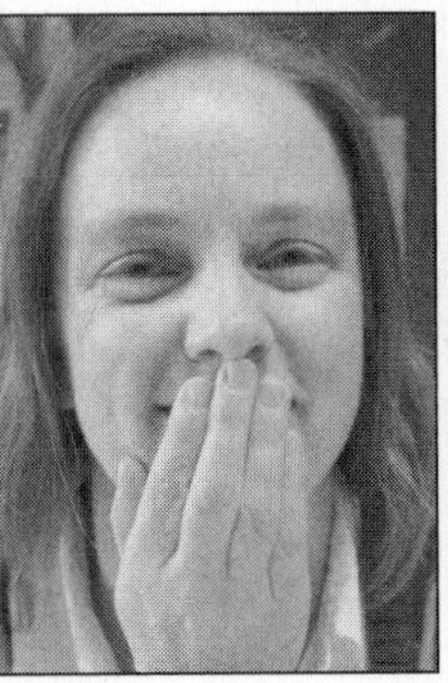

Good manners prohibit staying in prolonged eye contact with someone when discomfort creeps into an atmosphere of openness. In these conditions, a hand in front of the mouth warns that a distance has been introduced and becomes an excuse for the eyes to remain connected to the other person's.

The position of the palm of the hand also gives us some indication. A person who cuts herself off from her environment inverts the curvature of her wrist. This creates a break to take into account the latest possible objections before generally giving approval.

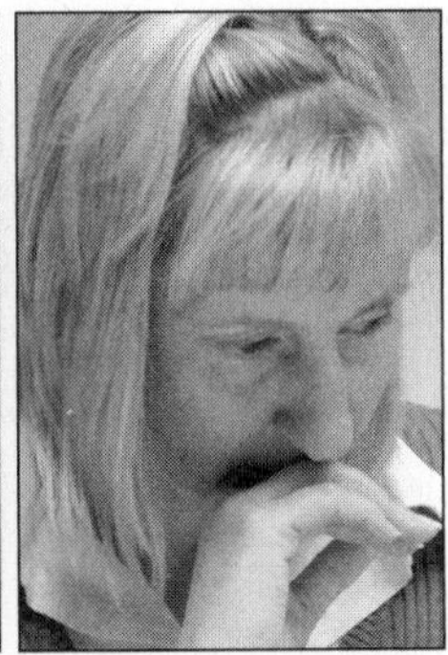

It is important to know that when a conversation is already full of too many distractions, the observed person in this attitude needs to turn inward to make a point.

Finally, the mouth is an obvious area of sensuality. A hand passes over the lips and the messages that come from them are generally very gentle: These gestures are not all unconscious. They are, above all, different from other messages. These messages are micro-caresses.

An openness, seduction.

The mouth is half-open and unobstructed. The lower palpebral fissures (muscles under the eyes) are raised high and are slightly rounded. This gesture is an overwhelmingly positive micro-caress. Let us note, just the same, that we are only interested in unconscious gestures for our discussion and that these signs of sensuality are not always unconscious.

Other gestures involving the hand and the mouth together are visible, such as, for example, when one says "Shhh!" by placing the index finger in front of mouth. But these gestures are too highly cultural to be discussed in this book. They are part of a system of learned signs and can therefore be distorted. Different from one group of people to another, these gestures are not of interest to our discussion. This question is addressed in Part Three.

The Jaw, the Chin, and the Hand

Hands, driven by nervousness, are placed on the chin. When an additional level of annoyance is identified, they will move to the jaw.

"This person irritates me."

"It annoys me to act this way."

The beard area tickles us, whether we have a beard or not, whether we are a man or a woman.[22] Itching is six times more likely on the right side of the face than on the left, which is hardly surprising since it corresponds to aggression that is provoked by another, and the representation of this lodges itself in the left hemisphere of the brain.[23] We therefore have a tendency to politely reject it by scratching the right side of the beard area.

On the left side of the face, nervousness is, on the contrary, the result of our own actions. We blame ourselves for having acted the way that we did, so we scratch. For example, a man scratches his left cheek when his wife reminds him that in order to get on the highway he must turn right at the intersection. He is irritated, very aware of not having a very good sense of direction.

Near our cheeks, where our teeth are strong and our jaw is powerful, aggression expresses itself without restraint, but near our chin, aggression gives way to caution and doubt gives way to questioning.

This man is doubtful. His situation is uncertain or ambiguous. He listens while scratching his chin. Other visible signs on the face will be indicators needed to know his real emotion, because doubt can spring up in many different circumstances.

A hand on the chin, if the wrist is bent or turned toward another person, generally signifies that this person is in a good mood. He has placed his hand on his face to try to put on a brave face but he is very open.[24]

ATTITUDES OF LETTING GO, OF RELAXING

Even more than the chosen arm, the position of the wrist is a guaranteed indication of mental attitude. The wrist tends to harden or become firmer, or will become stiff if the body is rebelling, regardless of the otherwise openness of the face.

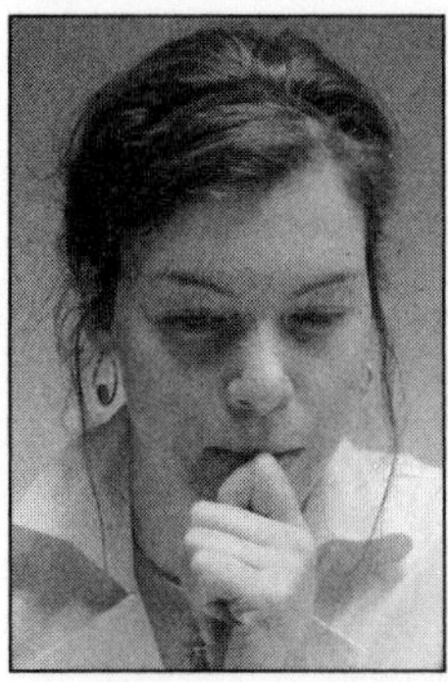 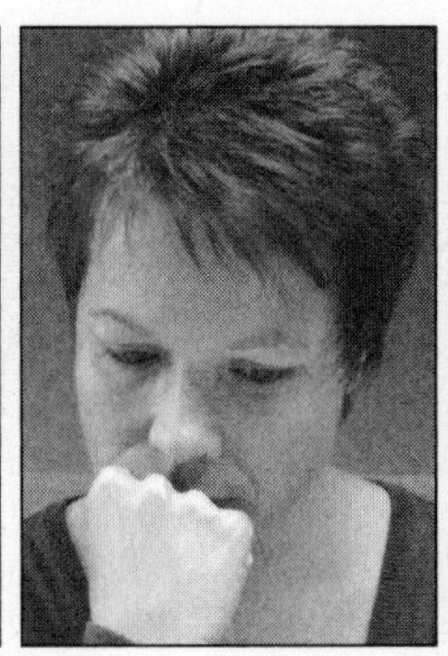  

The tension in these people is perceptible in the rigidity of their wrists.

When wrists stiffen, there is more tension in the body and it is visible in the joints.

The Hand and the Ears

The ears are often affected when spoken words have an emotional content. We pull on our earlobes when hearing positive words to help them sink to the back of our eardrums, and we block negative words with our hands. In this area more than others, it is important to observe the place that is scratched, because the meaning evoked can vary depending on the situation. We put our hands on our ears to avoid hearing what is not our business. We close our eyes to what we want to avoid seeing, and, likewise, we "close our ears" when a topic "irritates" them.

The left ear reminds us of our personal history and the inside of the right ear itches when the discussed events are more distant or external.

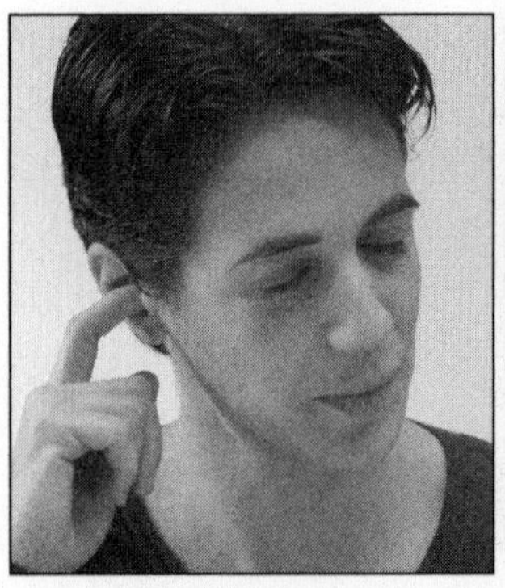

"I will not permit this information that is outside of myself and that annoys me to enter my ear."

"This information bothers me personally; I won't let it in."

The observation of hand movements around the ears reminds us of what Alfred Tomatis[25] established as the distinction between the right ear and the left. A child, in the first months of his life, hears the wavelengths of his mother's voice, and of women's voices in general, much more distinctly than those of his father. Deeper voices are detected later, around the age of six months. The right ear symbolizes listening to the outside world. Visual observations allow us to say with certainty that a person feels an itch in her right ear when she rejects problems that are outside of herself and that she does not want to take into consideration.

Touching one's ears gives off an impression of composure. There are thus situations when a person appears to be scratching an ear when she doesn't really feel an itch! The next time you scratch your ear, ask yourself if it is really bothering you! In fact, it is possible to observe this situation in the following photo.

Nonchalantly, the person who is scratching may turn away from the other person to think. This attitude is, of course, unconscious.

Be wary of this gesture![27] Let's admit that the use of the other hand would have been more logical. But this would be forgetting the secondary functions of scratching: to give off an impression of composure, to get out of a tight spot, to not remain passive without actually moving. The hand from the opposite side lets a person stretch, move away from the the other person, find an alternative to what is happening, a way out.

Itching in the ears also serves to reinforce positive messages.

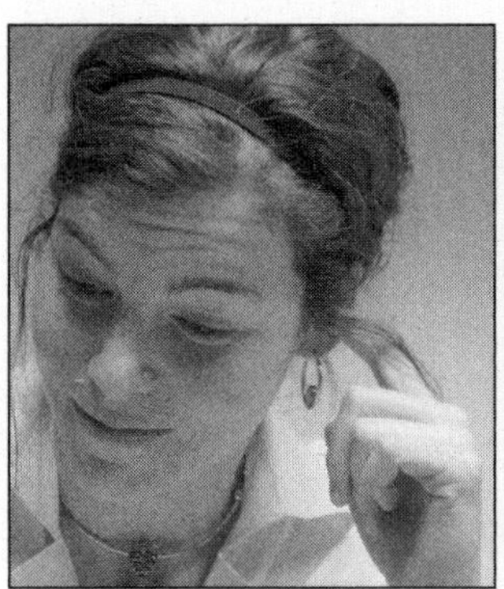

"What I am hearing pleases me." Personal involvement.

"I listen with pleasure to what someone is telling me."

Sometimes words flow into the ears. Scratching is then replaced by a micro-caress. The choice of the ear that is touched lets us determine if the information is personal or not, and the accompanying hand movement, if the person rejects or, on the contrary, welcomes it. All the other signs only indicate other nuances.

Scratching the body or the face is an expression of repressed emotions.

In order to understand which repressed emotion the person is feeling when they scratch, we must take into consideration:

1. **the side of the face that itches (right or left);**
2. **the exact sensory area where the hand is placed;**
3. **the choice of hand; and**
4. **the direction of the hand.**

CHAPTER 10

The Torso Is Our Armor

Repressed emotion is very visible on the torso. A hand that pauses on the neck, the chest, or the stomach makes it palpable. Emotion becomes a shield and all the more vivid when a person does not say what he is feeling. Nonverbal language therefore substitutes verbal language with remarkable efficiency on the torso. Like a butterfly choosing one flower rather than another, the hand is not placed by chance on an armpit, a breast, the chest. These motivations seem unconscious but their route allows us to get to the source of the present desire in the brain that directs it.

Emotions Blocked in the Neck

The neck is the royal way used by emotions to reach the brain. Chokepoints—and there are many—caused by negative emotion result in a "lump in the throat," and those caused by positive emotion result in "shortness of breath." But whether it is nice out or raining, micro-fixations, micro-caresses, and scratching let us follow the trail of hidden emotions on a person's body.

The hand goes to the neck to calm oneself down and let air through. This gesture conveys the "lump in the throat" phenomenon.

When a hand moves under the throat and presses into it, it is because a negative emotion is being repressed. In the picture above, the man in this position is discussing a controversial subject that makes him uncomfortable. His hand motion is unconscious but he would not have had this reaction if he were discussing a less controversial subject.

"I am the one wearing the tie, so I have the decision-making power. You better not forget it."

The neck is at the top of the body. People who grab their clothes here—their tie, for example, a true "organ of authority" from white collar to blue collar—show that they are "at the head."

The tie is kind of like, for the adult man, a substitute for the genitals on which he pulled, as a child, to reassure himself. Here are several observed examples: A young journalist is questioned by the chief anchor during a televised information bulletin. The news anchor does not fail to place his fingers on the knot of his tie several times, letting us understand that he finds the young journalist very sure of himself, a little too much so perhaps . . . A president of the French Republic during a difficult press conference reaffirms his authority with this same gesture. We can figure out, due to this gesture, that the question that has just been asked is more delicate than it appears, which is why he needs to reassure himself.

When people pull on their clothes, it is because the conversation is about to become "soft"; they get the feeling they have let themselves go a bit too much. People grab their collars for this reason.

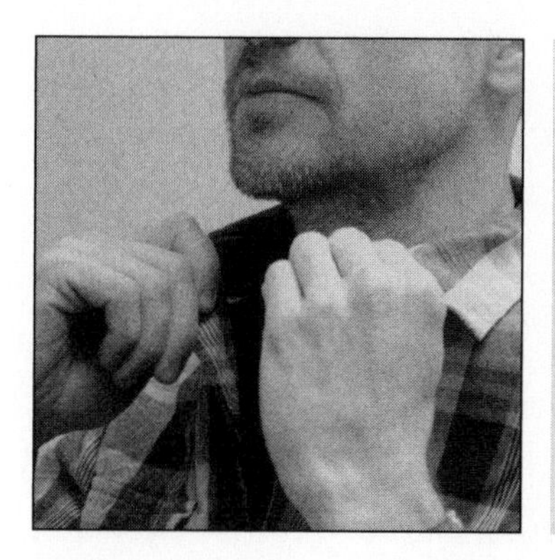

"I am rearranging my clothes: I am not just anybody and you should remember that."

The situations in which we pull on our clothes as if we want to smooth them out are always very serious and imprinted with dignity; these situations are not relaxed.[1]

The neck itches when our emotions are looking for a way out.

In the preceding situations, the brain gave orders to the hand to move toward the neck. But from the moment you scratch yourself, the relationship inverts. It is the neck that *asks* to be scratched. The person who pulled on the collar of his shirt could just as well have pulled on his jacket. The hand, governed by the brain, arranged for other strategies, but that is not true in the case of itching. The neck gives the order to the hand to intervene at this exact spot to relieve the itch. The hand doesn't have any thoughts of its own so it must inevitably scratch. Previously, the hand held a function; here it has become a tool for the body.

The Neck in Speech

The left side of the neck itches when we are creating a relationship with someone else. We are waiting for an opportunity to communicate.

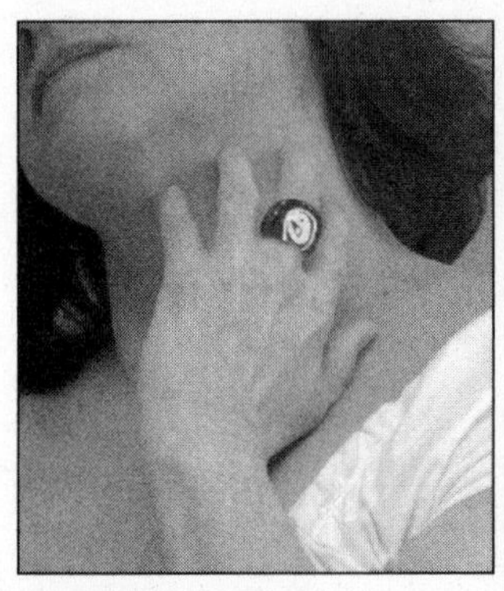

"I am going to talk about it as soon as I can."

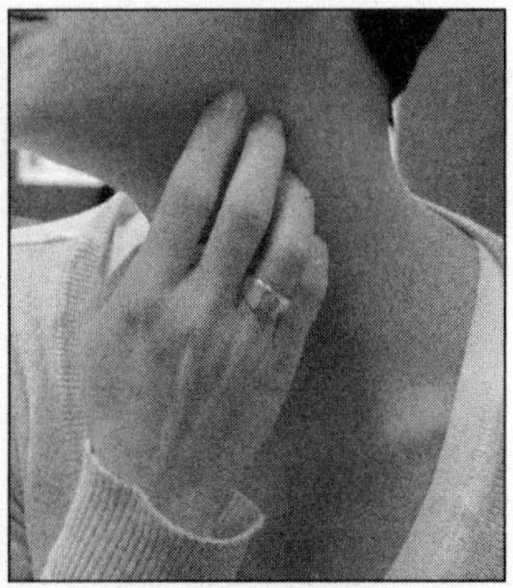

"I must pay attention to my wording."

These two people have things to say; they would like to speak. In the second situation, the right hand intervenes. It is not the most ergonomic hand. It crosses the body and protects it. This person will be more nuanced, less direct, and more willing to stake out her territory.

It is surprising to see at what point the context is different on the right side of the neck. On the left, the hand conveys the desire (prevented) from speaking, but the atmosphere is often good-natured; people seek to put their two cents into the conversation. When the need to scratch is felt on the right, serious people speak seriously to each other about things that, most of the time, bother them. The climate is rougher, and laughter, when there is any, simply allows the atmosphere to relax. The general context is tense, the words negative, and there are signs of closing up on the face and body over the course of the conversation.[2]

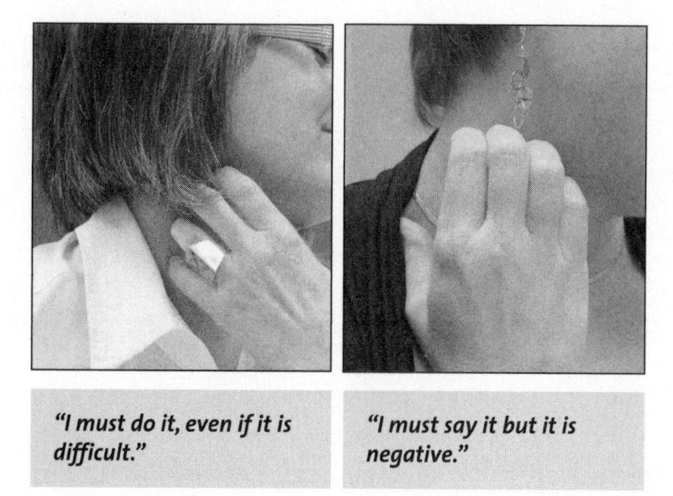

"I must do it, even if it is difficult."

"I must say it but it is negative."

On the right side of the neck, the general climate is symbolic of violence. This is less due to the current atmosphere of communication and more because of the words that trigger this type of itch.

The Nape of the Neck: To Say Something Indirectly

When a person feels an itching on the left side of the back of the neck, the atmosphere is often one of secrets. It is the right hemisphere—the one that creates connections—that has given the order, whether the movement is at the front or the back of the body. It is a matter of staying connected (left) but bypassing (behind) in order to advance—doing things in a roundabout manner. Some situations demand it or rather, to be more exact, some people think that they do. They believe that by bypassing something, paradoxically, they will advance quicker.[3] They could, for example, want to transmit a message without knowing how to go about it; or want to say to someone how much they appreciate them but are prevented from doing it too openly by indiscreet ears; or during an investigation, they might be ready to collaborate with the investigator but not know how to tell him that they know who the guilty person is without appearing to betray him.

"I have to pass my message on in a roundabout way."

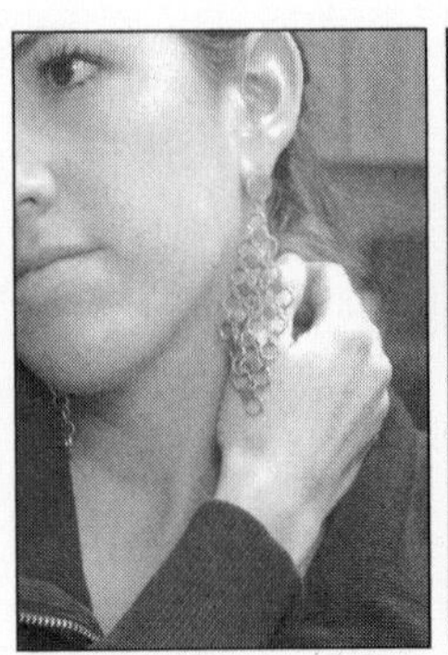

This indirect desire to get closer to another person often takes the form of a micro-caress at the left side of the nape of the neck. Excitement has given way to sensuality—the desire to speak and to move closer.

A person feels an itch on the right side of the nape of her neck when she does not want to communicate what is being asked of her. She searches for a strategy to get away. Scratching herself permits her to be diverted.

"I do not want to talk about it. I must find a way out."

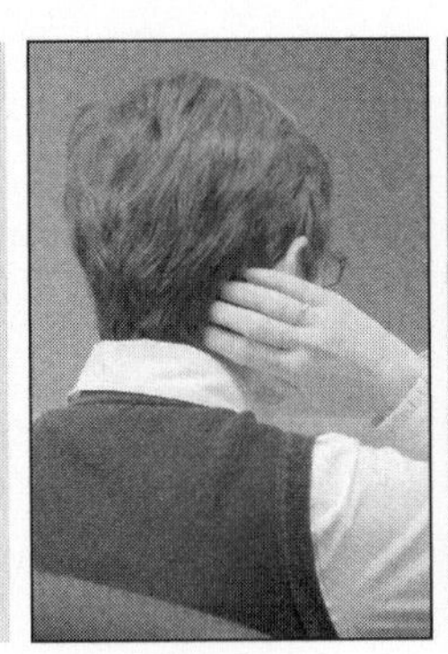

People scratch the right side of the nape of their neck when the context is negative: They are annoyed and do not intend to talk any more.

They are not always conscious of the emotional discrepancy that separates them from others. The same situation can be experienced calmly by one person while being taken badly by the other. This happens more frequently than one might think in professional hierarchical environments.[4] Unspoken things are implied simply because some things cannot be said, or rather because people believe that they cannot be said. Scratching is the red light that warns us to be more attentive to the person who scratches.

The Torso and the Chest: The Self as a Gift or as a Refusal

Hands are led toward the chest, the torso, and the armpits when a feeling of warmth is needed. This is the case with the singer who looks out at his audience, with the mother who sees her children leaving, with the person who implores you to believe him. These gestures are made from the heart of one person to the heart of another.

Hands connect on the chest, symbolizing the connection of the outside to the inside. But they just have to be separated a little to convey a whole other kind of message.

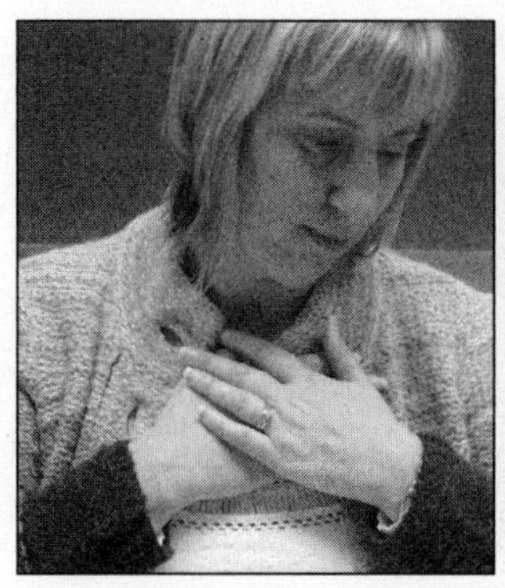

"I will keep you in my heart."

"I am proud of myself... Look at me!"

Awareness of the existence of the torso, the area of the ego, comes before our first lessons. An infant of six months, desirous of being held by his parent when he is in bed, will pull on his pajamas, in this area, to express this need.[5] This reality is also observed among preliterate people. Far from typically individualistic societies, the Papuans of New Guinea indicate "I" by pointing to their torso. The great apes themselves, whose brains began to form 400 million years before our era, share this behavior with humans.[6] Human beings do not learn that the center of the torso is the ego; they just know it.

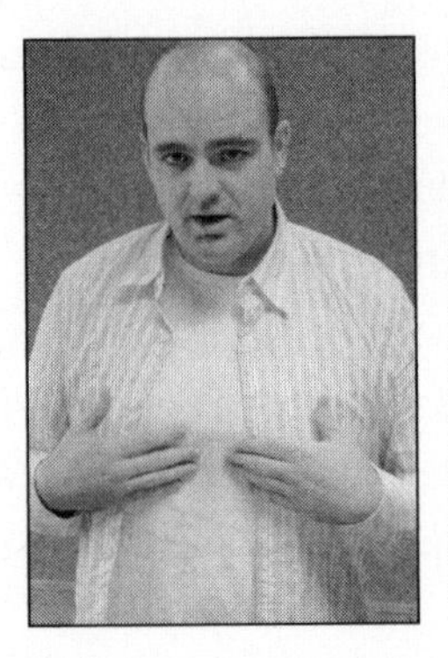

"Me."

Great apes strike their chests with their fists to show that they are dominant. The human says "I" while pointing to his chest. He does it consciously and unconsciously when he speaks.

Deciphering the expression "I" in the area of the chest becomes much more fascinating when the exact spot where a hand is placed is observed more attentively.

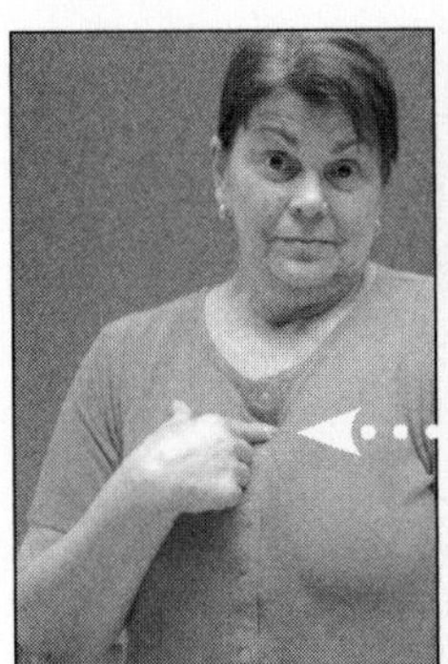

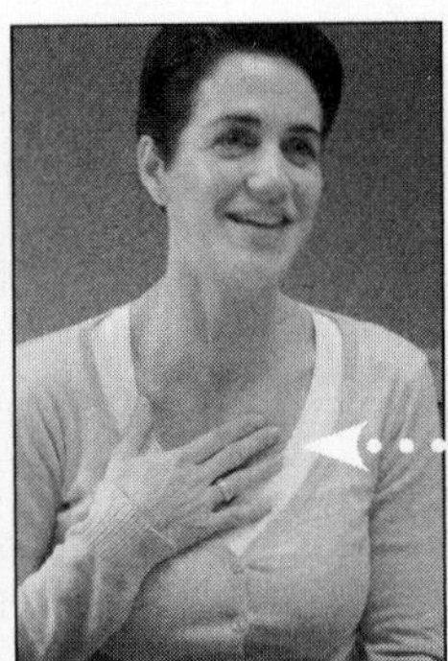

These hands are placed very high under the throat. These people consider themselves first; they put themselves in front, very high on their list. The lower the hand is, the more empathetic they are to others.

Unconsciously, in a relationship, people express "me," "I," "me myself," and "me . . . mine" with these gestures. The height of the gesture is always significant and conveys their level of self-esteem. The higher the hand is placed on the torso, the more they expect to be flattered.

People in situations we have observed, who have the sense that they must put themselves more forward, have a tendency to scratch their torso. For example, a man listens to one of his friends tell an anecdote that concerns him. He feels that it should be him telling the story instead because it is *his* story. It is possible that he scratches his torso and is showing his friend, with this gesture, that he dare not put himself forward.

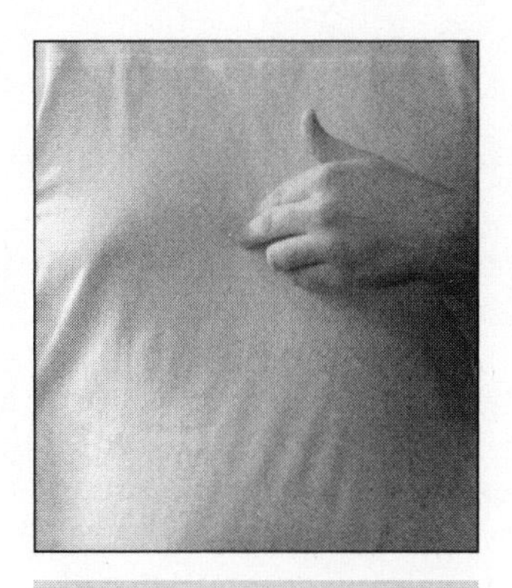

"I must put myself more forward."

In the photo above, this man scratches the area of the ego; he stimulates it because he has difficulty projecting his ego toward others.

The Breasts: An Expression of Giving . . .

Breasts produce and give. Feminine, they give milk and pleasure. The "gift" is thus present at the heart of every itch around the breasts, whether the person is male or female. Breasts are stimulated in all problems having to do with generosity: ours and that of others. It is around the breasts that a number of psychological conflicts connected to the idea of gifts are observed.[7]

With regard to the breasts, the left and the right of the body are not in the same boat. The left leads the person to his own history, to his own generosity, while the right, on the other hand, leads him toward the other, to what the alter ego demands, and that which cannot or does not want to concede to it. From the left breast toward the right, the hand glides from generosity toward its limitations.[8]

"I have had enough of giving. I am going to dissociate myself."

"I would like to get closer, to give more of myself."

The person who feels an itch near her left breast is living an internal conflict. She would like to give more but cannot resolve to do so. That is why, without there being a physical cause, she scratches herself. The breast is an erotic area but here it loses its sexual vocation. This connection is more fundamental.

Connected to the left hemisphere, the right breast has a different status. An itch is felt when a person perceives that she must give more, whether it is because of her role, her function, or her "mission," but she just doesn't want to. In the specific case of the photograph above to the right, this woman is listening to another speak about the status of women. Everything divides them: social rank, ideas, personal image. This woman is invested in a trade union struggle, the other in fashion. They are even more separated by a real gap in generations and see society generally in a different way. The woman on the left cannot stand what the other person is saying. She disengages herself by scratching.

We also feel itchy when we are alone! In fact, we are never really alone. The people who matter to us are present in our thoughts and our imaginations. The same principal cerebral areas are activated, whether we carry out an action or we imagine it.[9] What would be more surprising is if we didn't feel itchy when we were alone!

The Abdomen and the Pelvis: Materiality

Halfway between the top of the head and the toes, the stomach that is stroked, caressed, or scratched is stimulated when a discussion turns to possessions, ownership. A person who places her hands on her stomach is often proud of what she possesses, but it can also be that she is envious of what she does not have.

The Stomach: Possessiveness

Pregnant women caress their stomachs more or less consciously, thereby coming in contact with their babies. Other than during these specific periods, they touch their bellies less frequently than men do, tending more to forget about their stomachs. Men, on the contrary, especially if their stomachs are prominent, are not afraid to caress them, discreetly or not, in public. Satiated, their hands linger there, thereby conveying their satisfaction. Thanks to this area that is positioned at the center of the body, they impose their presence in the middle of a group or on another person. People who stroke their stomachs always want to be perceived as central characters.

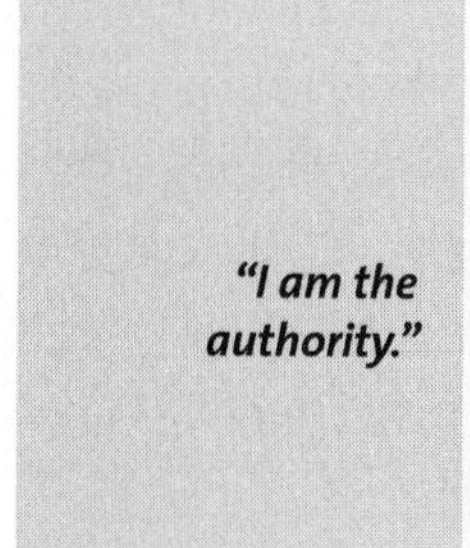

Hands on the hips also convey authority. The body stands like this to symbolize authority. The beltline is in an area at the center of the body that shows ownership and power, what the tie seems to represent on the level of speech. Again, as always, pants might coincidentally be pulled up simply because they have fallen down slightly! We don't always have to look for another explanation at all costs. Observing people lets us see rather quickly the difference between when their pants are falling down and when they want to show their authority.

"I pull up my pants to show you that I am the authority."

"I wear a tie; I am the one who decides what to say."

The stomach is at the center of our possessions. The person who touches it is proud of his own. The hand placed on the stomach makes a path from one to the other. A miser does not stroke his stomach. He is too afraid that you will take what he owns from him. He doesn't brag about his possessions; he does not show them off. The man's hand, in the photo on the following page, touches the center of his stomach, near the area of his navel. He is not afraid to be or to become, during this micro-caress, the navel of the world, to say what he thinks, or to take the place that he feels is his: in the center.

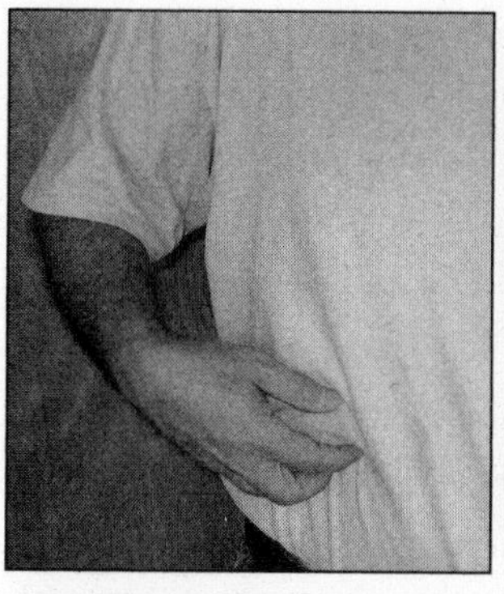

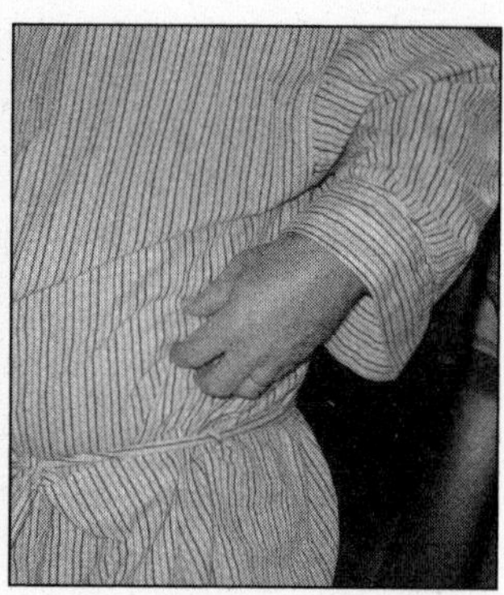

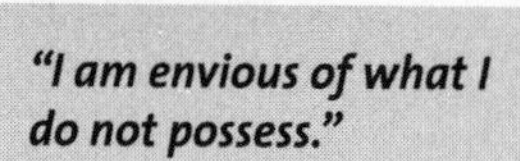

"I am envious of what I do not possess."

"I am proud of my possessions."

A person who feels an itch near his stomach, whether at the center or to the left, is proud of what he has but seems to defend, by scratching, this pride. He feels what's at stake with regards to the specific possession and scratches because he is excited. This situation is approximately four times more frequent among men than among women.

The hand goes toward the right side of the stomach when a person is in front of possessions that are not his or because he feels dispossessed: His things have been or are going to be taken away. For example, a man notices his neighbor getting into a new car that is more beautiful and more powerful than his. He says to him, "Ah, you have changed your car?" while touching the right side of his stomach. He is not openly conscious of it but his body already knows that he is jealous.[10]

The Pelvis

The pelvis is the area of sexuality par excellence. It has a specific status since a hand will not settle there without deviating from the rules set by good manners. For this reason, it would be logical to think that the hands would avoid the pelvis altogether, but certain observations cause us to be more circumspect. Women do not pass their hands over the central area covering their genitals, while, though not common, this has been observed in men. A little boy reassures himself by pulling on his genitals and masturbating; this is a normal phenomenon.[11] Some men also comfort themselves unconsciously by stroking their genitals. They do it on two occasions: either, when in certain countries, in the presence of the fairer sex, or in the hierarchical universe in which the connection to virile power is a form of approval. In these contexts, scratching the genitals allows him to assert his strength, his virility, his dominance. When two men are face to face, the one who touches this area shows the other that he is allowed to do anything he wants, that he is the boss. We might ask ourselves what problem is hidden behind this unconscious desire to show off his strength, but that is not the object of our discussion.

It is also important to note that this gesture is not very different from touching the knot of the tie, in white-collar circles[12] . . .

The hand is placed on the neck when dealing with messages that are connected to what must be said or kept silent.

The torso is the area of the ego. It is linked to all the issues of the assertion of being.

Breasts are linked to the giving and the refusal of a gift. The left and the right have, according to this point of view, quite a different status.

The stomach and the pelvis express materiality. The hands are placed there in all matters of ownership and they show desires as much as fears in this gesture.

CHAPTER 11

The Back: "The Other Side" of the Body

The back is a symbolic area that has become popularized for having a bizarre reputation. From the person who *talks behind someone's back* because he is not brave enough to face her, to the one who *gives the cold shoulder* because he gets fed up with having *taken everything lying down* because everything was *put on his back*, to the one who *went behind his back* and the one who feels he's been *stabbed in the back*, the back often having *broad shoulders*. It is not really the most pampered part of the body, and the hand, in these conditions, generally goes there to avoid facing something. But here again the rule has its exceptions, because once again, the two hemispheres split up the left and the right side of the body.

The Trapezius: Holding "Too Much Weight"

The equation is simple: back = can't face it = run away. These messages are as easy to interpret as they are difficult to see when the other person is facing us!

At the top of the back, the trapezius is stimulated as much by concrete tasks as by more abstract ones. It contracts when we move the large Normandy wardrobe, concrete, but also contracts when the project seems too heavy "to carry," more abstract. The white-collar worker leaving work occasionally massages his trapezius muscles to relax them even though his pen is the only heavy thing that he has had to carry! In reality, he "carries" responsibilities, decisions that "weigh heavily." It is not surprising, then, that under these conditions, he needs to massage his trapezius at the end of the day.

The left trapezius does not have the same status as the right when faced with some burden. It is scratched when things are too heavy to carry but the desire to "bear it," to "hold up," is real. The contradiction between the desire to do and the awareness of a task's weight expresses itself as an itch.

"I want to help, but it is difficult to carry."

Different from other areas of the body, the trapezius is easily touched by both hands, so the unconscious choice of one hand over the other plays a role in the reading and interpretation of the gesture.

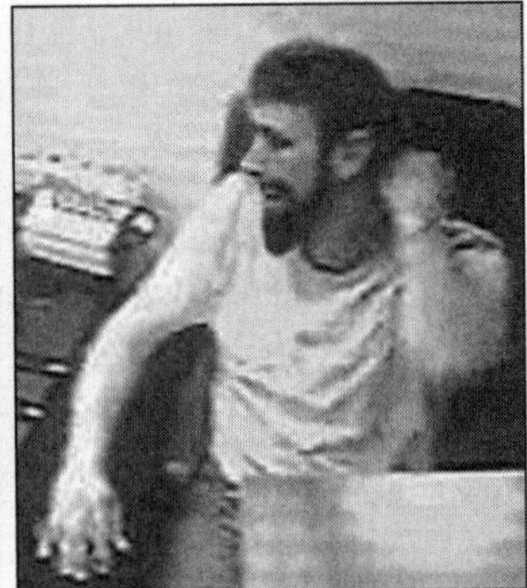

In the photo on the right, taken from footage of a police investigation, the person is innocent but knows who is guilty. He is also likely, in the eyes of the investigator, to be guilty himself! He asks himself what to do so that the investigation can move forward without becoming a "stool pigeon," "informer," "snitch." How far is he obligated to collaborate? He is facing a matter of conscience. His body shows that he has decided to cooperate. If not, he would not be experiencing an inner conflict and would not be scratching himself. He resists, still carrying the weight of responsibility on his trapezius that he has not yet transferred to the investigator, but it is only a matter of time, of opportunity. In the photo on the left, the right arm crosses the body and protects it, while in the other, the arm that is the closest to the itching, intervenes spontaneously. In fact, this man's collaboration will be spontaneous.

A person risks more by dissociating from the action to be taken when cerebral energy is directed toward the right trapezius. The general context is difficult. "It weighs too much!"

"I don't want to have to do it; it is too heavy."

Here, very concretely, this man disengages from the scientific hoax the woman to his left is describing.

A person disengages when faced with the weight of things. He puts the events, the situations, outside of himself. He is no longer as involved as when the left part of his body was engaged in the action.

The body is profoundly honest. It knows what is good for it and that what is good for it is also good for the whole human race. It is programmed to adapt to situations in everyday life and every one of its micro-reactions testifies to this.

The Shoulder Blades: Giving Oneself Magnitude

Underneath the trapezius, our shoulder blades help our arms move by giving range to gestures. A person feels an itch in her shoulder blades when she would like to hurry but she feels stopped in her tracks. From this point of view, the right and the left shoulder blade really distinguish themselves.

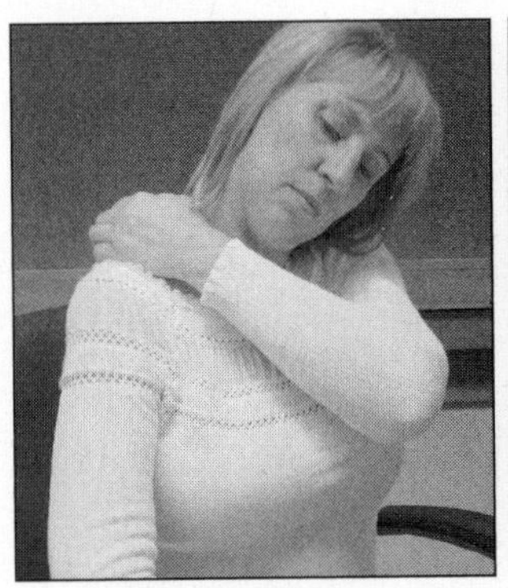

"This demands too much effort; I don't want to do it."

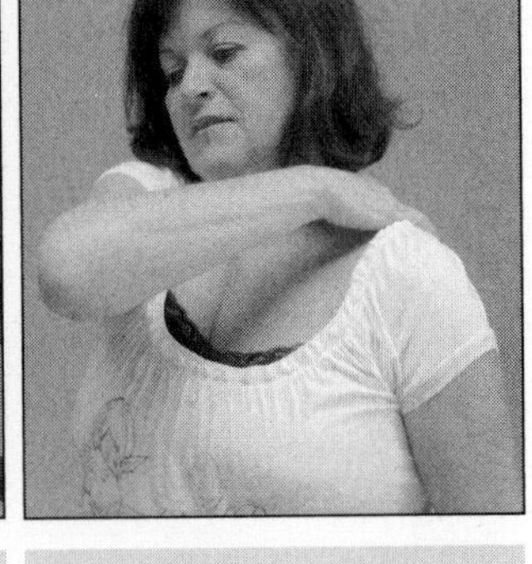

"We have lost enough time. We must hurry."

The left shoulder blade helps ready the arm that is necessary for the effort to work. Annoyed by a boring speech, a person who wants to interrupt can scratch herself here. Without fear of caricature, one can say that frequent scratching of the left shoulder blade is peculiar to hyperactive types.

An itch of the right shoulder blade occurs in very different situations, even opposite ones when a person is in a hurry to disengage. For example, a woman asks her friend, "Would you give us a hand painting our house tomorrow?" and he answers, "Yes, that's a good idea!" while scratching his right shoulder blade. He says yes because he is afraid of disappointing her but his body disengages, moves away. Deep down, he feels, without having clarified it in his mind, that he does not want to do it. Our knowledge of neurophysiological mechanisms explains this thought process.[1] Concretely, you can be more or less assured that this friend will find some frivolous pretext to put her off.

The Center of the Back: Existential Flight

The back is at the heart of being, or rather at the back of the heart of being! When a person feels an itch here, it is because he is looking for a way to flee in order to not engage.

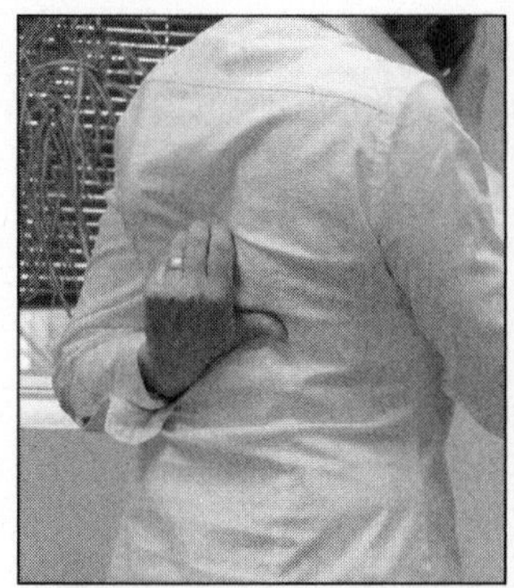

"I do not want to engage in this interaction, or even be here."

The two people above would like to get away. Their hands disappear from the other person's view in order to take refuge behind their backs; the hands are only a tool in this operation and could be replaced by any object. Some people, leaning against a wall, even scratch their back against it.

The Flank: Reacting Quickly

Lower down on the back, the hand can also move to the flank and the kidneys. At the flank, this is an expression of desire, but not so if on the kidneys.

The kidney is considered, from a nonverbal perspective, the area closest to the spinal column.

The flank is considered, from a nonverbal perspective, the side of an individual's back.

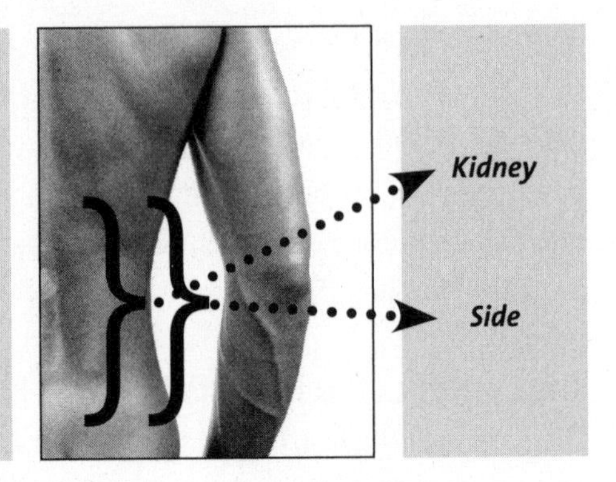

The left side is, from the tips of the hair to the toes, related to connections. Driven by the right hemisphere, the left hand strokes the left side, and the left side that summoned the hand because "it itched" responds to a desire for physical contact.[2] The person scratches himself then in order to get rid of[3] or soothe an emotion that is too strong.

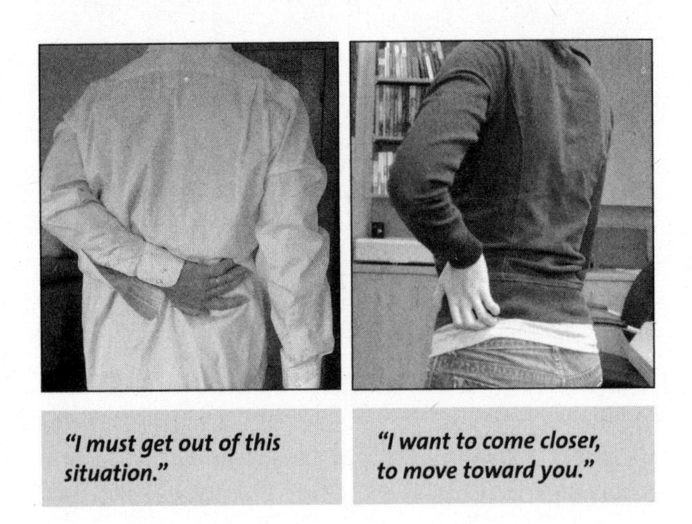

"I must get out of this situation."

"I want to come closer, to move toward you."

Some metaphors or sexual allusions are sometimes used in verbal speech along with this type of scratch[4] or micro-caress. Scratching gives off the impression of composure.

A human being feels an itch on the right side when he would like to leave, not physically, but rather to flee from a situation that, at that time, is generally negative. Simply changing the subject of conversation, for example, is sufficient to make the itch go away.

The Kidneys: The Fundamental Structures

When hands are placed on the kidneys, the weight of the world is implied. It is a heaviness that has a primarily existential cause.

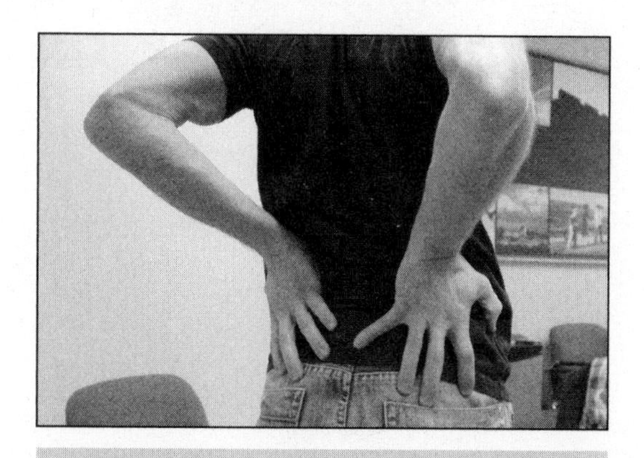

"The situation is difficult."

The kidneys are supported by the hands when faced with too much weight. The situation is so weighty that it could well cause "a back strain." The weight is not of the same nature as that felt in the trapezius area; it is instead an existential nature that the kidneys support. This heaviness affects the whole structure. When a person feels an itch over her right kidney, she decides to free herself of this weight by leaving. Take, for example, this exchange between two friends:

> "We should buy a sailboat together, don't you think?"
> "Good idea!"

The person scratches himself at this suggestion, helping us understand that the joint purchase is without a doubt not such a good idea. The weight of the commitment pushes him to run away rather than to participate in this shared purchase. Scratching tends to lessen the physical fear and recklessness of buying a boat. Let's not forget that scratching ourselves makes emotional areas atonic.[5]

A representative of the administration cannot stand what a social worker is saying and turns away from him while scratching himself.

Scratching allows us to get away, to give off an impression of composure, and, as in the photo above, to disengage from the conversation. Therefore, it has a pacifying role.[6] Here, the man moves away by scratching himself: His body becomes the actor and he does not have to voice his discomfort since he is physically experiencing it.

When a person feels an itch on the left, she is hiding the gravity of the situation that her body feels from herself. Example: Jack must organize a large demonstration and needs Catherine's support, who is not there; he says, "Well, that's funny, Catherine has not called me!" His burden is heavy but he doesn't want to flee. With his hand over his left kidney, he would like to hasten her arrival.

The Area of the Buttocks

Near the area of the buttocks, the weight of things, their price, and their materiality express themselves fully. The muscle in the buttocks bounces back, very obvious and very useful when we need to run. Strong itches that are felt there therefore prevent the desire to run.

The anal area delivers very interesting messages that are not always scatological. It is more taboo than the buttocks. Some causes that are purely physiological, like hemorrhoids, etc., can lead the hand there despite our discussion of itching. This is why we must take into consideration the verbal side of an interaction. Normally, people who discreetly scratch themselves in this area always speak of material difficulty and how much things cost. For example, during a family reunion, a brother says to his sister, the mother of three adolescents: "We could all go to the South this summer; there are package deals that are not that expensive. " The woman's hand, that disappears surreptitiously and discreetly behind her back indicates it would only be "not that expensive" for her relative. "Not expensive . . . my ass!" she thinks perhaps.

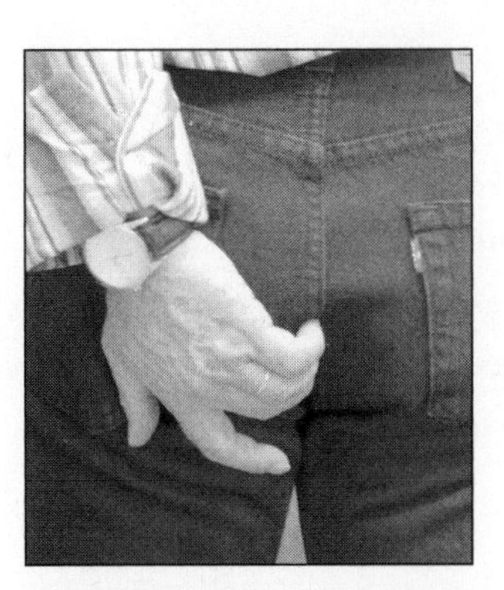

"I will not be able to give what they are asking of me. I don't have the means; this poses a problem for me."

Why does the hand go to the rear when material difficulties are brought up?

It is not possible to remember the entirety of one's own childhood. Now, without a doubt, we should look for the implementation of this itch between the ages of one and two years old. On the other hand, it suffices to have a child remember the strategies put in place in order to "potty train" him. For the first time in his life, at a transitional period in his psychomotor development, the child will have power over his parents! They are so happy when he makes his first "poopoo" in the toilet, that they are full of praise for him: "He is so nice, he left us a nice gift . . . he must leave this kind of gift in the pretty toilet more often . . ." The child understands that he has the power to make "gifts" each time that he wants to, by releasing his sphincter or not, and that giving these gifts brings power. He also discovers that he can refuse to do it and thus deprive his parents. Fantastically, the anal area is invested with the archaic connection to "material gifts." Later, everything points to this when dealing with money we cannot give, caught between the desire to give and the impossibility of doing so, the memory of this archaic situation leads our hand to this part of our bodies.[7]

The hand goes to the back when a person would rather leave than face something. From this perspective, the right and the left of the body have very different statuses.

The hand goes to the back during difficult situations, but the specific area that is touched allows us to understand that the person does not always flee from these difficulties.

CHAPTER 12

The Limbs: To Act

The arms are called upon for action. The brain sends them blood, and their electrodermal temperature increases, thereby allowing them to protect their owner in all difficult situations. At the same time, they are the links to affection and when we "take someone in our arms," our emotional investment exceeds the simple physical action. To take someone into one's arms is to experience an impulse of the heart. The arms and the forearms are not used in the same circumstances. Their action is regulated by the management of joints, thanks to which we become "articulated."

The Shoulders: For Support

The shoulders are not called upon without evoking an appeal to generosity. They "offer a shoulder" and symbolize solidarity.[1] Thanks to them, a person who has "wide shoulders" has his hand on the wheel. Shoulders are situated too high up on our bodies for our hands to go to them without a very specific reason.

More or less visible, depending on our specific morphologies, a very interesting small piece of bone, the acromion, is found at the top of the shoulder. The hand moves toward it when "hierarchy," "superiority," that which is "larger" is evoked . . .

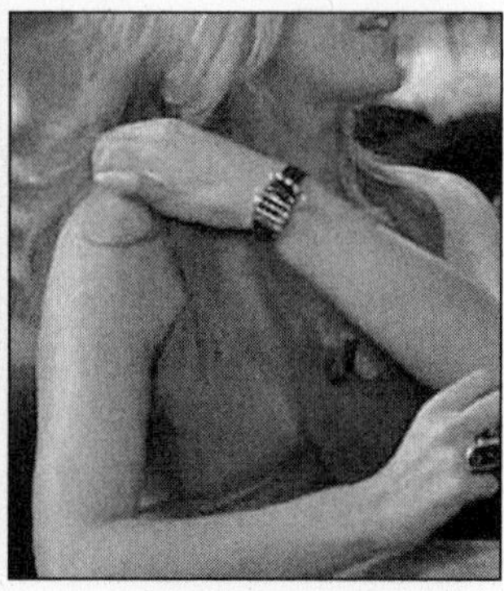

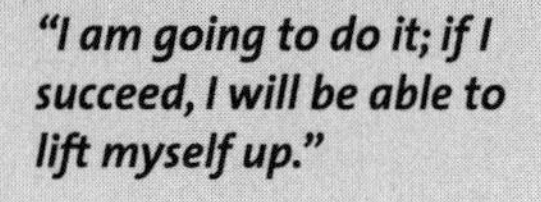

"I am going to do it; if I succeed, I will be able to lift myself up."

"I am afraid of not being up to what they want me to do."

When a person manipulates his left acromion, he is expressing his worry of hierarchy. He will have to surpass himself, be the bigger man than usual, but he has doubts.

In a filmed situation in the photo on the left, a person listens attentively to an investigator. She prepares to take a polygraph test (lie detector) that will clear her. While the investigator shows her how the device functions, she massages her left acromion mechanically, as if she could have done something else but didn't. Her body, or, more precisely, her limbic system, which is in direct contact with her body, has already anticipated the results and knows that she will come out stronger from this ordeal. Without that, her hand would not go to her left acromion. She stays in contact with the investigator and indeed, the device will prove her innocence.

It is very astonishing to see at what point the body, before the mind, is conscious of events to come. Scratching is the most immediate response but often precedes concrete awareness by several days.

A person who places her hand on the right acromion is dealing with something that is beyond her. She does not feel up to it. This situation can also happen when a hierarchical authority figure is present and puts her ill at ease. On the following page, on an American television show, a TV presenter is placed in a difficult situation, in spite of herself, with her co-presenter.

The left shoulder is the shoulder that helps. A spot tingles, directed by the brain's right hemisphere, signifying that the person feels like intervening, to support another.

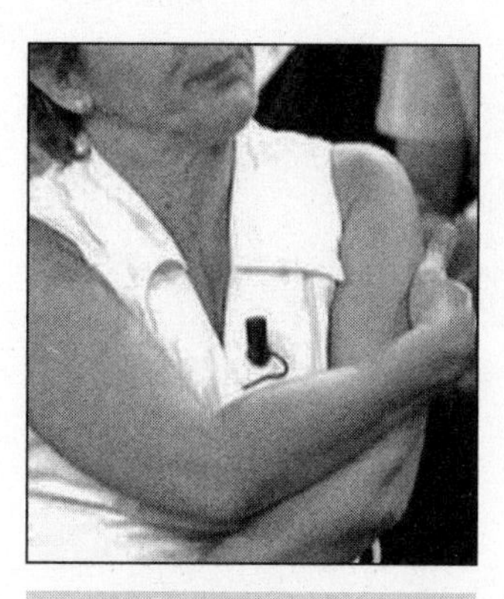

"I must bypass this problem in order to get closer."

The closer the itch is to the front of the left shoulder, the more the desire to immediately engage, to move forward with a helping attitude, to cooperate, is stronger. It is often because we dare not act that we scratch, thereby postponing any real action while still seeming active. Itching can also be felt in other places on the shoulder. On the back, the interpretation of this gesture is somewhat different.

When an itch is felt in the area behind the left shoulder, the principal difference is the atmosphere. Adversity forces us to find a roundabout strategy to achieve our ends. It is not enough to suggest it alone; we must truly bypass the problem, recoil in order to advance. A person scratches himself then with the opposite hand. Here, it is simply a question of limb flexibility.

Body messages of the right shoulder are of a different nature.

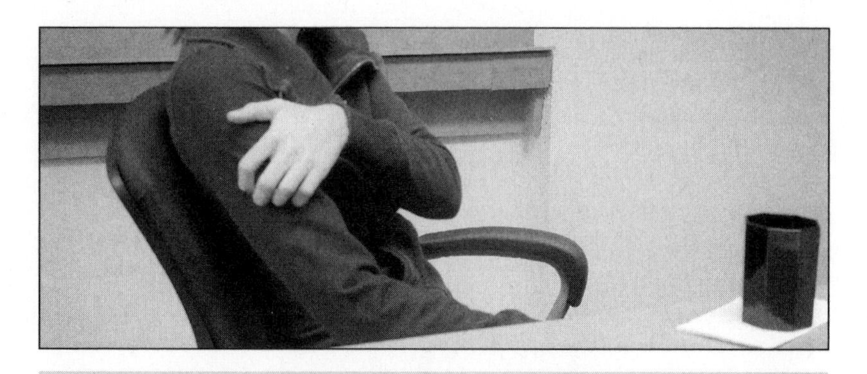

"I would like to stay out of this, so I don't have to help."

When the itch is on the right shoulder, a person feels that she has an interest to assume responsibility associated with helping, but she doesn't really want to help. If she directs her hand behind her shoulder, in a certain sense, she is giving in. This itch is classic when seduction is put at the heart of the communication process. In situations where one person is trying to seduce another, the one who refuses to participate in this game of emotional connection turns away with his hand. In the photo above, a person is trying to convince this woman of his good faith. Faced with the verbal stream of the person speaking to her, the exterior itch allows the young woman protect her body and throw the interaction off.

The Armpits

The brain, thanks to our thoughts, mobilizes the appropriate body areas.[2] Take for example a passerby to whom someone says: "Can you help me?" Desiring to do so, the passerby sends energy into his arms but he notices that it is unfortunately impossible for him to help. He therefore scratches an area associated with helping (the shoulder) and expresses without saying so his incapacity to "help." In fact, our hands take refuge in our armpits when we are powerless to help or to do.

Between the left armpit and the right, it is the context that especially changes which armpit is being scratched.

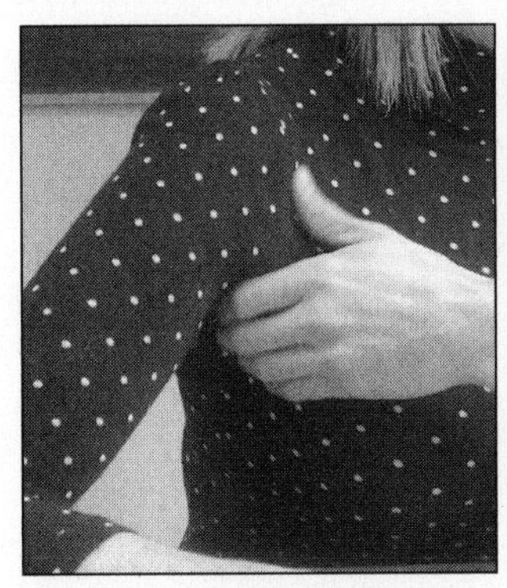

"I am powerless in the face of what is happening to me."

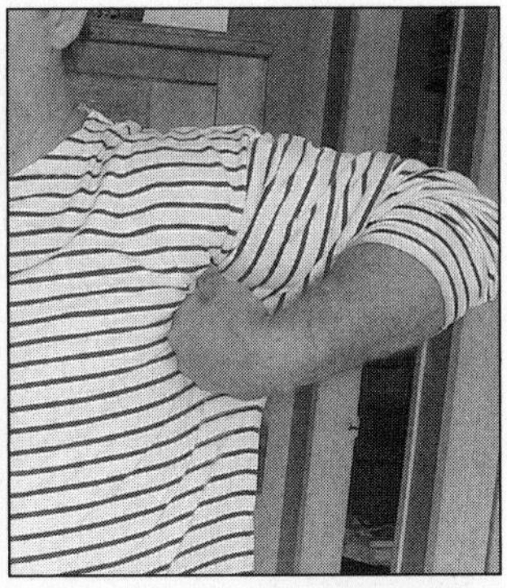

"I would like to help you but I don't really know how."

An itch in the right armpit shows an incapacity to act and takes place in generally negative contexts. Powerlessness is very poorly experienced. In the photo on the left, a woman who is guilty of stealing scratches her right armpit. This attitude is rarely observed in people who are innocent. The itch is there because of her conscience, which she recognizes. In the photo on the right, a man whose friend has asked him, "Will you come help me move in this weekend?" scratches his left armpit in a sign of powerlessness. His inability to give his friend a hand is real. A part of him feels like saying, "I'll do it!" but another part of him knows that it will be impossible. During this episode, the electrodermal temperature of the body part responsible for the action—the arm—has increased, mentally preparing him for action. By scratching himself under the left armpit he gets relief, and at the same time he stops the mental process that pushes his body to try and help.[3] The next time you get a "tingly" feeling in your armpit and you go to scratch yourself, ask yourself what thoughts come up.

The Collarbone: To Open Oneself Up

The collarbone, from the Greek *eteocle*, was defined by these ancient people as the key to the heart.[4] An itch at this spot, whether it occurs on the left or on the right, expresses generosity, the desire to give.

"I am ready to help."

"I have an interest in giving more."

People stroke or scratch their left collarbone in all situations in which they would be willing to give more than they are being asked to. For example, a son asks his father, "Dad, can you lend me $50?" The father gives the money to his son, who usually doesn't ask him for money. The father would have been prepared to give him more because he feels that his child is worried about money, and he doesn't know what's wrong.

When an itch is felt on the right collarbone, generosity is tinged with an interest to protect or reassure, and a distance is created between the two people interacting.

Biceps: The Emotional Connection

The hands move toward the biceps during emotional events. Their connection to the world is never very concrete. Concrete is what the forearms are good for. The arms, on the level of the biceps, have a mission of emotional proximity. Which arm that is used is dissociated from our interpretation.

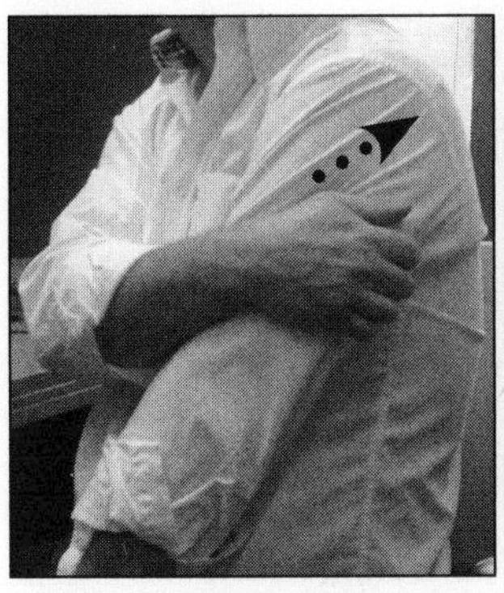

"It will be necessary to bypass this in order to get closer."

"I am trying to get closer."

The left arm is invested, touched, moved, turned, or pursued each time the expressed sensibility is highly sensitive. There is never an emotional exchange, a desire for possible affection, without the hand, at one time or another, settling here. It often moves toward the other person, going part of the way to meet him.

When the outside of the left arm itches, the nature of the person's desire is paradoxical: It protects and conquers at the same time. This itch is frequently observed in the political world. Present in all verbal jousting, it is visible when we try to convince someone in a roundabout way, to make him enter our bubble, to lead him toward ourselves.

The right arm is stronger than the left, whether we are right-handed or left-handed.[5] It is also more tonic since the left hemisphere uses many more dopaminergic neurotransmitters than the right.[6] When an itch is felt on the right arm, the situation is often negative.

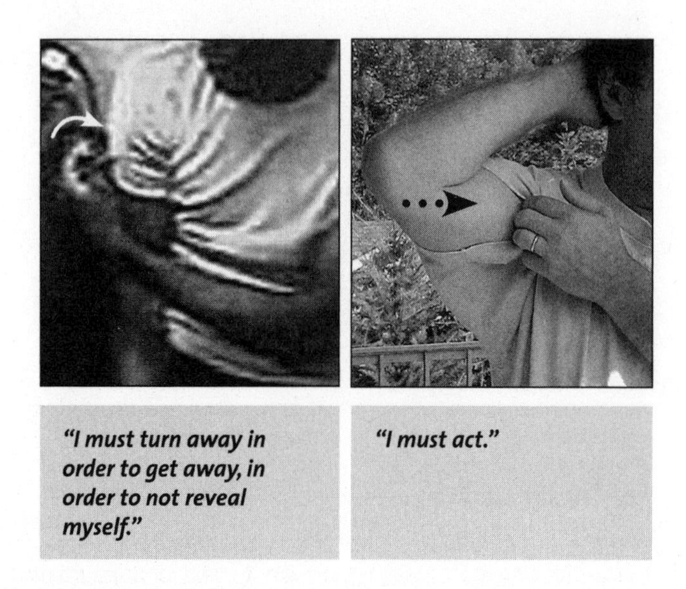

"I must turn away in order to get away, in order to not reveal myself."

"I must act."

When a person scratches the inside of his right bicep, his body opens toward the other person. This is because he has the desire to open up in the conversation and to get closer, which is shown by scratching.

An itch on the outside of the right arm expresses a need to protect oneself. If the feeling were clearer there would be an outburst, but generally people shut down and smile instead. In these situations, they have a tendency to keep their arms solidly glued against their bodies, as if they have something to protect or defend. This is the case with the man in the left photo above: For now, nobody knows yet that he has committed a theft for which he will be declared guilty. He runs away, turning away, like the arm that he scratches.

The Elbows: The Joints of Relationships

The joints give flexibility to the body. The brain moves the hands there each time that the ability to be or an interest in being flexible is questioned. The elbows allow the association of the arms and forearms in a common dynamic. The left elbow and the right are like two terrible parents who are not always in agreement but who have the same concerns.

"If I tried, I could change my attitude to make my relationship with this person easier."

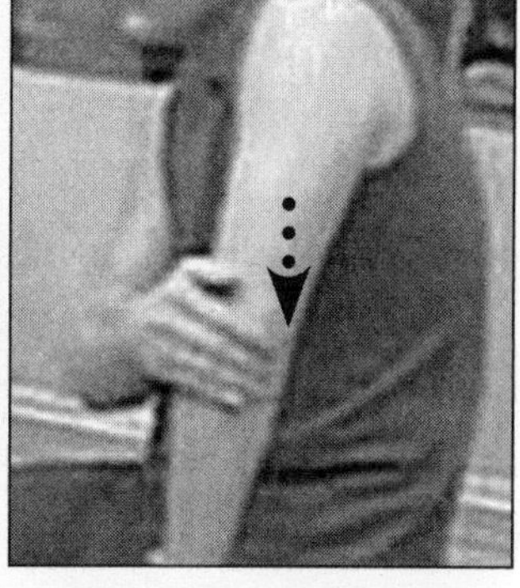

"I feel like changing my attitude in order to get closer, but I must protect myself."

When someone scratches the inside of the left elbow, the need to become flexible, to change the rhythm of the relationship, is tackled. Here is an example: A child of separated parents noticed small red spots appear in the fold of her elbow when she had to go to her father's house for the weekend. The little girl could not fold her arms, which prevented her from hugging her father and his new partner. These red spots disappeared when she returned to her mother's house. We must ask ourselves: What if it wasn't just a coincidence? The brain and the body simultaneously find unconscious strategies, sometimes unexpected ones, when faced with the conscious inability to deal with difficulties. No longer able to fold the elbow also means no longer being able to find the flexibility to move toward another person, no longer wanting the "I" and the "you" to agree. When a person scratches the inside of his left elbow, he is saying to himself in essence: "If I dared, I would go to his aid; I would leave in order to speed things up because I want to." An itch in the fold of the left arm expresses the desire to take an emotional step toward another person. It is always very heavily yet pleasantly emotionally charged.

The outside of the left elbow is also managed by the right hemisphere, which remains the hemisphere of connection for both sides of the arm. The person who scratches herself here is trying to adapt emotionally. She chooses a roundabout way to communicate because her reconciliation cannot be direct. The fact that it is the left elbow that is scratched lets us conclude that the body, although unconscious of it, has already found a way to bring the other person toward itself.

The right elbow does not have the emotional character of the left elbow. Managed by the left hemisphere, which is tied to the outside world, it is more in control and not invested in the same kinds of concerns. It connects the doing of a project with its concrete realization.

"I must change my relational strategy to get out of this situation."

or

"I prefer to run away rather than change my relational strategy."

"I must find a strategy to make the other person stick to my project, to my idea . . ."

Someone who scratches the inside of the right elbow is trying to get closer to " striking a deal," connecting two or several things together.

As far as the outside of the right elbow is concerned, the problem is symmetrically inverted. The person does not feel capable of being in the relationship. She is being required to have a flexibility that she does not have. She does not see how she can improve the relationship, change its character, give it more strength; she feels instead like retreating but does not know how. She therefore remains unfeeling when faced with the problem since she places it outside of herself.

The Forearms: To Take Action

The forearms are halfway between the emotionality of the arms and the practicality of the hands. It is not for nothing that we roll up our sleeves to get to work.

The left forearm symbolizes concrete connection.

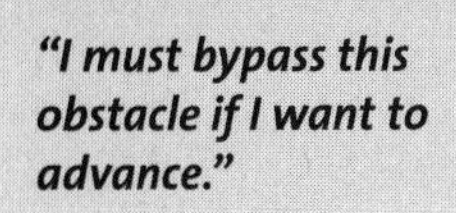

"I must bypass this obstacle if I want to advance."

"I want to conquer this obstacle."

A person who places his hand on the interior of his left forearm feels the desire to intervene. The movement is fluid, spontaneous, and the fact that this is the internal side suggests the concrete openness of the other.

A person who places his hand on the exterior side of his left forearm is divided between two commitments. This itch is characteristic of internal ambivalence. He feels like doing something, concretely achieving something, but also feels the necessity to develop an indirect strategy. It is also possible that this itch is caused by the fact that he dares not get closer to the other person.

On the right side of the body, controlled by the left hemisphere, itching is more thought out, less spontaneous, but also more strategic.

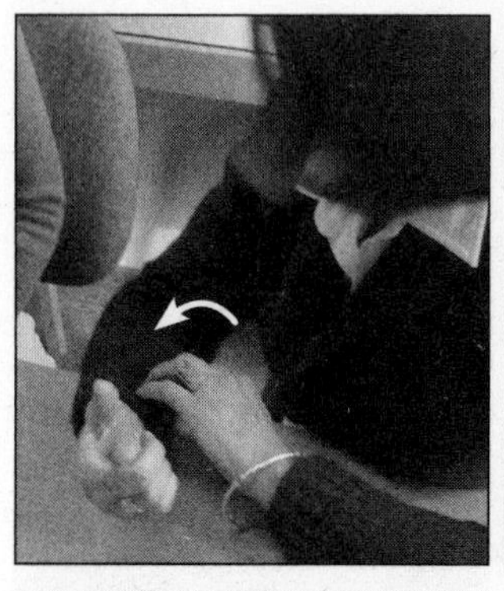

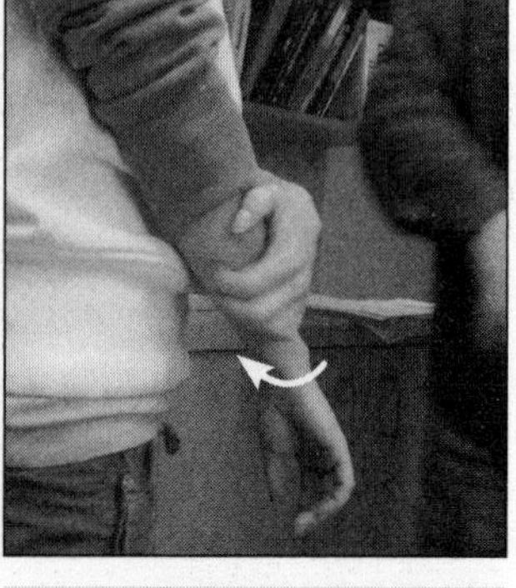

"I must get closer concretely and strategically."

"I must get out of this situation."

When a person places her hand on the interior of her right forearm, she feels it is in her interest to act. It is difficult to say from just this sign if the wish or interest is the driving force, but the action to carry it out is generally seen from a concrete and strategic point of view.

If a person places his hand on the exterior of his right forearm, he protects himself. No longer looking to confront, on the contrary, he wants to get away from external aggression. The general atmosphere of the conversation is marked with aggressiveness.

The Wrists: To Concretely Change Direction

The wrists are by far the most flexible and mobile of human joints. Different from other muscles or joints of the arm, they can move just as well forward, backward, and laterally.[7] People who have more nuanced thoughts often have very flexible wrists, while those who are more uncompromising have more rigid wrists. The thought activates and the wrist twists; the thought subtly changes and the wrist relaxes. It is used as soon as there is a change in direction.

"I want to do this."

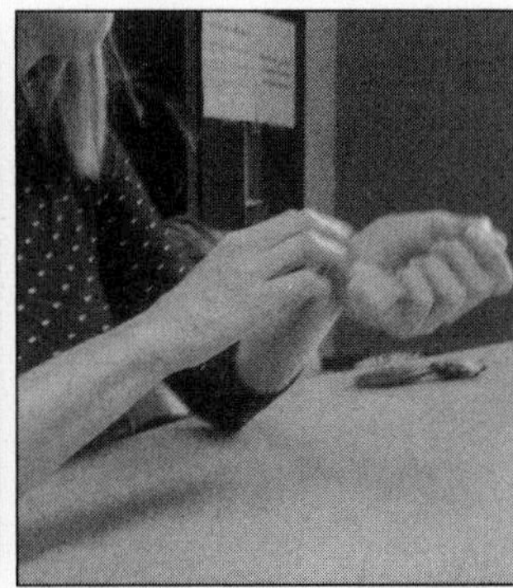

"I invite you to come closer." (Change in direction)

The left wrist is the wrist of concrete opportunities. An itch on the inside of the left wrist means that the situation presents itself in a positive way. In one observed case, the itch occurred during the following exchange. An employer asked his assistant, "Would you be willing to take care of this task?" and she answered, "I'll have to see!" An experienced eye knows that she will acquiesce without a doubt because she scratches her wrist while turning it outward. The task in question has an unseen nature and implies new responsibilities. It is positive excitement that has generated the itch.

In the case where a person scratches the outside of his left wrist, he is still invested but the nature of his thought is different. He has an idea at the back of his mind but must bypass a problem for the sake of efficiency.

The right wrist expresses a concrete change in direction. The notion of commitment is present. Here, too, is the question of flexibility.

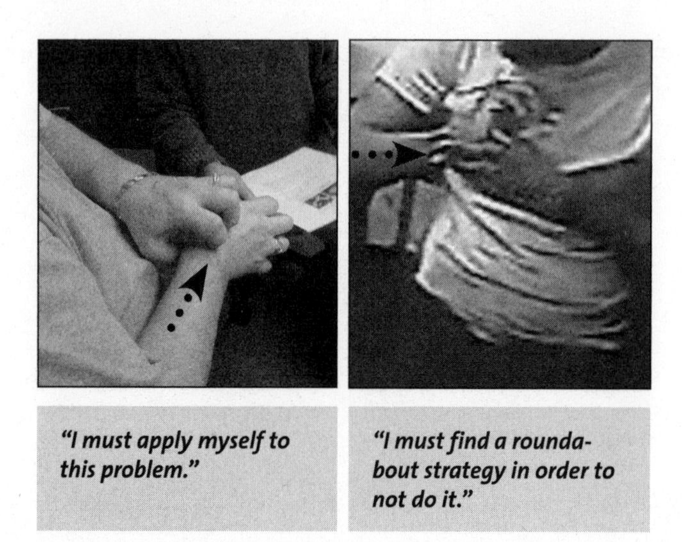

"I must apply myself to this problem."

"I must find a roundabout strategy in order to not do it."

When a person scratches the inside of her right wrist, she expresses her concern or her duty to "act otherwise" and this is not always due to a cheerfulness of heart. The will to act guides her choice.

On the other hand, if she scratches the outside of her right wrist, there isn't the same flexibility with changing in direction. The contexts in which this gesture is identified are more often contexts of adversity. They are negative.

The Legs: To Leave and to Flee

The legs allow us to move and connect us to each other spatially. They say "yes" by approaching or "no" by running away. Conversation exchanges are all subject to this law of the lower body which advances or moves away, and handles the impulses of the brain that decide whether or not to welcome information or a new emotion. The brain thus summons the hands to the legs each time that agreement with an idea, a project, or a person is called into question. Once more, the hands give us information on the nature of this desire, often before the person becomes aware of it himself.

The Top of the Legs: The Social Link

Without regard to the incongruity of language, it would be appropriate to say that the left leg symbolizes the heart because it is solicited as soon as a human being tries to spontaneously approach another person, free from all calculation. The desire to "go out with," to "go with," or to "go steady with" makes us put our left leg forward.

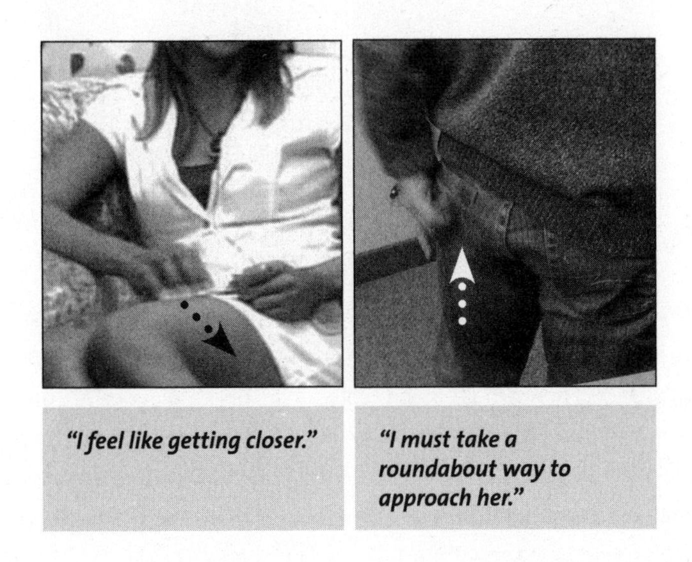

"I feel like getting closer."

"I must take a roundabout way to approach her."

The photo on the left shows a woman who is speaking to a man on an American TV reality show. Her tone is detached but her nervous hand on her left thigh is already anticipating the real connection that there will be between them.

If this movement is made at the back of the left leg, the same desires, the same feelings, express themselves but we think that the connection can only take place in a roundabout way. The hand goes behind the body because it cannot move forward openly, as if everything must remain hidden. A general expression of mischievousness or discontent imprinted on the body allows us to get this general sense.

The right leg, directed by the left hemisphere, expresses its engagement in movement. The left hemisphere is "harder" than the right: Its unconscious strategies are imprinted with pragmatism, willpower.

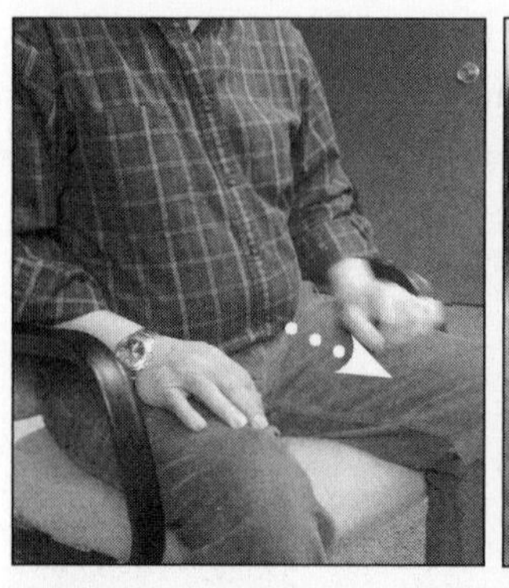

"I must approach strategically."

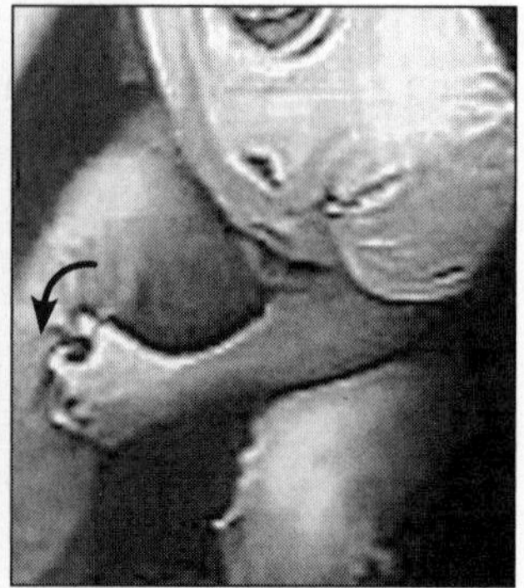

"I no longer want to participate in this exchange."

When one feels an itch on the right half of the body, the conversation is often negative or difficult. Information is treated by the left hemisphere with more distance. For example, an employer asks his employee, "Are you going to commit to this project?" She responds, "I will think about it" and scratches herself. She does not say "yes" spontaneously but questions herself in a hostile atmosphere. The necessity, rather than a desire to do the task, provokes the itch on the right.

A person who touches the back of his right leg expresses his desire to escape from a situation. For example, during an investigation, an innocent man who knows who is guilty avoids questions and, while appearing participatory, conveys, by scratching himself, his desire to escape. He is trying to make an honorable exit without being obligated to deliver compromising information.

The Knees: Being Up for It

The knees are manipulated more when in a seated position because then they are within range of the hands. Each knee has a specific purpose. The left is at the heart of reconciliation. It has the same function in the leg as the elbow has in the arm, the difference being that it tingles in accordance with the spatial emotional bond. Questions will arise like: "Will I be up for it?" or "Will I be capable enough to do it?" or "Will I achieve it?" The knee unfolds when we desire to be bigger and folds when we must bow in front of another.

"Will I be up to this project that pulls at my heartstrings?"

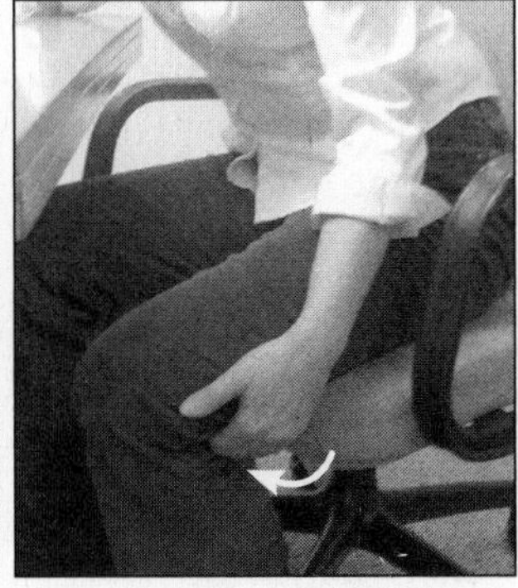

"I will need to go in a roundabout way to be up for it."

The front of the knee itches when a part of a person—that wants to be up for whatever even though the person herself is afraid—would like to involve itself. For example, a woman asks her friend, "Will you come with us on a walk this Sunday?" and she answers, "I will think about it," while scratching her left knee. She thinks about it indeed, but she especially tries to convince herself that she is capable of doing it because she feels like it. Otherwise, she would not have unconsciously chosen her left knee. She scratches, she doubts, she therefore needs to be encouraged, to make herself be up for it . . .

Here is another example: A specialist interrogating an innocent woman about a theft notices that she scratches the back of her left knee in a recurring manner. He knows that the knee goes back to the feeling of not of being "up for" something and deduces from this that the woman has a hierarchic superior, someone "above" her. The fact that the itch is located at the back of the knee makes him understand that she is trying to bypass something. He questions her superior and discovers very quickly that it is he who is responsible for the theft. She hesitated to give his name.

When we must show that we are up to it, that we are the largest, the best, the strongest, it is the right knee—the one that deals with performance, our will—that we touch. The person says to himself then, in essence, "I am afraid that I will not be up to this challenge, but that is a question that I do not have to ask myself; I must get involved." When the right part of the body is touched, the situation is even more conflicted and conveys adversity.

"I must be up to this challenge."

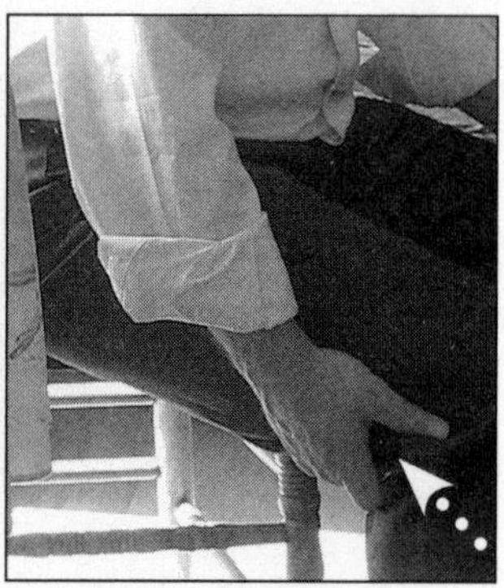

"I will not be up to this challenge; I must escape!"

The man in the image on the left must make a request. That is what is making him uncomfortable. This image contributes, with numerous others, to remind us of the universality of itching.

The back of the right knee expresses very different problems from those of the back of the left knee. People who scratch themselves in this spot are persuaded that they are not up for whatever. Faced with adversity, they try to escape. Their body moves off-center in order to not be totally present in the conversation. They think: "I must get out of this situation that really makes me uncomfortable."

Let us follow along the leg to get to more and more concrete spheres.

The Tibias and the Calves: Moving Around

If you find yourself in a meeting that must end at 4:00 PM. one Friday afternoon and that at 4:10 PM. the formal discussions continue, watch how the people behave. It is quite possible that you will notice one or two people pull up their socks. The socks had already fallen down at 3:30 PM., but at that time, nobody wanted to leave the meeting, but at 4:10 PM., yes! The hands are directed toward the bottom of the leg when a person shows the need to move around. The tibia and the left calf are sought out when, in one way or another, a person must move more quickly, accelerate his movement.

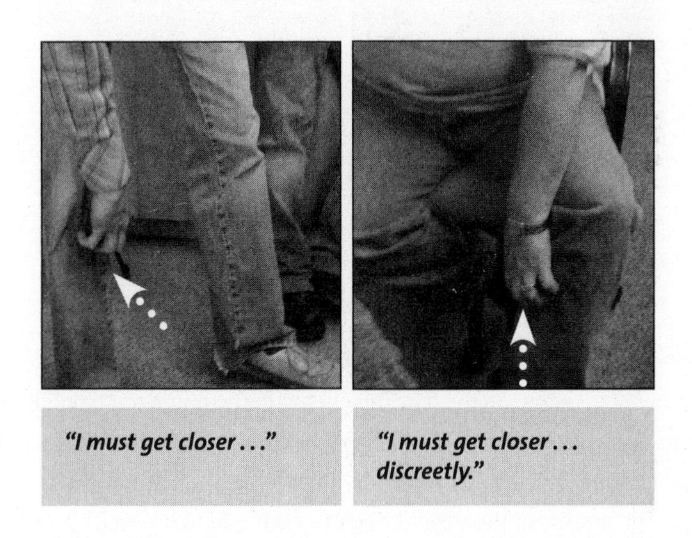

"I must get closer . . ."

"I must get closer . . . discreetly."

The brain sends more blood to the area of the calf and the tibia, producing vasodilation, when one must act or move faster. And if there is itching it is because nothing is happening, because the person is not moving when they should be getting a move on.

On the back side, concrete difficulty needs to be spatially and psychologically bypassed. In the second image, the man looks at one of his colleagues while scratching the back of his left calf. The left hand crosses over his crotch rather than going around the body on the right. This suggests that he finds the relationship rather friendly and would not look negatively on making a closer connection. The impulses that have triggered his desire to scratch himself are not seen consciously. On the other hand, they will emerge in his consciousness either after a period of introspection, or very naturally in the process of reflection.

From the left to the right tibia, the situation is not radically different.

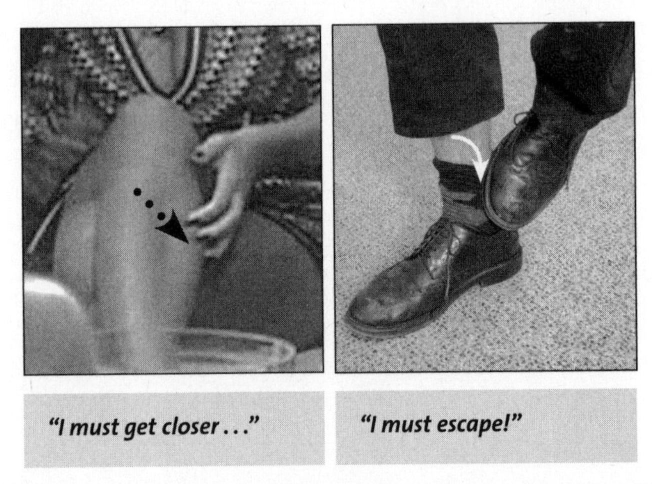

"I must get closer . . ." *"I must escape!"*

When the hand is placed on the right tibia, the interest to act is colder, less emotional, than when on the left. The person in the photo on the right uses a quick and concrete strategy to avoid losing time. He is, moreover, not entirely conscious that he is scratching with his other leg, too busy thinking about escape. The energy of the upper body can continue to be used to other ends while one leg scratches the other. This homeostatic movement conserves energy.

The Ankles: To Concretely Change Direction

The ankles are the only joints of the leg that allow movement from top to bottom and laterally at the same time. They are appealed to when concrete changes of movement are called for. Connected more directly to the genitalia than other parts of our body are, they are also one of the rare parts of the body whose movement is often sexual.[8]

The left ankle connects the tibia, the calf, and the foot; it is indispensable for walking and "to not lose one's footing." When the hand reaches for the interior of the ankle, the human being expresses that he is grappling with a concrete desire to change directions, that he wishes to get closer.

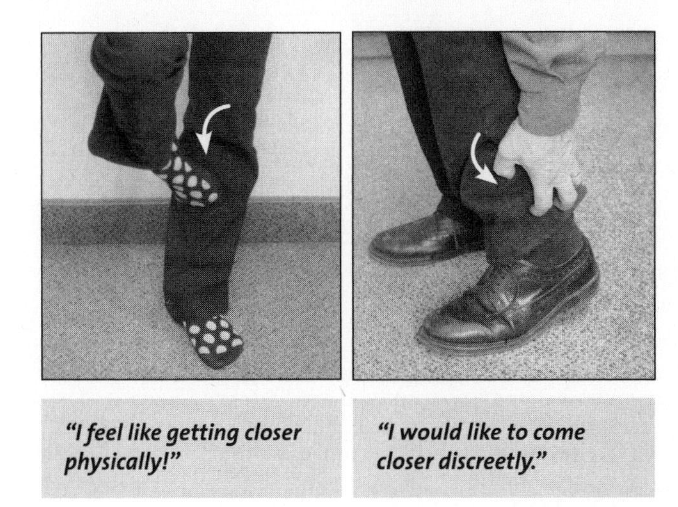

"I feel like getting closer physically!"

"I would like to come closer discreetly."

A person who scratches the back of her ankle thinks, in essence, "I would willingly change the direction of our relationship in order to get closer to you," but the gesture is more hidden. She strongly and concretely would like this connection, which sometimes has a sexual nature, to happen. The more open the angle of the foot, the more real the desire for openness.

The significance of "taking another direction" is different with the left ankle than with the right. If the hand lands on the right ankle, the relationship will be more rational, logical. The atmosphere of watchfulness is more felt.

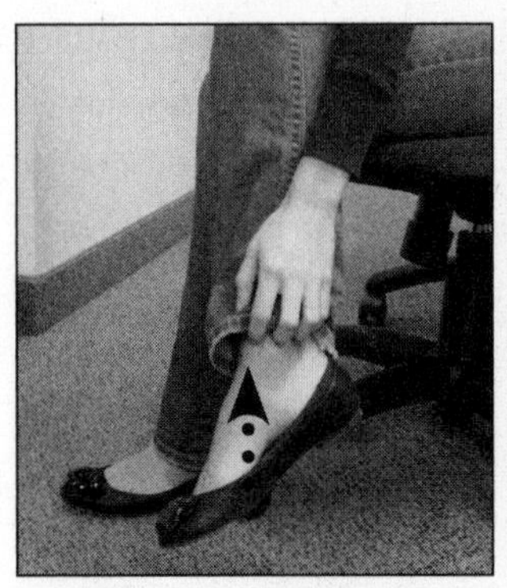

"We must take another approach to advance."

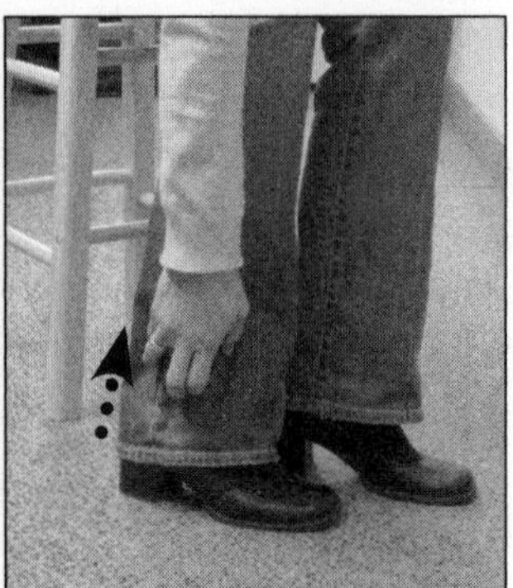

"I must find a way out."

When the right ankle is sought, the relationship is placed in an unknown atmosphere.

On the back of the outside of the ankle, an itch is felt when the change in direction imposed on the situation or relationship is pushing us to retreat, to get away.

Itches are, on the body, the voice of repressed emotions.

Thanks to scratching, emotional tensions are managed and the body recovers its homeostasis.

The arms are sought out if it is a matter of physical action, of concrete intervention.

Emotional tensions connected to flexibility in face of changes in direction arise in the joints.

The legs are the functional tools used by human beings to move closer or to go farther away.

CHAPTER 13

Taking Matters in Hand

With the benefit of hindsight, we can say that this narrative traces the journey of the neocortex and the emotional system joining forces against each other on the battlefield of the body. The neocortex would like life to go smoothly without turmoil. From this perspective, it smothers strong emotions. But emotions have existed in the brain for millions of years. It is not a matter of dislodging them. With a sudden movement of wrinkles, the heartbeat, and other "scrapes," they organize an active resistance against the neocortex. They propagate in hands that have been made clammy and moist. The neocortex commands the hands to block emotions by not moving, but it is always too late: Emotions have already left visible traces of their rebellious spirit on our hands.

To Pinch: The Edge of the Hand or the Fingertips

It is time to "take control" concretely. The brain gives orders to the body, to the hands, in this case, to intervene, but what happens is that sometimes one person's needs conflicts with those of her partner. Faced with the desire to take charge of decorating the house, ordering parts of a file, planning a vacation, for example, nothing says that a colleague, a partner, or a spouse will also not want to "take charge." The arrested need is tangible.

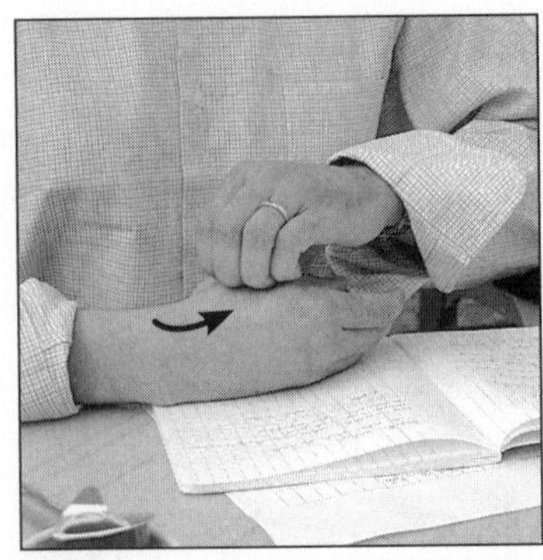

Left grip: "I feel like taking charge myself." (Spontaneous reaction.)

Right grip: "I must take charge!"

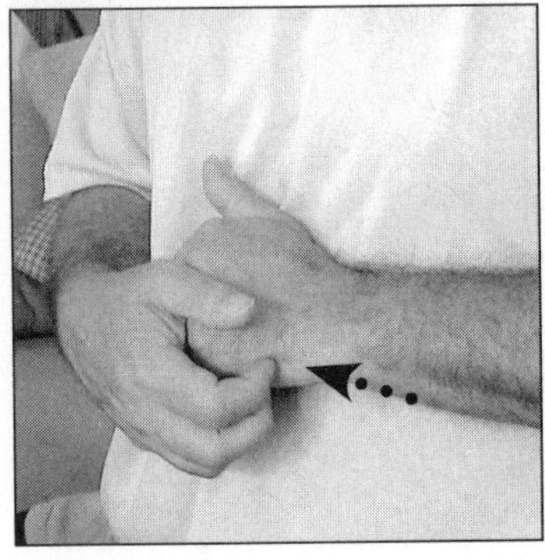

Edge of the left hand: "I would like them to ask me to do it."

Edge of the right hand: "I must take care of this without putting myself forward."

A person feels an itch at the edge of her right hand when she must act concretely but she does not dare get involved. If the itch is at the edge of the left hand, the situation is more emotional.

When it is the edge of the hand that is scratched, the wrist is less fluid; it is held against the body. The person would like to act concretely without putting herself forward and is more concerned with discretion.

It also happens that it is at the knuckles where tingling is felt. The hand then closes almost into a fist. The joints are bony and hard, and there is always a lot of roughness when they are touched or scraped, regardless of whoever's hand that is being considered.

If the itch is felt at the fingertips, a person is eager to implement what is being discussed. Moreover don't we say: "I have it at my fingertips"?

The nature of the motivation is the principal criteria of distinction between the left and right hand. Impulse, spontaneity, and the desire to act are the masters of movement concerning the left hand, while control, need, and necessity are the masters of the right hand. The context is generally more positive when the left hand is involved.

The palms will be scratched each time a more general thought, more intimate and more hidden, occurs to someone. The person does not want to show his desire to intervene. This unconscious phenomenon can emerge in his consciousness after a bit of introspection.

The Successive Circles of Discovering the World Via Our Fingers

The symbolism of the fingers is not tied to verbal language. Babies, for example, if they cannot reach some object they would like, scratch themselves exactly like adults do, even at an age when they are still not capable of resorting to verbal language to communicate their needs. The great apes scratch themselves like human beings do. It is not among them either that verbal language leads to one part of the body or another. Finally, video footage of preliterate people collected by researchers and available for observation has convinced us of the universality of itching. Again, we must admit that a more universal phenomenon than that connected to a culture dependent on its forms of expression are in effect.

A child's discovery of his fingers provides several rich indications about their role in communication. The child discovers his fingers one after the other at the rate in which he invests in the world. They appear in his drawings, moreover, very late.[1]

The index finger, which permits him to be the master of his own actions, to take, to point, to say "I," is discovered first, and this is universally so. The child points when he is about to use his first structured words.[2] After that, the middle finger corresponds to relationships. The child realizes that next to "I" (index), there is another (middle finger). Then, after "I" and the "other," the third realization that will appear in the child's mind, the ring finger, is the first structured group: the family. The pinky finger is the outermost finger of the hand; it is therefore the link to the outside world. With adults, it is scratched when harmony with the outside world is called into question. In this arena, of the body and the hand, let's not forget the finger that is the most useful of all, the one that is opposite, in its topography, the other four: the thumb. It does not have the same status as the other fingers. It is in fact an extension of the arm. It is the "self," quite simply. The infant finds it naturally in the course of his intrauterine life and already sucks on it in the mother's womb. With dogs, for whom the awareness of "self" does not exist, the thumb is not separate from the paw. On the other hand, with apes, who possess a true consciousness of self,[3] the thumbs are articulate and entirely separate from the fingers.

The cerebro-motor development in children seems to indicate that the discovery of each finger corresponds to that of a concentric dimension supplementary to its own existence. This process is implemented during the discovery of the body in relation to space. Relationships with others are questioned each time an action takes place around the fingers.

THE DISCOVERY OF THE FINGERS AND THE WORLD

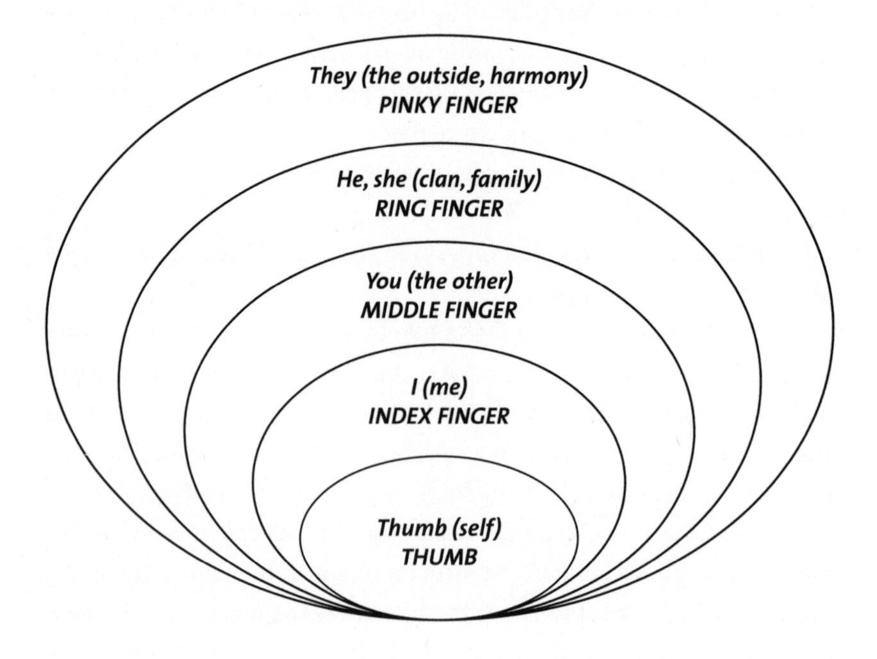

The Thumb: The First Relational Circle

The thumb is indispensable for picking things up. An itch in the thumb is a great deal like that of the grip. When it is the only finger involved and the index finger is separate, there is a desire to intervene without trying to put oneself forward. That is the case, for example, with the person who, when having a drink with some friends, wants to take the last small salmon canapé without everybody seeing him, so he scratches his thumb unconsciously. He doesn't really feel like putting himself forward.

The gesture of hiding a finger in the other hand is even more interesting since the finger represents a dimension of ourselves that we want to make disappear.

The person in these video stills is trying to keep a low profile.

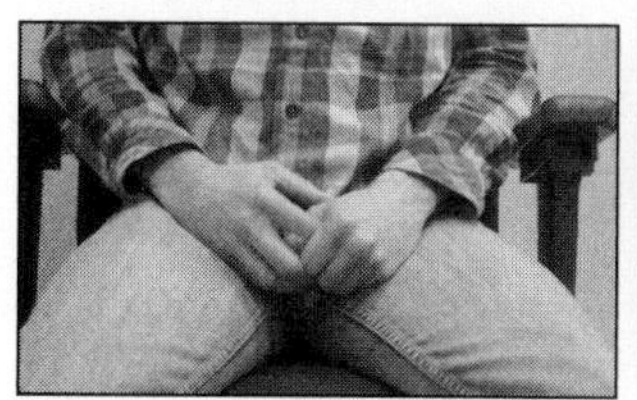
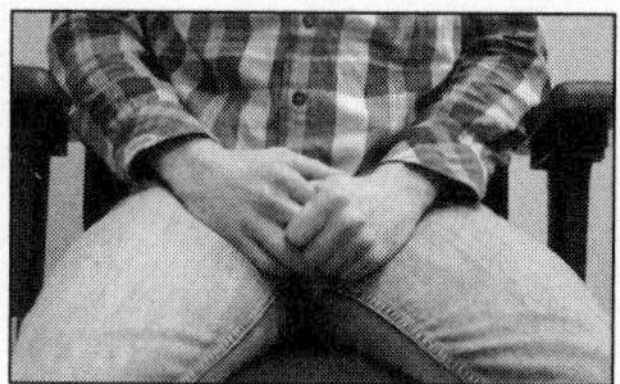
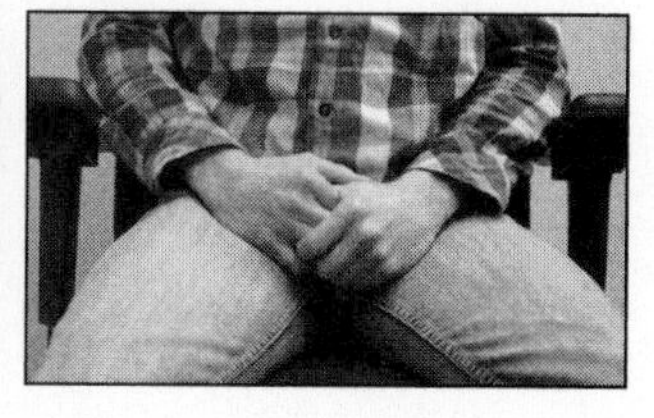

The hidden fingers testify unconsciously to the desire to protect himself. He puts the part of himself that he wishes to conceal in his hand. I bet you won't be able to find someone who can describe their achievements proudly while adopting this posture.[4]

A baby discovers his body by beginning with the elements nearest in order and then those farther away. He discovers, moreover, his environment at the speed with which he becomes conscious of his body's details. These first impressions remain and are reinforced over an entire lifetime. Here, we put the body in relation to the space that surrounds it. In this context, a person can scratch one finger when she wishes to act or intervene positively or negatively by projecting herself in a concrete, relational way, but she can also hide, squeeze, or grab a finger with the other hand when she is trying to protect or hide a dimension of her interaction that she doesn't want to share with the people around her. That is true for each one of the fingers.

The Index Finger: The Second Relational Circle

The index finger is the finger of assertion, the one that someone who wants "to speak" uses to put himself forward. This behavior is not acquired. It is seen in the child who points at an object before even knowing how to speak. An ape also shows what he wants with a pointed index finger, and he cannot speak either.

"I must intervene!"

The index finger is pointed when we are trying to put ourselves forward. This is universally true.

Each time a person feels an itch on her index finger or she puts it forward, as in the photos above, it is because she has something to say and she wants to intervene.

When the index finger is held tightly, it is spontaneity that is held back. When it is the right index finger, the person would like to move forward, to say "I" in a more assertive way.

While scratching, the finger has a tendency to tighten and in more than 80 percent of cases, the index finger moves up rather than drops down, thereby conveying the person's will to remain dominant in the exchange.[5] The great apes scratch themselves with their index fingers when it is a matter of hierarchy or dominance.[6]

If the index finger is hidden, the situation is completely different.

"I hope they will not ask me my opinion."

This person hides the index finger of one of his hands as he hopes he will not have to intervene. The finger which ordinarily says "I" is trying to disappear.

The Middle Finger: The Third Relational Circle

With the hands, it is always a matter of taking something concretely. There are hundreds of ways of doing this. The person who "takes" to the road does not use the same cerebral connections as the person who "takes" a glass or the one who "takes" his lover because he is "taken" with her.

The videos where we see people scratch their middle fingers show problems having to do with intimate relationships, with the desire to physically, sexually, "take," often as it is a question of taking control of another. The hand allows us, in fact, to control what we take. If the index finger permits us to say "I" in a general way, the middle finger permits us to say it in all the situations where we find ourselves in a relationship of an intimate or dual nature.

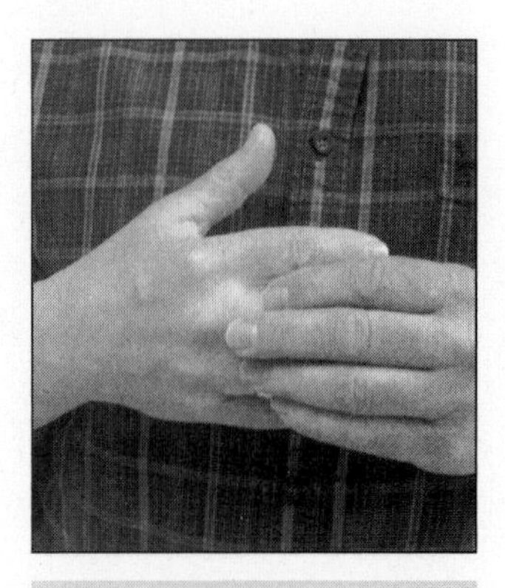

"Let's protect this relationship!"

The middle finger sends us back to the dual relationship of closeness. The hidden finger (the relationship) is protected by the opposite hand.

The hand has a tendency to take the finger that it hides to protect it. For example, a woman asks one of her friends for news about her husband: "And Jenny, is everything OK?" By seeing her suddenly hide her middle finger, she understands that she does not want to discuss this subject that is of an intimate nature to her.

The Ring Finger: The Fourth Relational Circle

The fourth finger is the finger of the group, the fourth way of saying "I" and entering into a relation with the world; it symbolizes the clan. It is on this finger that the wedding ring is placed, a symbol that the relationship between two people has become a social reality. When this spot itches, the connection to the group is questioned. Faced with the desire or the need to create more of a connection, to improve it, we feel it on our left fourth finger, while in a threatened relationship, we feel it on the right fourth finger.

The fourth finger can also be hidden by the other hand when, rather than putting it forward to intervene, it is appropriate to protect, hide, or keep it to ourselves.

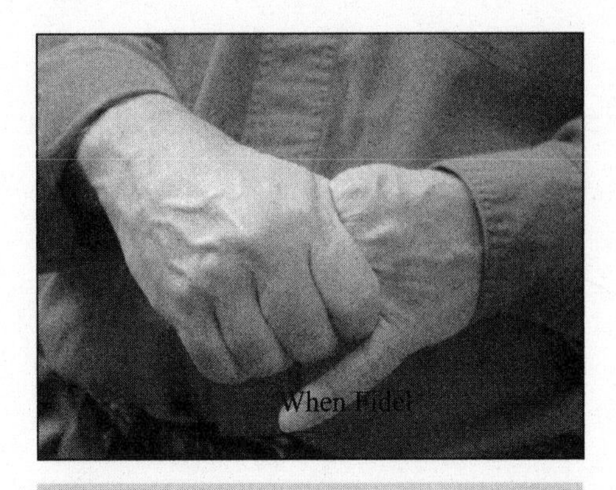

"Let's protect the group."

If the fourth finger of the left hand is hidden, it is because the person does not want to talk about his family, his intimate clan, which he feels does not concern others. His reticence brings even more a kind of restraint or reserve.

If the fourth finger of the right hand is trapped, the situation is more negative and the defense of his world more substantial.

When Fidel Castro speaks about his relationship with Che Guevara. What he says was without a doubt not known to the outside world; it belonged to the two men, and his hand closed to protect the secret of the social agreement made.

The Little Finger: The Last Relational Circle

The little finger, which is the outermost finger of the hand, is scratched when harmony with the environment, the broadest relationship, is not respected.

An itch on the left little finger signifies that there is a desire to spontaneously modify the order of things to create more harmony, while for an itch on the right, on the contrary, the left hemisphere, the more analytical and controlling, is called upon to reinforce the established order. In one case it is a question of reinforcing harmony, in the other it is about defending it.

It is still possible that when facing the outside world, the person who wants to protect himself, to maintain a balance or keep his relationships tidy, grabs one of his little fingers with his other hand.

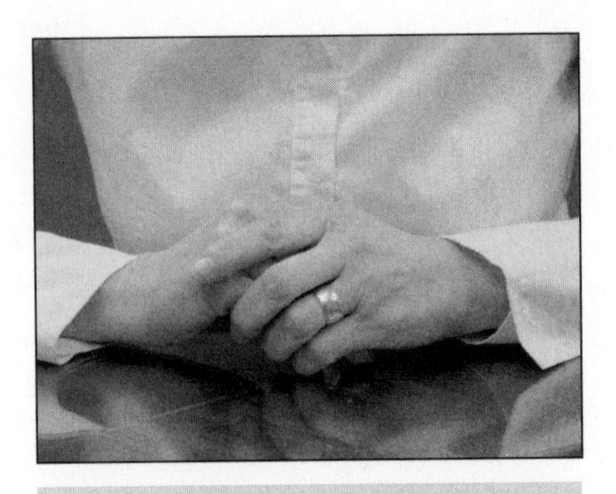

"Let us protect this harmony against the outside world."

This micro-fixation is the expression of our anxieties, of our fear that something will be thwarted . . .

When it is the left little finger that is held, the situation is always more positive and good-natured than when with the right little finger.

When One Hand Takes the Other Hand

Certain emotions can shake us up. If we feel that they do not concern anyone but ourselves, our hands form a loop, a shield against the outside world. When a hand is inside the other, our entire body forms a block. Certain positions testify to this shutting down; others only show modesty, but all of these gestures, largely universal, are unconscious.

Crossing Our Hands: Different Facets of the Self

Our hands do not go one inside the other when we are alone in our living rooms, in the comfort of our private lives, but rather in the presence of others. The wrists' position indicates the hierarchical situation of the person being spoken to; it reveals the pace of the relationship. The wrists are either vertical (raised upward), horizontal (parallel to oneself), or down (turned toward the floor). The nature of the relationship is expressed by their height. It is possible to feel superior, equal, or inferior to another person.

In these illustrations, we must take into consideration for the time being just the position of the wrists, and not that of the hands.

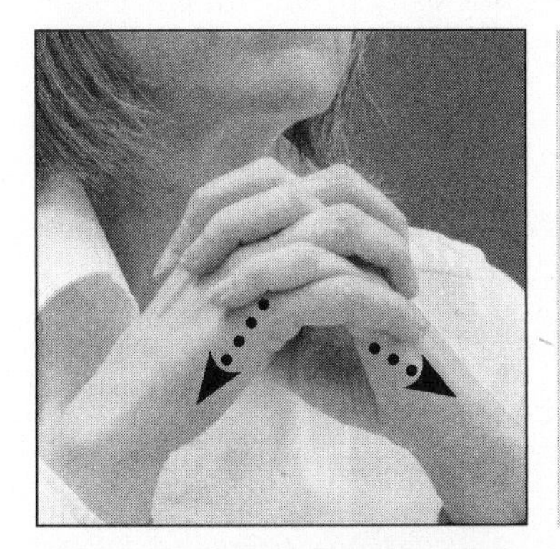

WRISTS POINTED UPWARD

This woman projects, at this exact moment, the image of someone who is superior.

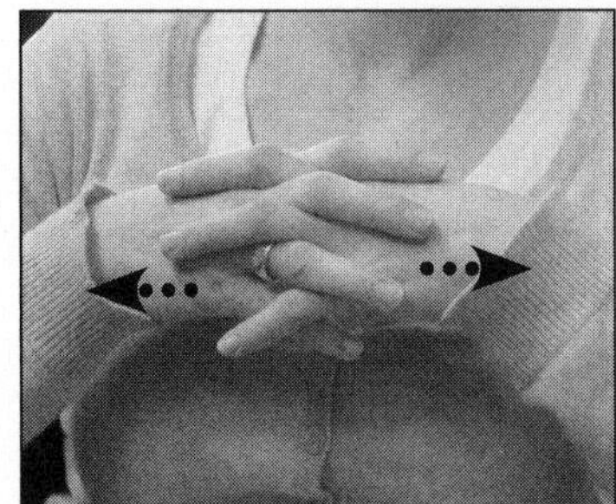

HORIZONTAL WRISTS

This person here maintains an equal position with the other person.

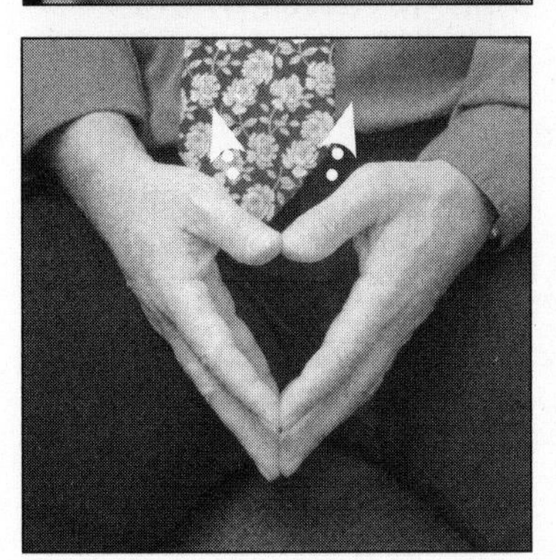

WRISTS POINTED DOWNWARD

This man, at this exact moment, puts himself in an inferior state or in a state that prevents him from moving forward. His wrists hide him by pointing toward the ground, as if he has to hide himself.

Wrists do not have a particular reason to point up. A person whose wrists are pointing up is trying to take the upper hand in an interaction. For example, the one trying to speak always has his wrists raised toward the sky, his hand or index finger lifted, while a willful person always points his wrist up with his fists closed. This verticality shows that he is not putting down his guard. Wrists placed one on top of the other try to convey, unconsciously, the person's influence at that exact moment. Observe any situation where two people are having an exchange, debating. If there are hierarchical differences between them, the one who has his wrists pointed upward, vertically, shows or is trying to show his superiority.

A person whose wrists are horizontal is at the same level as the person to whom he is speaking. This natural movement leads him toward the other.

The wrists can take a third and last direction: toward the ground. The person thereby shows that she is listening. If she speaks, it is never in an assertive manner.

From the ironic French expression to "Have courage, and flee" to the Napoleonic strategy that says that the best defense is a good offense, the configuration of the hands, all of a sudden in love with one another, is a good indicator of unconscious communication methods.

Certain people favor some crossings of their hands, simply because they let them feel more present in their body. Behind the states of the body, there are states of thought. When thoughts are recurrent, gestures also become repetitive in their own way.

The Hands Closed One Inside the Other: "I Protect What I Stand For."

Knowing that we could return to our foundations at any moment is the condition of a satisfactory exchange. The creation of a bubble with our arms, into which we can re-center ourselves, is part of this process. This loop allows us to feel comfortable during stressful situations. Different variations of this gesture convey just as many states of mind.

Crossed Fingers

A person whose hands are intertwined and whose wrists are vertical seems strong. His dominance speaks through his body language.

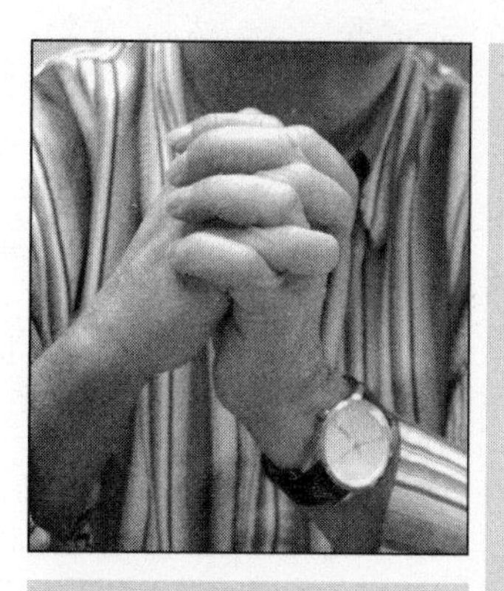

"I am dominant in my established position."

FINGERS CROSSED WITH THE WRISTS POINTED UPWARD

The fingers are intertwined, indicating a closing-off and stress.

The wrists are pointed upward; they are therefore in a position of dominance.

One of the wrists is bent, indicating flexibility in the interaction.

"I am dominant in my position, but I am not inflexible."

Sometimes the index finger crosses the hand. The person thereby affirms his authority. The index fingers are pointed toward the sky.

When the wrists are horizontal, the status of authority has transformed into a more egalitarian relationship. It is stress that brings the hands together.

When the atmosphere is relaxed, the body does the same. Wrists in a vertical position soften and find a horizontal position. A person whose hands are locked into each other horizontally with their fingers intertwined puts himself in a bubble. This position, which we often observe at the beginning of a meeting in the professional world, shows a desire to change and open up, but people take another position as soon as they begin to speak, so as to leave behind the previous position. If they do return to that position or if they stay in it while they are speaking, it is because they are sharing information they do not want to with other people. They are not in a cool and rational exchange but in a dynamic of contradictory debate.

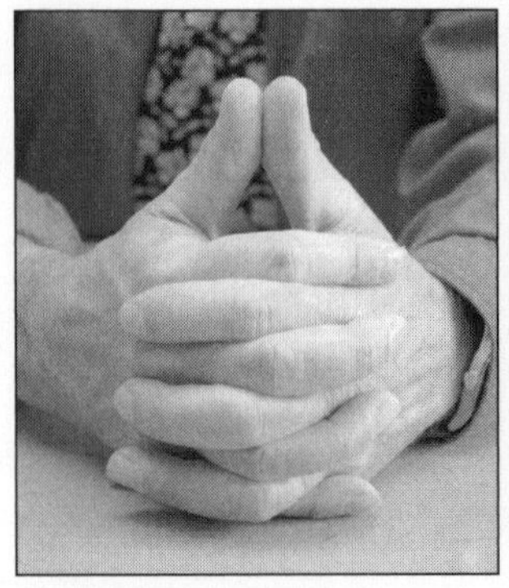

"We are in an equal relationship. I am stressed."

Desire to move forward.

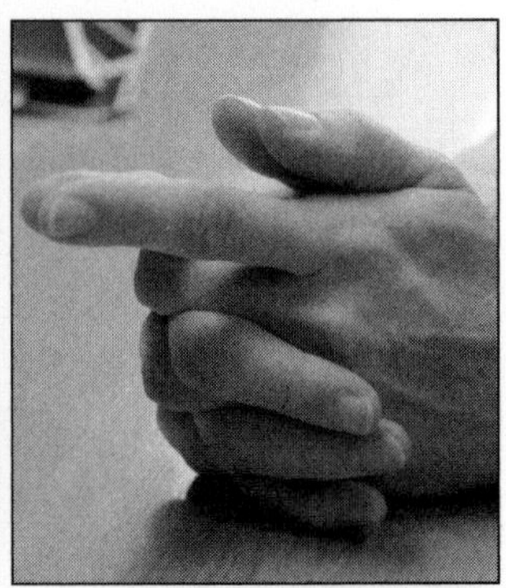

"I have something to say or to defend." Atmosphere of confrontation.

The more the hands are squeezed together, the more that uneasiness is evident.

When the wrists are pointing down, the same stress remains. The person is waiting for the other to take the situation into their hands. The body creates a block with the hands and moves forward.

"You can go there, but I will not put myself forward."

HANDS CLOSED AND WRISTS POINTING DOWNWARD

This man is on a hierarchic rung that is below the other person's. This is one of the rare positions when the hands are closed without aggressiveness.

The person who holds himself in this position does not take control of the direction of the conversation but waits for the other person to do it. He is often standing. We see it with people who are seated, like at the doctor's or specialist's office, waiting for test results or results from a study or analysis of some kind.

With a Finger of Aggressiveness: Pointed Fingers

It frequently happens, in unrestrained exchanges, that the fingers are held on the inside of the hands. This attitude is noticeable in scenes where the noise level is very elevated and where a disagreement is expressed without restraint.

"Let me call you into suspicion."

HANDS CLOSED AND FINGERS POINTED

This man is sure of his facts, and he has something to say in this generally conflicted atmosphere. The fingers held in a horizontal position, as if they are bristling, express aggressiveness.

Tense fingers show more aggressiveness than those that are folded. The hands are therefore like porcupines whose sharp needles can prick, simply to protect themselves. In the photo above, an American politician defends his record in front of a cutting journalist, after having lost the election.

Fingers Crossed Back

Sometimes the fingers turn inward, their tips going back toward the center of the body.

"I feel divided, but I have to decide."

The person doubts his choice. He must decide but he questions himself about his responsibilities. He is not yet ready to share his decision because he does not know what he wants.

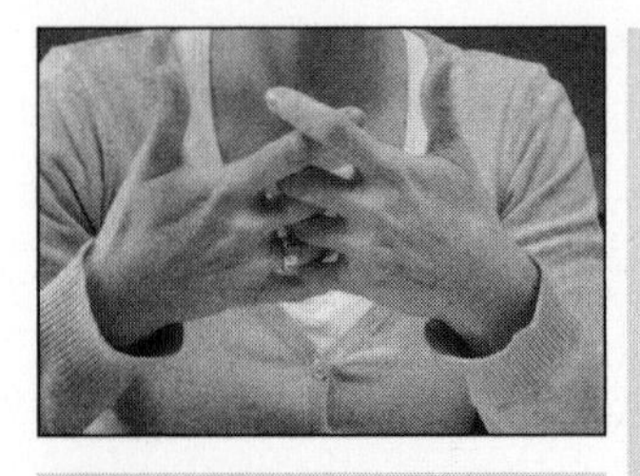

"I feel divided. For the moment, I am keeping my decision to myself."

This gesture expresses guilt or a feeling of uneasiness. The person hesitates between two options. If you could hear what she is saying, she would say things like, "Yes, I agree, but on the other hand . . ." She is facing a dilemma.

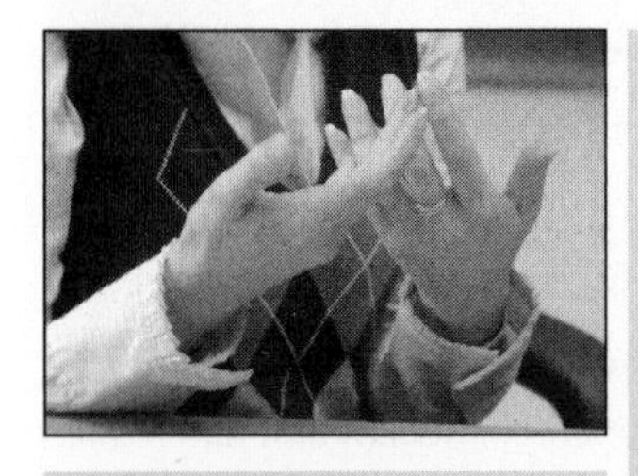

"My position is ambiguous and I am going to tell you why."

In this situation, the body has a tendency to twist. This person, feeling powerless, is really upset. Her shoulders lift up; her palms make a movement toward the other person. She would like to tell him what is in her heart, to confide in him.

In a situation of negotiation, if a person's fingertips are turned toward you, it is because he is in the midst of convincing you. If it is the other person who is in this position, he is in the midst of being won over to your cause . . . at least partially, in any case.

The Hands in a V: "I Protect What I Know."

The person who thinks that he has abilities that others don't places his hands one against the other and points toward the sky with his fingers.

"I know, and I am going to explain it to you!"

HANDS IN A "V" POINTING UPWARD

These people are unconsciously making the form of a pyramid with their hands; they believe themselves to be more competent than others and want to show it. In this position they seem very erudite.

"I know and I am going to explain it to you!"

This position does not convey sharing. The person KNOWS and she will respond if someone asks her a question, but she expects nothing from her listeners. On the contrary, it is she who expects to provide benefit to them, in small doses, with her knowledge. Her arms do not move toward them. This is, for example, the position of a preacher on the pulpit whose mission is to deliver the word of God. He is the custodian of an important task, and he conveys it as such. In this position, people are always calm and serene, possessors of the philosopher's stone at a small cost.

In the image on the right, the person holds her wrists up high to the sky. Her posture reinforces the meaning of her words and gives them a serious tone.

If the wrists are horizontal, the person puts his- or herself on the same level as others and desires to find solutions together as a team.

"Let's move forward together; let's share with each other."

HANDS IN A HORIZONTAL "V"

These people hold their wrists horizontally: They are no longer alone. They are going to do, or propose to do, something with another person; their hands are up for the task.

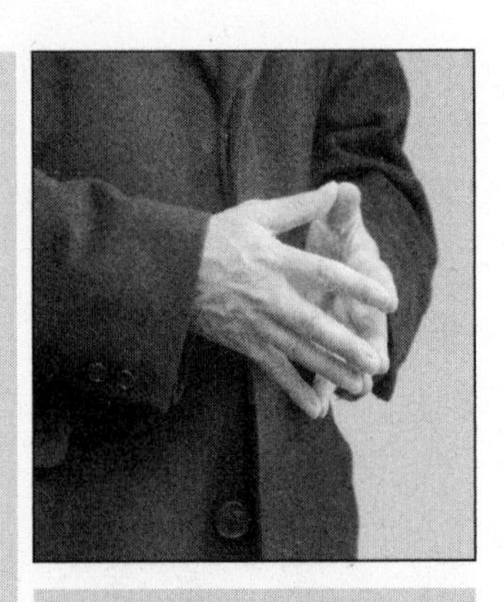

"Let's move forward together; let's share with each other."

The person who squeezes his fingers tight against each other in a horizontal position is showing (even if it is not consciously) a strong presence, an authority. Television presenters frequently use this gesture, as if to say: "I know, but I am not here to put myself ahead; we share the information with each other."

When wrists are pointed downward, the person seems to be saying: "Above all, do not ask me to put myself forward because I can't." He is very conscious of being, in a certain way, the center of attention. Otherwise he would not have his hands in a "V," but at the same time he is powerless or incapable of being the leader in the present situation. Paradoxically, this position is often the one used by natural leaders who are placed in situations where they cannot assert themselves.

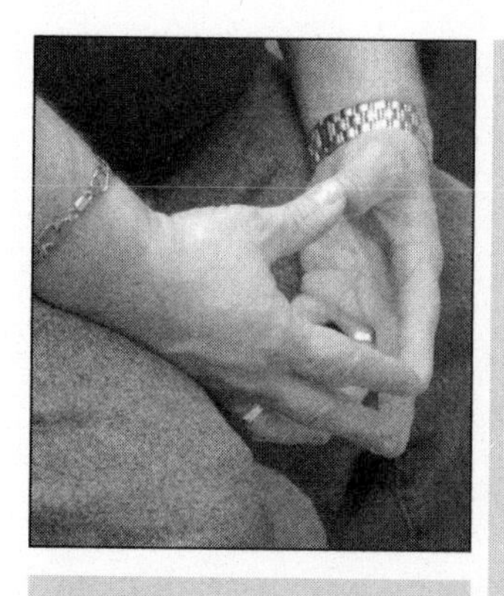

"I cannot put myself forward."

HANDS IN "V" POINTED DOWNWARD

These people have the sense that they are central to the exchange but absolutely cannot put themselves forward.

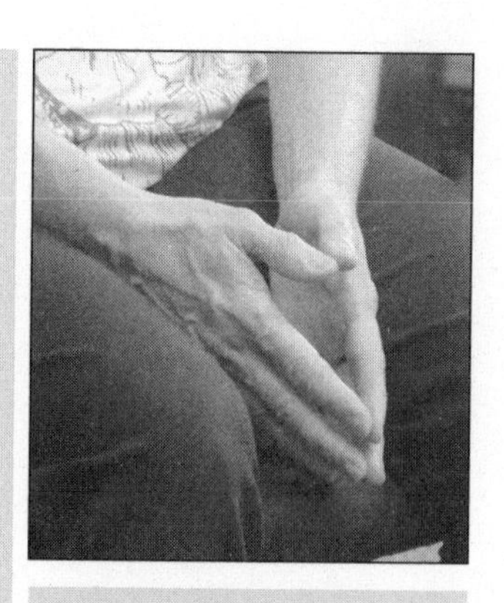

"I cannot put myself forward."

Hands Clasped: "I Protect What I Choose."

When a person clasps her hands together, she is putting pressure on them, one against the other, that corresponds to the pressure that is in her head. The intention will be different depending on the configuration of the wrists and this gesture will have different significances according to the body area where it is being carried out.

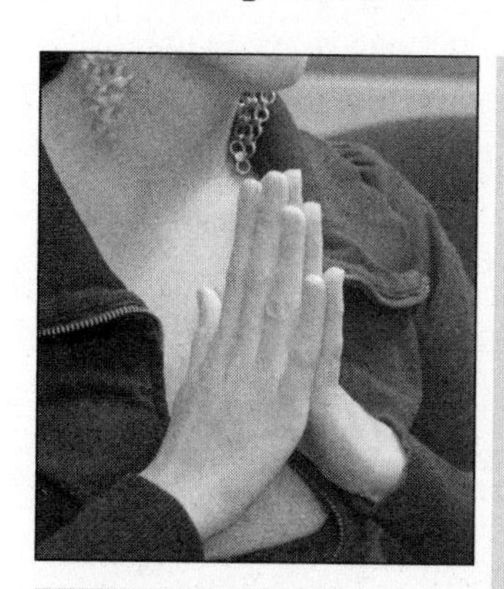

"I have to decide!"

CLASPED HANDS POINTING UPWARD

These people must make a decision. They are going to do it in a rather harsh manner, to the detriment of the other person.

The one on the right places her hands in front of her mouth because she is going to have to speak.

"I must decide; how should I say it?"

A person clasps her hands in a horizontal position when she is troubled and she is going to have to choose, to decide. She re-centers herself, weighing the pros and cons.

This attitude is most often observed when the atmosphere is tense. If the gesture is made down and up, up and down, with tense fingers, the interaction may seem cordial, but the situation often conveys a conflict that is under the surface.

"I would like you to understand what I am trying to say."

HANDS CLASPED HORIZONTALLY

This person tries to make it understood to the people she is talking to that she must make a decision, all the while remaining connected to them.

The lower the wrists move, the less the person is trying to put herself forward. Choices are going to have to be made and the decisions do not depend on her. Her index finger moves toward the ground. The hands, generally between closed thighs, will be hidden because of this fact.

Washing One's Hands: "I Look for My Place"

Psychology experiments show that people feel the need to wash their hands after having fabricated some lie for the experiment! But they are washing their hands without them being dirty! These movements are therefore the same as those that are made under the faucet.

If the wrists are pointed upward, it means that the person who is washing her hands is dominant in the exchange. She has news that is difficult to announce, and she does not know how to go about it, especially because the message is negative.

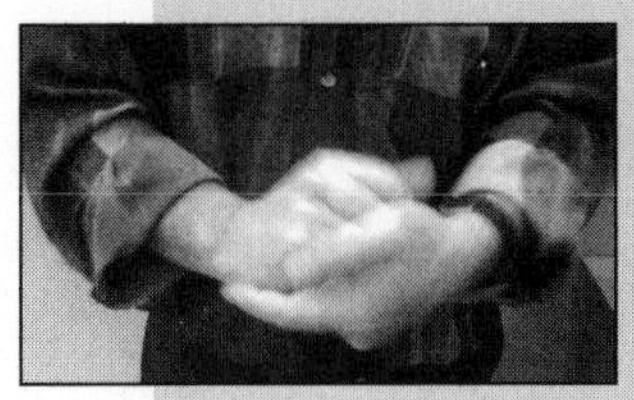

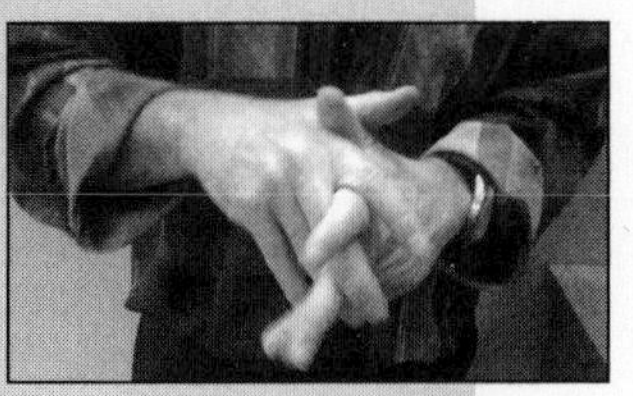

This sequence of photos of hands pointing downward being washed takes place over two seconds.

Here, a journalist is asked what he thinks of radio slang. Wanting to defend his colleagues who speak slang, he is quite uncomfortable and answers by "washing his hands"; they slide together, one inside the other, like two snakes. By making this gesture, he looks for a way to bypass the question in order to answer correctly. This sequence of photos ends with the fingers tensed and pointing in the other person's direction. That is the sign that beyond the hand washing, his state of mind is detached, filled with unease and aggression.

This gesture can also be made between the legs. During an investigative interrogation, hand washing pointed downward is seen among guilty people (those who lie) but not among innocent ones. The former's hands point down toward the ground and hide because they are far from dominant. They vigorously rub their hands against each other in search of an escape. Note that we are not saying that this is the gesture of a guilty person, but rather of someone who is uncomfortable, who does not know how to respond to a dominant person.

- The hands hide inside each other when we are trying to create a distance.
- The nature of this distance is visible in the configuration of the hands.
- Each finger has a specific functional role. They are held by the opposite hand when concerns connected to their symbolic functions are encountered.

“The idea that mental activity, from its simplest aspects to its most sublime, requires both brain and body proper became especially compelling. I believe that, relative to the brain, the body proper provides more than mere support and modulation: it provides a basic topic for brain representation.”

—Antonio Damasio
Descartes’ Error

“I move external objects with the aid of my body, which takes hold of them in one place and shifts them to another. But my body itself I move directly; I do not find it at one point of objective space and transfer it to another. I do not need to look for it. It is already with me.”

—Maurice Merleau-Ponty
Phenomenology of Perception

PART THREE

When the Body Thinks Out Loud

The human being is a creature of emotion. Sociable, he suppresses those emotions that he does not want to transmit but that a specialist can detect in an itch or an asymmetry of any feature. But not all emotions are meant to be suppressed. Some of them, on the contrary, are even amplified, again thanks to body language. The role of certain gestures is to help those outgoing emotions emerge, to highlight them. We are no longer talking about facial or body gestures, about all those moments when the hand, at the body's command, relieves an itch before sheepishly returning to the other hand. No, we are talking about sweeping gestures now, of those that allow the human being to affirm his humanity.

Gestures speak; they speak because they say more than words can by being more precise. This is the law of success. A person wants to be understood and he will be beyond his expectations.

CHAPTER 14

Gestures Also Had a "Big Bang"

Gestures have a function: to support our speech. They put conviction into a conversation and facilitate us getting closer to each other. But first, why and how did they appear? Until their origin has been explained, it will be useless to try to understand what gestures say.

Who Would Have Bet on the Longevity of the Gesture?

One day, spoken language appeared, and that day who would have bet on the longevity of the gesture? Against all odds, gestures, which should have disappeared with the appearance of words, proliferated instead!

Gestures should have disappeared because their primary function was to describe. From the moment spoken language appeared and it began describing reality with unequaled precision, gestures should have been replaced by the new instruments of progress: words. Now, look around you. We are compelled to recognize that this is not what happened. The hand moves, during an interaction, about every six seconds, which means that it makes ten gestures in a minute if the atmosphere is of an average emotional intensity. A person who participates in conversation for three hours a day and who will live for seventy-five years will make nearly 40 million unconscious gestures over their lifetime! These gestures tell the story of what is unconscious. In a certain way, they are all of the life of that which is unconscious. This is a considerable godsend that we are unaware of, and its deciphering is crucial.

Gestures have not disappeared because their function is not to replace words! They have not replaced them for three principal reasons:

1. Words were not numerous enough to replace gestures overnight. There must have been some grunts before "It is possible that it will rain today!" became well articulated. For centuries, gestures and words were acculturated and existed together, jointly.
2. Words did not replace gestures because of the relevance of body language. A person who says, "It is possible that it will rain today!" can smile and thereby attest that it is time for the harvests, or make rapid gestures to express the necessity to protect himself from the rain, unless his arms, in the bad weather, don't drop from fatigue. In short, body language is essential to providing nuances, subtleties, and for this reason, not only have gestures not disappeared, but they will never disappear. Their role will develop even further.
3. Gestures are indispensable to speech in a situation of exchange and allow us to synchronize with other people. These gestures are unconscious but necessary. Children who are born blind make gestures. They have, however, never had the opportunity to see somebody else make them.

As astonishing as that might seem, gestures that we make when saying, "Pass me the salt!" are inscribed in our genetic heritage!

Current gestures are inscribed in our brains at three stages. Let's take a tour around the house.

The First Generation: The Proto-Gestures of Dominance and of Sharing

The first gestures have undoubtedly helped place hierarchy in a group. It is by being recognized as dominant that human beings, and before them the great apes, and before them small monkeys . . . made themselves known as such. The fact of standing up in order to claim dominance and be on top is an attitude identifiable as much with monkeys at it is with children. It is interesting to see that the joy that is obtained from "winning," and therefore "beating" someone, accompanies gestures of recovery. These are part of our genetic heritage. They are made without having really been learned.

In every attitude of victory, the body gets bigger. These attitudes are more ancient than modern man.

Great apes raise their arms before hitting the ground to convey their joy. These gestures were then refined to become totally human and function outside of the contexts that they were born in. For example, when someone has a drink, the more he respects the person with whom he is drinking, the more he will drink.[1]

Attitudes of submission that lead to bowing, making oneself smaller, and lowering the eyes also appeared, forming the first words in the body language alphabet. The non-human primate bequeathed the attitude of dominance to the human primate. Hundreds of centuries later, this is still present in our genetic makeup.[2] The dominant person lets himself touch the other person, like the dog who puts his paw on his fellow dog that he dominates. Humans did not have to learn this reality; we knew it all along.

In all the attitudes of dominance, the dominant person is the one who lets himself touch the other.

Certain individuals do not like to be touched, often because they do not agree or recognize the other person's supremacy. This behavior is inherited from the animal world.

In the hierarchically coded universe, touching is always done by the dominant party. In fact, it is not in good taste for someone of an inferior status to touch a person higher up. Moreover, he will not do it.

In this first attitude range, a person unilaterally imposes a code of communication on another. But sharing gestures, passed down by non-human primates, also emerged before spoken language. The ape who wants to be deloused will indicate this by placing his hand on the part of the body that he wants his fellow ape to groom. A human being makes this gesture when his hand is tenderly placed on his body, guiding the other person's glance to where his hand stops.

This unconscious strategy of making a connection is again a genetic gift from non-human primates to *Homo sapiens*.

With humans as with animals, this unconscious but very real strategy often has sensual connection as a goal. The hand leads the glance where she wants him to go, without anything having to be said.

This young woman leads the glance to the nape of her neck.

This woman covers her chest with her hand, leading the gaze where it would not otherwise have gone.

The woman in the photograph on the left[3] isn't thinking: "I am going to put my hand on my neck to lead your glance to where my flesh is softest!" Her physical attitude is unconscious.[4]

The first proto-gestures belong to a universal category, appearing in every animal kingdom. They are still nonverbal behaviors today, but other categories have appeared as the human brain evolved.

The Second Generation: The Gesture at the Origin of Spoken Language

For a very long time, the only serious theory that explained the jump-start of man from his cousin the ape consisted of the acquisition of bipedalism. Standing, it was thought, allowed the descent of the pharynx and the larynx in the throat, making the emergence of spoken language possible. But for this theory to be true, it would have been necessary for the cerebral area of language to appear where only the emotional cry of the ape had existed previously. But the area of speech did not develop there. The baby who cries because he is hungry does not activate the same cerebral area as the child who says that he is hungry. An emotional cry and language are not connected. Human speech appeared, in fact, in the cerebral area occupied by the body language of the great apes![5] Speaking with the use of an organ is one thing; having something to say is another! The larynx and pharynx, without the intelligence that gives meaning to language, are not of much use.[6]

The most serious hypothesis today consists of the theory that by standing, *Homo erectus* made his hands available for other things than maintaining balance,[7] notably for relational interaction.[8] The cerebral area controlling gestures became an "area of words"[9] at the rate that it was able to make its gestural "gutterality" understood.

Apes communicate among themselves with "ritualized gestures," like delousing, for example, and pointing out objects that they want to obtain. Their movements are urgent, demanding. They do not make these exchanges for pleasure, as humans do. Children fabricate, in an innate way, a category of gestures not understood by even the most evolved of apes: those of sharing, also known as "declarative gestures." They are able, from the age of a few months, to point their fingers at a cloud or the moon, for example, without any other expectation than to share the event.[10] These gestures are particular to human beings.

The Clear Distinction Between "I" and "You"

Verbal language and body language are connected. It is a signal of a young human being about to speak when his index finger dissociates from his other fingers to designate things. The index finger is the gestural area related to that of speech. And, in fact, the area of the dominant index finger becomes warmer just before we say a word.

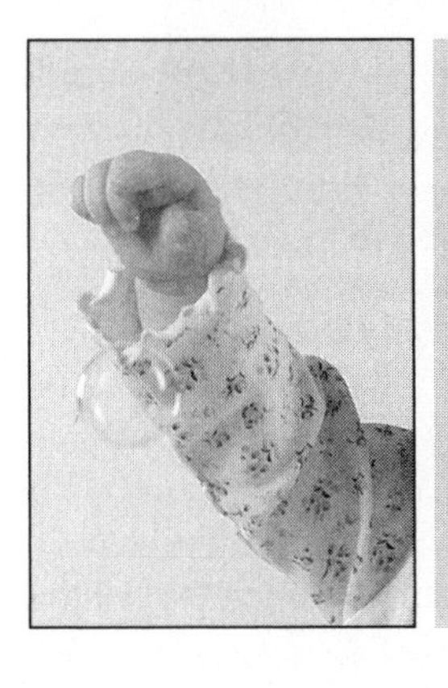

The baby shows his hand first (on the left). Then one day his index finger will dissociate from the other fingers (on the right). He will then be on the way to pronouncing his first structured words.

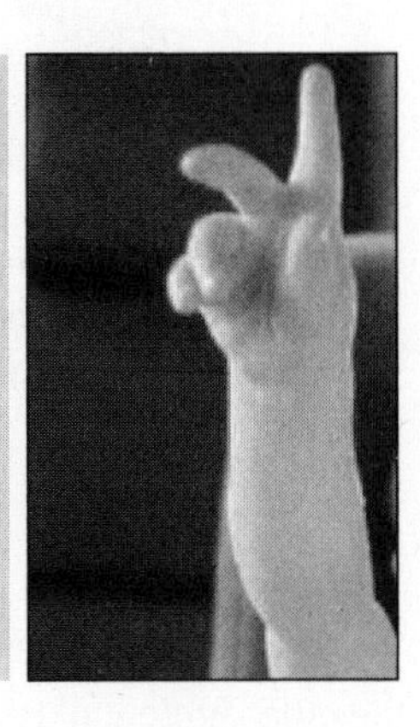

Gestures designating "me" and "you" are without a doubt the origin of a number of other words once the cerebral difference between the self and the other is established. At four years old, a child discovers the difference between "I" and "you." He understands that his thoughts are different from those of another, and thus his interests are too![11] This is the last stage of the consciousness of self. This discovery will have an enormous impact on his communication as an adult.

"I." The human being uses his index finger in order to share. This gesture is his own.

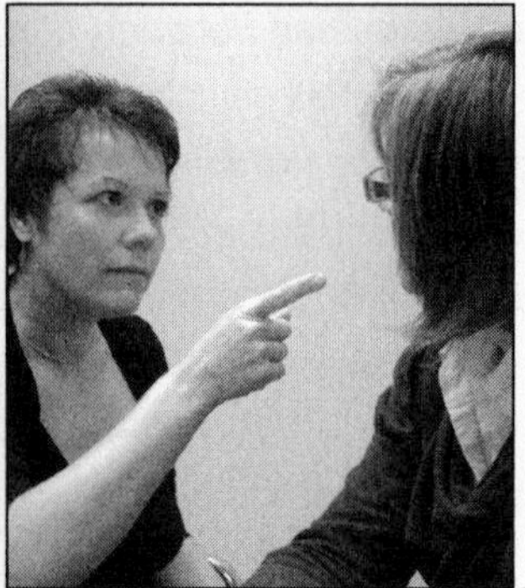

"You." This person designates the other. This accesses human intersubjectivity.

Understanding the difference between "I" and "you," between the self and the other, profoundly transforms what an emotion even is, because from the point when a human being understands that what he feels and what he tells another person are two different things, the emotion will be on one side and the expression of that emotion on the other.

We Must Not Confuse the Emotion That Is Felt With the Emotion That Is Expressed

Human emotion is fundamentally different from animal emotion for one simple reason: Human beings know that an emotion is an emotion![12] Our upright position allows us to use our hands for other things than maintaining balance. They have become entirely separate tools that we can, to some extent, watch as they act. By giving orders to our hands, we have created distance from ourselves. The two following gestures illustrate this property of the human mind.

"Shh!" In the photo on the right, the woman's posture is completely free from the injunction of the gesture. It even conveys complicity.

Normally this gesture is coercive and indicates that it is forbidden to speak, but in the photo on the right, the gesture has lost its prohibitive, negative character, even if it continues to indicate "silence."[13]

Gestures will not be automatic expressions of emotions, but will rather qualify them, sometimes even color them differently. This realization gives birth to conscious gestures. The intentional decision to make one gesture over another is born.[14] The hand and speech become accomplices. It is the hand that holds back speech and thoughts hidden behind the emotion.

"I am keeping this thought to myself so as not to laugh."

"I am keeping this thought to myself to give myself time to reflect."

"I am keeping this thought to myself for modesty's sake."

"I am keeping my anger to myself."

The hand is the human being's accomplice in face of emotions. Body postures can substitute for words: a hand coming in front of the mouth and a glance addressed to another person, so vivid that he understands that he must look behind the gesture. Our hands, mouths, and eyes are controlled by our thoughts. Communication begins to exist, accentuated at multiple levels.

The mouth represents the oral; the hand leads the glance there. A sensual attitude.

"The way I look at you must let you know that I have more to say that I won't." The index finger is the finger that says "I."

If gestures really support words so much that they end up substituting them, it is because human beings who observe each other know that silence is itself a carrier of communication, that they don't need words in order to speak and understand.

The Third Generation: The Word Triggered the Outbreak of the Gesture

The symbolic will be born, and even explode with the appearance of the structured word. Gestures, too. The human being begins to speak. He becomes capable of predicting, anticipating, connecting events and ideas with each other, and in this context the development of language takes on a metaphoric character. A man or a woman said, one day when the sun was high, "The atmosphere is heavy!" and made themselves understood even if the words "atmosphere" and "heavy" had never been used together before, because a gesture, a body posture, was able to illustrate this metaphor.

"The atmosphere is heavy!" The gesture and the facial expression of this woman let us visualize this image and feel the evoked atmosphere.

Metaphors go one step further than gestures.

The emergence of speech inevitably leads to the question: How are people who do not know each other able to communicate so easily?

Thinking about them, a person can evoke themes as abstract and immaterial as the human mind, space, time, life . . . with perceptions and definitions that are invariably different from those of other people, and yet he can make himself be understood very well! Gestures are not strangers to this phenomenon.

Human beings understand each other for two reasons:

- Words are concrete!
- Gestures reinforce the concrete aspect of dialogue.

Words Are Concrete!

Everything that is not concrete is not understood by the human mind and will be forgotten. It is on this model of concrete realities that abstract realities are built. Here is an example: A growing baby drinks milk. His mother drinks him in with her eyes. Then he will start to eat food, eager to taste earthly food, to devour life, to savor every moment, to bite off as much as he can chew, all the while paying attention to not eating too quickly for the sake of his health. As an adult, weary of chomping at the bit, he will feel the desire to nourish himself with other things, to not swallow or gobble up just anything, and not allow anyone to intervene with his choice to fuel some controversy. Life is too short, and ten seconds have been taken from him since you read this paragraph.

Descriptions of life inevitably pass through a succession of metaphors. Are they necessary? Yes, it is impossible to do this without them. They permit us "to speak of one thing in terms of another."[15] By imagining ideas, we make them concrete.

Take the example of the human mind. It is difficult to conceive of a more abstract reality, and yet consider these few sentences:

"I find it difficult to work today."
"His mind is absent."
"Be careful; he is fragile."
"You must treat him with care."
"He is all washed out."
"I've gone a bit soft in the head."
"He's a bit rough around the edges."
"He had a breakdown," etc.

The mind is evoked as if it were an object, a machine, a concrete reality. This is not a choice; it is a necessity to make ourselves understood. This explains a phrase like "Time is money." Transformed in this way, time is no longer immaterial, but it is closely quantified and takes on another dimension. No communication escapes from this reality.

Metaphors inscribe reality spatially. The top is always designated as positive and the bottom as negative. Happiness is at the top. This explains why we are in top form, that we are with the angels, that we must raise our spirits, get back on our feet, that a child must raise his grades in school otherwise there will be hell to pay at home, why depression makes us hit rock bottom, why when things can't sink any lower they must go up. The dominant is at the top, the dominated below; health is on top, sickness on the bottom. To be healthy is to live life standing up; to be sick is to lie down, like the person who pauses momentarily to lie down during a poker game. In short, these metaphors not only explain reality, but they also use our acquired experiences to make them material.[16]

An exchange of words is invisible; it is made concrete by the use of metaphors, indispensable for making ourselves understood and sharing the immaterial. But all this would not be so precise if words were not accompanied by gestures . . .

Gestures Reinforce the Concrete Aspect of Dialogue

The metaphoric work that makes most immaterial facts concrete would not be complete without gestures. They help convert ideas into material things. Look at these several examples taken from real situations.

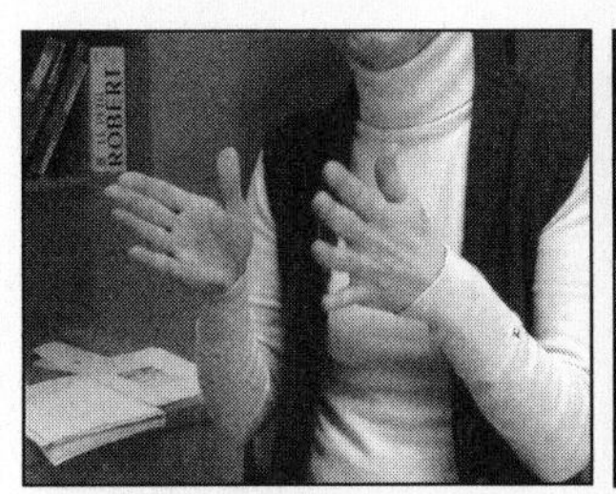

"We must try a more radical solution."

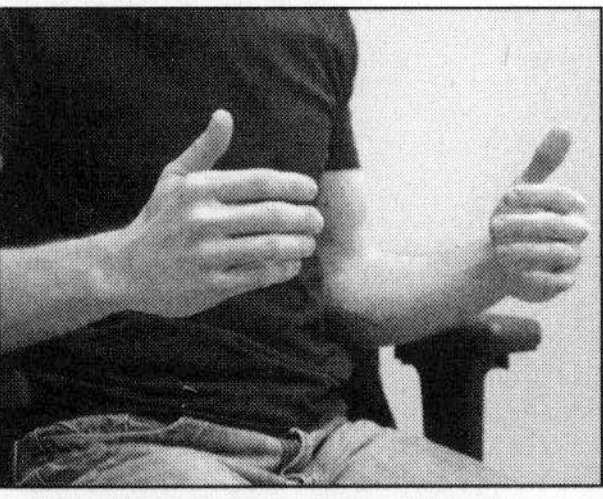

"There are language barriers."

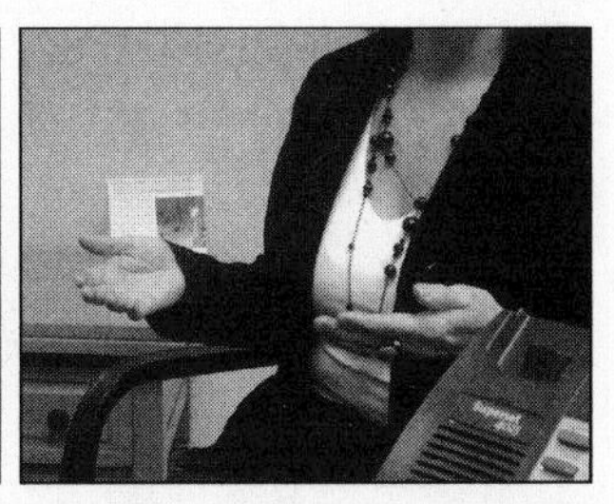

"We have given all that we can give."

These different gestures support speech. They do more than illustrate reality: They give it its consistency. They are not necessary for reflection but are indispensable for sharing. Human beings, when they are alone, do not make gestures. These are intended for others during interactions. They compress the thought addressed to the other person.

In the image above on the left, "the solution" becomes an item in itself, one we can hold in our hands. The woman indicates this in her gesture so the person across from her can imagine it. In the middle photo, concrete language barriers get in the way of communication. Finally, in the image on the right, the woman holds in her hands, in an imaginary way, what she has given. Her movement makes this gift tangible. We do not make a conscious effort to understand these people yet we understand them better thanks to their gestures.

Between people who are trained to observe nonverbal gestures, these movements are said to be semi-conscious rather than unconscious, because they are made without thinking, but it suffices to hear, "Well, you are making gestures!" for the awareness of body language to emerge. Nevertheless, these gestures are most often spontaneous and unconscious. This is the case with the gestures below.

Gestures are unconscious. People speak and forget that they are making them, but they can become conscious of them at any time; they are thus semi-conscious.

Gestures are an expression of the collective unconscious. They are, in a subliminal way, universally understood because the same gesture made by different people always conveys the same thought.

If certain people never make a such-and-such gesture (this happens), it is because they "never" feel the emotional tonality associated with it. Calm people, for example, never hit their fists against tables, not because they do not know how to do it, but rather because the gesture's emotional tonality is not in agreement with who they are. On the other hand, all people who hit their fists against tables are universally expressing anger.

The nature of gestures has changed over the course of time.

Modern gestures appeared with the emergence of speech. They have diversified it profoundly.

Gestures that were used for speaking have been replaced by those that allow sharing.

Today, two large categories of gestures coexist:

1. Those that are conscious, indispensable for understanding each other and intended to describe. They replace speech in certain conditions (interactions with strangers, in noisy places).
2. Those that are unconscious and that clarify speech. These are by far the most numerous.

CHAPTER 15

Today, Four Types of Unconscious Gestures Coexist

Gestures allow ideas to integrate themselves into conversation. They transform abstract ideas into intangibles. This is one of the general conditions of a verbal exchange of good quality, a necessary formality of understanding each other well. Ideas, thus transformed and singled out, begin to come alive in conversation.

In these images, the people seem to be holding something that we cannot see. Ideas (events, relationships, emotions) are transformed into tangibles.

All of our dialogues necessarily take one of these forms. Four kinds of gestures, indispensable to communication, express them:

- figurative gestures describing events;
- symbolic gestures characterizing relationships;
- projective gestures expressing emotions; and
- engram gestures making speech more fluid.

Figurative Gestures Describe Events

Figurative gestures are descriptive. They illustrate material realities so that the other person can visualize them. For example, a person makes a gesture with his hands and says, "He had to dig a hole more than three feet deep"; another person wipes his forehead which is actually dry while saying, "The sun is blazing hot"; another uses his hands to make an outline of an umbrella; and another describes the fish that she saw jump next to her fishing rod.

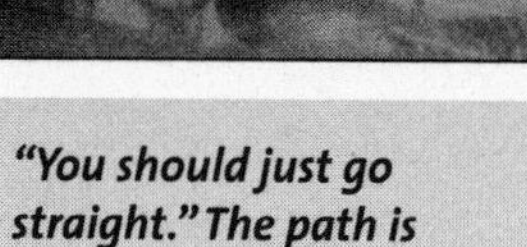

"You should just go straight." The path is shown.

"Call me!" The telephone is shown.

"I caught one this big!" The fish is shown.

A good communicator always makes many gestures. His descriptions—exact because they are imagined—contribute to making what he says vivid, accessible, and therefore concrete and real.[1] He puts images in our heads, giving a material basis to events. The abundance of his gestures expresses his engagement, his enthusiasm, and the actions described in detail become all the more interesting to follow, to listen to, to watch.

Symbolic Gestures Characterize Relationships

People who think that gestures are cultural in fact evoke symbolic gestures.[2] Their origin is cultural. These gestures are born in a specific environment and develop there. For example, a person learns, while playing basketball, the gesture that signifies "time out" (when a break in the game is called). One day, he makes this gesture in another context without realizing he is saying, "Let's stop!" This gesture has then become a physical expression independent of the universe in which it was formed.

Symbolic gesture meaning an interruption of the game.

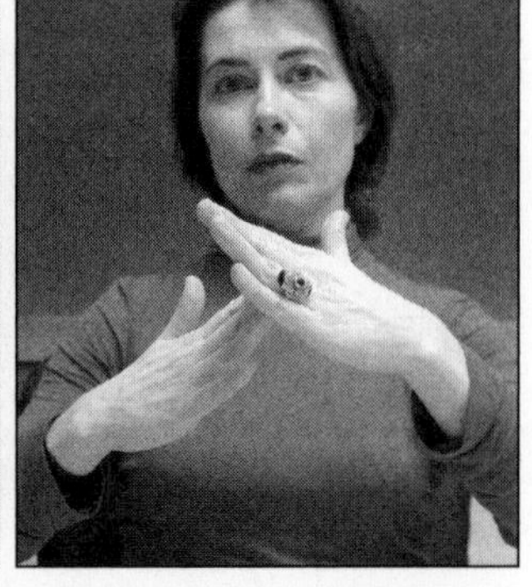

"Cut" or "pause" or "time out."

The birth of these symbolic gestures is associated with the construction of mental states. Inner calm generated by their practice can be reassuring, simply because emotions, information, and motor skills are interconnected in the brain.[3]

Rituals always create new gestures. To identify them systematically would be, in the context of this book, laborious and not very interesting. It suffices for us to know that symbolic gestures that are learned methodically in a context will then be exported and performed, often unconsciously, in a context other than the one in which they were created.

Professions in which noise or distance prohibits verbal exchanges like, for example, scuba diving, aviation, carpentry . . . are particularly conducive to the creation of conscious symbolic gestures.

"It's all good."

"Nothing is going well."

These gestures are made inside and outside of their contexts. Raising your thumb existed before aviation and diving, but pilots, by popularizing the gesture, gave it a second life. In the same way, the gesture of the thumb turned toward the ground performed by Roman emperors in arenas to condemn plebeians is found again in all countries where movies have popularized it. The day television will have conquered the planet with standardized programs, the symbolic, cultural character of gestures will become truly universal.

"Great!"

"Everything is OK."

"Excellent!"

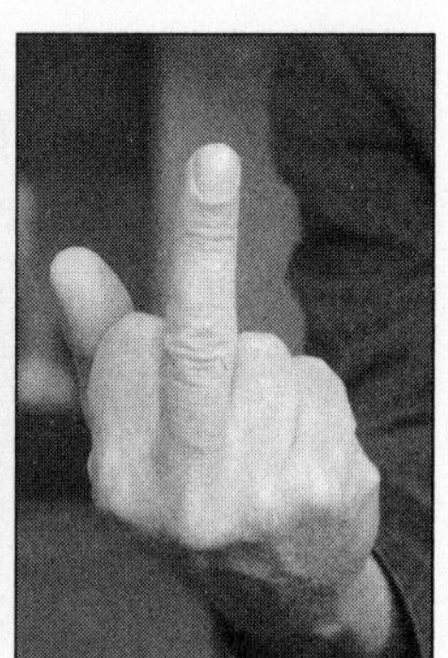

"Screw you!"

All gestures are still images. They freeze time to crystallize the relational state that they evoke. There are about 200 or 300 of them.[4] They are initially cultural, but can be widely understood across the planet. Emotion conveyed by the face at the same time that a gesture is performed generally allows us to recognize its significance, even if it seems initially incomprehensible.

Projective Gestures Express Emotions

Gestures that express emotions are by far the most frequent. Even if they are fewer and less developed in primates than in human beings, these gestures are common in both species. They transmit messages of the heart. Our hands that move in the air talk about our interiority. An arm gesture involves the whole shoulder, sometimes even the head, and if we look closer, the entire body is actually completely involved in the communication.

Projective gestures are many; they are in fact the most numerous, but not the most difficult to decipher, because the same principles apply to decode them. In an interaction, your arms are projected in front of you. Nobody really thinks about it but the direction of the wrists is not at all the same depending on whether a person wants to open herself up emotionally to another person or not. Observe:

"Let's talk to each other."

The palms of this man's hands include the other people in his bubble. This is the gesture made when taking someone in your arms.

"Leave me out of this."

The palms of this man's hands place the other people outside of his bubble. This is the gesture used to push or repel a person or an object.

Observing the wrists is sufficient to understand if a person's state of mind has changed.

Projective gestures are the most frequent and the most revealing in every state. In the rest of this book, we will decipher them scrupulously because they speak of emotions with accuracy. Suffice it to say, for the time being, that knowing a certain category of gestures allows us to evaluate the emotional state of the people who are speaking.

It remains for us to discuss engram gestures. Up until now, all the gestures evoked served to communicate. This last category reveals gestures that produce thoughts.

Engram Gestures Make Speech More Fluid

A baby, born blind, has never seen his parents make gestures; however, he will also make them! Gestures are indispensable for producing thoughts during a conversation. We make them even when we speak on the telephone![5]

Conversation differs from solitary reflection on one fundamental point: Another person gives his opinion, and it is necessary to take it into account because we must constantly integrate the contents of his speech into ours. Gestures stimulate the cerebral area intended to produce continuity in conversation.[6] People therefore talk by making gestures that are neither projective nor symbolic, but rather repetitive and quite brief.

Four different kinds of gestures reflect our relationship with reality. The same gestures, in appearance at least, have a different meaning depending on the situation being described, the relationship being symbolized, the emotion being related, or the speech being made.

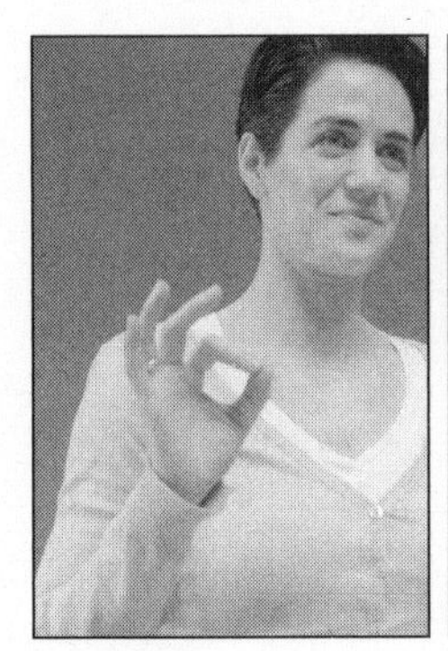

"It's OK."
Symbolic gesture.

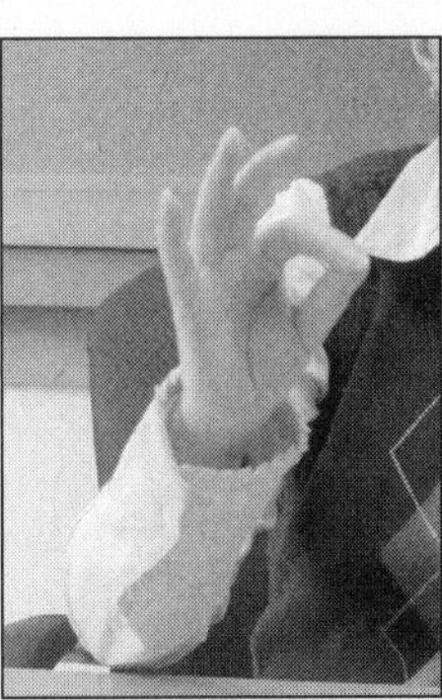

"That's exactly it."
Figurative gesture.

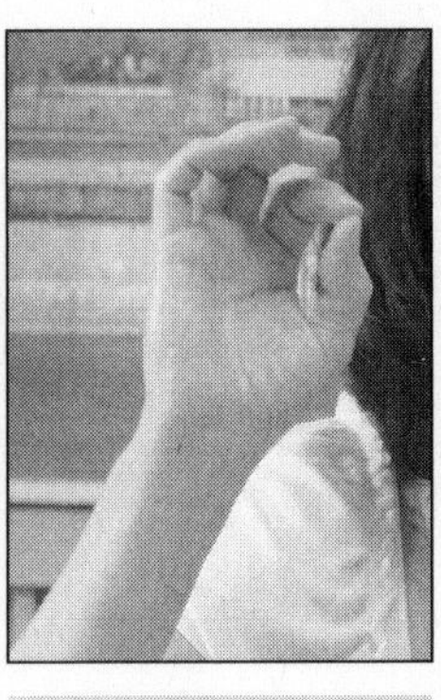

"That's what I wanted to say."
Projective gesture.

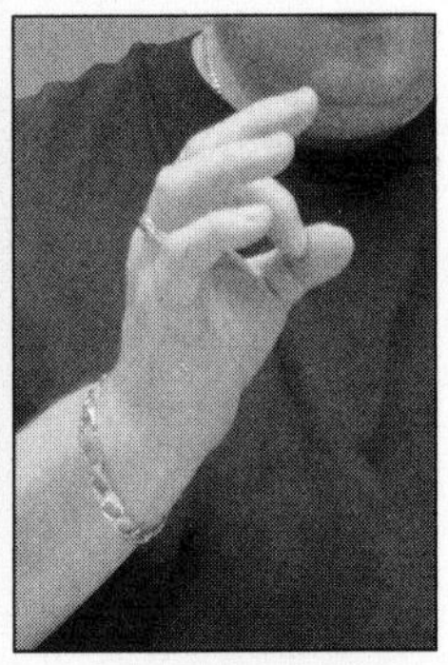

"I am searching for some detail."
Engram gesture.

Engram gestures are performed to stimulate the cerebral area in which speech is produced. It appears in conversation each time that a person is looking for the right words.

In fact, the same gesture can have several dimensions. It is found that 90 percent of gestures have an emotional dimension; we will therefore focus all our attention on them.

- Gestures allow us to modify our thoughts in order to better transmit them.
- Gestures function by making our thoughts concrete:

1. by describing situations (figurative);
2. by specifying emotions (projective);
3. by characterizing the state of a relationship (symbolic);
4. by making speech fluid (engram).

These four types of gestures can be utilized together in the same sequence of communication.

CHAPTER 16

The Wrists Give Their Informed Opinion

Gestures, beyond their general dynamic, all have one point in common: They convey the presence of emotions. They are visible in a particular segment of the arm: the wrist. Associated with the face and the body, the wrists move closer together in conversation and reveal rich indications about the emotional nature of the relationship. Five different configurations convey five types of very specific relationships.

"I am torn."

"We are connected."

"Let's move forward together."

"There's you, and there's me."

"Not for me, thank you."

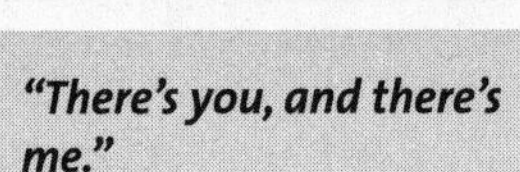

"I Am Torn!"

Normally, when a relationship is harmonious, the body presents itself as one unit. But sometimes the wrists point outward, as if one part of the person speaking is outside of the discussion. In fact, even if he does not say so, he is thus showing us that he is not totally connected to what he is saying, that he is divided. This gesture is often made when a person does not know what to decide.

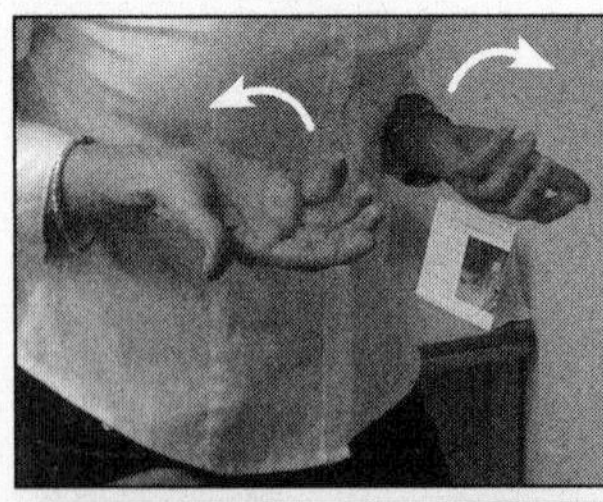

"I don't know; I am torn."

These people don't know what to do; the palms of their hands go outward.

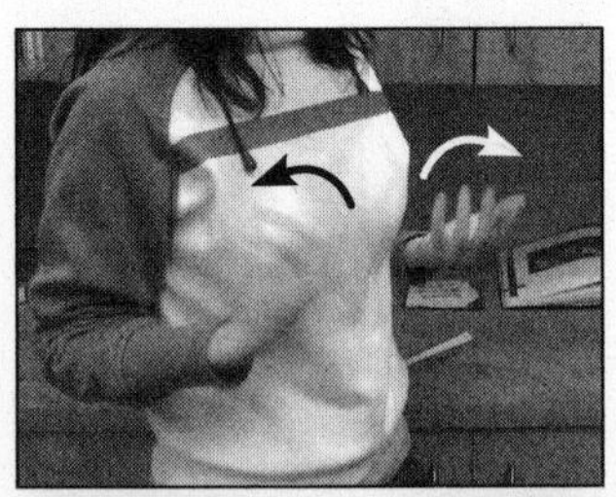

The person feels incapable of choosing, of deciding between one thing and another: His wrists extend outward. This is quite evident in the image on the top left on the previous page. In the other images, only the position of the wrists allows us to understand these people because what they are saying is certainly less clear. The palms of the hands say what a person doesn't always say—for example, that he is not totally in agreement with either the other person or with himself. Whether he expresses it verbally or not, his wrists do show this. And if he claims that he agrees, part of him does not! This is what happens, for example, if you are the spokesman of a group that has made a decision that was not yours. You have solidarity with the group but are in disagreement with their position at the same time.

In this mental attitude, the ring finger and often the little finger are separated from the other fingers of the hand. Both their motor functions are managed by the same principal nerve. Look at these other images.

Her wrist is turned outward; therefore her hand moves toward the outside.

The person is so divided that she seems to place herself far from what she is saying, as if she did not have the right to say it or she did not want to get involved. If the wrists of the people you are talking to are in this configuration often, this is part of their bodily heritage[1] and can correspond to a personality trait. This repetitive gesture indicates the fear of taking up too much space. Let's be clear: Here, it is a matter of people with whom this gesture is recurrent. Anybody can make this gesture at one time or another. We must therefore listen more attentively to what the person is in the midst of saying.

"I Totally Agree With You!"

A person is unified when his whole body engages in the same dynamic. Gestures are carried out with more roundedness, the wrist more relaxed. For example, a person who describes a wine and explains its qualities will say that it is round on the palate, easy to drink, and glides down the throat. His gestures will be in harmony with his speech and his wrist "will form one body" with his whole being as he expresses himself. It is also with sweeping gestures that your friends welcome you and share with you without a second thought.

The hands move back and forth incessantly between two people to facilitate their communication. The direction of the movement clearly translates into a willingness to improve the exchange.

The general position of the hand faithfully describes needs and desires. Here, the wrist is neither constrained nor rigid. The people are trying to attract each other, to return to themselves or to go toward the other; they express their feelings. They are not hiding and other indications on the face or the body should show this. This is the position of giving.

"Let's Move Forward!"

The person who wants to move forward or move faster gives his body the configuration needed to act and put himself in motion. His wrists are placed like those of a runner, offering the least wind resistance, thus permitting the discussion to move forward. These gestures are very pragmatic.

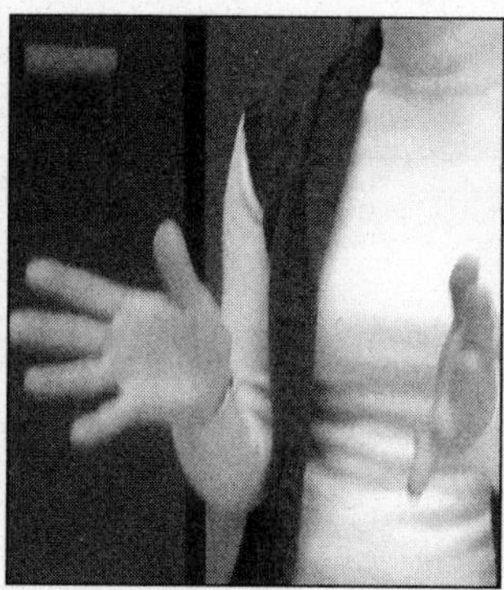

These people, by their gestures, show that they want to move forward and faster. The rest of their body is no longer languid, demonstrating the same desire.

Gestures are sharper and show the direction in which the person wants to go. The fingers are not always tense but are more so than in the preceding configurations, simply because these wrist positions convey action.

Be careful not to confuse these gestures with figurative gestures describing square shapes. Here, we are in the emotional domain.

"I Want Some Space!"

The wrists can convey our desire to extricate ourselves from an exchange, to distance ourselves. Even if the tone of the discussion is muffled, we indicate, with our wrists, that we do not place ourselves in the same bubble with the other person. The self is distinct and different from the other.

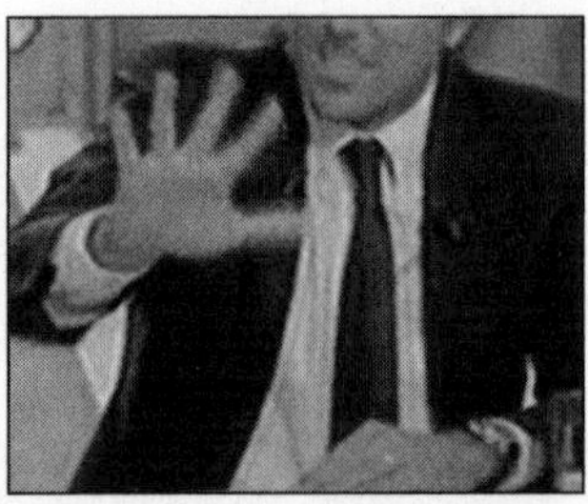

The palms of these people cut them off from the other person.

This gesture is frequently seen with police who stop drivers and ask them for their license and registration. It has even become symbolic, since one can see it on customs signs while crossing certain borders. In everyday life, it is performed much more unconsciously but the meaning is the same. The person who places his wrists in the direction of another person in this manner shows him, without necessarily telling him aloud, that they are of a different opinion and that they shouldn't mix everything up.[2] Phrases like, "One moment!", "Calm down!", "Wait your turn!" or "Don't ask me that!" are often present on the verbal level at the same time. But this gesture is even more interesting when the words are muted, because the wrists help us understand that the person does not want to proceed. Behind a façade of closeness, this creation of distance is real and can, on occasion, become rejection.

"I Reject!"

The distance taken from the other person and complete rejection are expressed by the wrists being very close to each other. It is simply the lack of flexibility in the joint—the wrist appearing locked—which prevents seeing the distinct configurations of the wrists more clearly.

Some differences are visible all the same, notably the position of the thumb. It has a tendency to pass under the other fingers to push the hand outward even more.

The thumb passes under the other fingers to push the hand outward.

Gestures blend with emotion that is visible on the face. A person often has difficulty hiding his nervousness or his annoyance. This is the only hand position out of five that is often so aggressive.

The position of the wrist is so graphic that even when someone is on the telephone and the person he is talking to is thousands of miles away, the nature of the interaction is understood.

"I am torn."

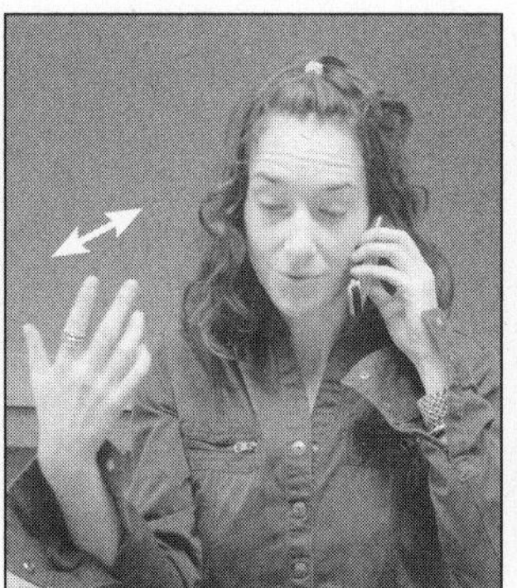

"We are connected."

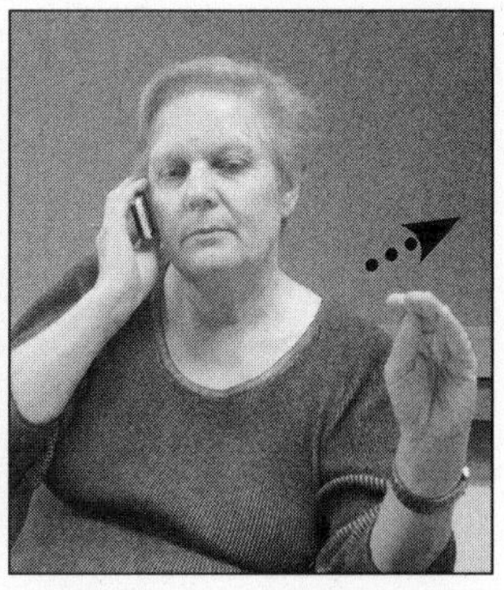

"There's you, and there's me."

Thanks to the wrists, the brain speaks through the hand.

Thoughts are transmitted to other people through hand movements.

The orientation of the wrists expresses the engagement of the body. It allows us to know if the other person is engaged in what he is saying or if he sets himself apart from his speech.

Five different wrist positions characterize five states of engagement.

CHAPTER 17

Discord Between the Head and the Hand

A person is a whole. He doesn't use a hand; he is the hand that he uses. The hand transmits the intentions of the brain into space. "Perched" in his brain, the person is trying to convey true messages, but at the same time, he does not want to say everything. He wants to keep to himself what he was not able to stop from thinking but which risks leaking out in his gestures! So he reins in his body so that he does not transmit his unconscious thoughts. But how can he do it? In the heat of a discussion, he is too concerned with finding the right words and appearing intelligent to continually pay attention to the choice of hand that occupies a certain space, to the position of his wrists, or, still more revealing, to the axis of his head as an extension of his hand. But his thoughts leak into his hand and is quick to "tag" his most unconscious thoughts in space.

A Person Is at the End of His Right Hand

Most gestures are made unconsciously. Holding car keys, pressing an elevator button, or jingling the change from the bread bought at the bakery in our pocket are small, unconscious gestures,[1] but that does not mean that they are made randomly.

The right arm, whether the person is right-handed or left-handed, is the active one.[2] Alert, the left hemisphere, and with it the right side of the body, becomes more active. It organizes things in order one after the other and introduces exactness into reasoning[3] so well that when the right hand moves around more than the left hand, the person is consciously expressing himself in a rational way.

Below, two people communicate with their right arms. The preceding lessons should help you decipher these photos.

This man uses his right arm (vigilance) and he looks more with his left eye (openness). His face is asymmetrical (ambivalence) and his wrist opens in our direction (connection). If he speaks of his discomfort, this is congruent with his body language, since his ambiguities are written on his face and his body.

MOVEMENT OF THE RIGHT ARM

Rationality

Vigilance

Discursive logic

Rigidity

This woman uses her right arm (vigilance) and looks more with her right eye (creating a distance). Her right wrist reinforces the established distance. If she says that everything happens for the best, we must understand that in reality things are more complicated than that.

A person is completely present in her gestures.[4] If she only uses her right hand in her interactions, it is possible that she is not able to relax. This will be the case, for example, with a candidate at a job interview or when someone is tackling a complicated issue. The issue does not allow for relaxation but helps the person stay focused. It is therefore not a question of putting someone on trial who has difficulty with being spontaneously at ease. Also, let's not forget to question our own attitudes and to ask ourselves if, by any chance, our lack of simplicity is not the principal cause of the other person's tensions!

A Person's Left Arm Talks About Him

In a conversation, it is common for people to use their left hand even if they are right-handed,[5] which shows that gestures are not carried out according to the logic of the dominant hand.[6] The left hand is directly tied to the right hemisphere, the hemisphere of spontaneity,[7] when we are resting and on auto-pilot because we are tired. Consider the example of someone who has misplaced his keys. Distracted by something else, he has placed them—probably with his left hand!—in a logical place dedicated to storing things but different from his habitual place. Tired, on "auto-pilot," his right hemisphere did the work without him being conscious of his actions.

Patrick Vertischel, a neurologist by profession, brings up the case of one of his patients, who is incapable of passing information from one hemisphere to the other.[8] This man walks into a bakery, asks for bread, and pays for it. What happens to him next is a misfortune that we might find comical in other circumstances. He places his money on the counter with his right hand, but his left hand takes it back! The man, realizing his mistake, takes the money from his left hand with his right hand, and places it on the counter for a second time, but the left hand takes it back a second time! The third time, the man puts the money down, blocks his left hand under his right armpit, and leaves the bakery!

This little anecdote, like the story of the misplaced keys, expresses two very important traits specific to the right hemisphere:

- It reacts spontaneously. The man took his money back automatically, without thinking.
- It responds to simple messages, like, "Do not leave your money!"

The left hand is that of spontaneity. People who speak while agitated do not filter the information that they transmit or economize certain cerebral efforts.[9] Those who communicate solely with their left arms register less structured information and put more confidence in what they feel than in what they rationalize, and they let themselves go. Their energy is directed toward the left side of their body.

The left arm is the arm of spontaneity. All of the visible signs indicate the openness and the well-being of this woman.

MOVEMENT OF THE LEFT ARM

Spontaneity
Impulsivity
Interior relaxation
Tiredness

This man's left arm shows impulsivity. He looks tired. He is on "auto-pilot" and no longer sorts through information.

When energy is sent to the left side of the body, people communicate with more spontaneity, but also with more impulsiveness. This knowledge is not used to its full value, without a doubt because it is not yet well established in the scientific community. But let us look at an example.

In 1967, General Charles de Gaulle took a trip to Canada. He planned to begin his journey in Quebec, the province that is predominantly Francophone. To most French people, he was just on an official visit to Canada; however, Quebec is like the other provinces because it was first a French colony 400 years ago. Named New France at that time, it then joined with other provinces and territories to form Canada.

When the head of the State of France arrived in this immense province—that seven million Quebecois, fighting for four centuries so that the French language would survive on the North American continent, call their "nation"—he met a fervor that overwhelmed him. He spent three days there and, after a trip that led him from Quebec to Montreal by the Chemin du Roy, was profoundly touched by the warm welcome that he was given. He marked the end of his journey with a speech that would make French-Canadian diplomacy so uncomfortable that de Gaulle would be invited to return to France immediately. In front of the crowd that had gathered at the foot of city hall in Montreal, he, in fact, said a sentence that will remain engraved in history books and will journey around the world, surprising protocol and rallying the majority of separatists who came to hear him: "Long live Quebec, long live free Quebec!"

A number of analysts have since asked themselves if de Gaulle had planned to say this audacious phrase, but our societies are so established in words that a nonverbal deciphering of the historic moment has never really been carried out. However, if we interpret the attitude of the head of the French State by comparing it to those that he expressed on other occasions in different circumstances, a very interesting phenomenon is observed. As much due to his military training as well as his personality, de Gaulle held himself very straight. His body could even be called rigid. Now, the moment he delivered this memorable sentence—he was behind two microphones and spoke directly into the microphone on the right—his cerebral dynamic changed, his body switched to the left and it is with his left hemisphere that he said: "Long live free Quebec!"

"Long live Quebec..."

"...long live Quebec..."

"...free!"

The body does not switch to the left without a reason. De Gaulle was not a man to make dramatic gestures. He always spoke in a very erudite manner. If his body switched to the left as he changed microphones, it is because very strong emotions guided him. No one will really deny it. But it is shown here clearly with nonverbal indicators.

Every time that the left side of the body and the left arm participate in an interaction more than the right side and the right arm, we can conclude that the person is very emotionally responsive.

People express themselves more with one hand than with another as a function of the cerebral energy that moves through them and thus shows whether they are spontaneous or, on the contrary, more in control of themselves. But if we observe the axis of the head in line with the hand that is utilized, this delivers still other messages.

The Head and the Hand: Connected or Not

When we look at another person, our gestures contribute to transmitting our thoughts. A person who is sure of what she is saying holds herself very straight; her gaze is direct; her gestures convey her thoughts with precision; and she is in full alignment with the axis of her neck. Her head bends to the side of the hand that is being used to communicate.

These people's heads bend toward the side of the hand that is being used to communicate. Their relationship with the other person is therefore harmonious.

When the head bends to the side of the active hand, the person communicates as one unit. He is totally present. The agreement between the unconscious choice of hand and the position of the neck is sufficient to make this clear.

Let us compare this series of photos to the previous one.

These people's heads bend toward the opposite side of the hand that is making gestures. Their relationship with the other person is not harmonious.

In this situation, the people seem fine, but in their heart of hearts, they are keeping a distance. They are not lying and they are not in disagreement with the person they are talking to, but they must defend a position that is not theirs or communicate with someone they don't care for. The position of their head is not congruent with the hand that is being used to communicate. Their heads and their bodies are going in one direction and saying one thing while their arms are going in another and saying something else, thus showing their refusal "to go toward" since their body is divided between the central axis (spine) and the peripheral (the arms).

These messages are all the more interesting to decipher if the people are smiling, as in the photo below. In fact, their smiles are not totally sincere because their eyebrows are drooping down toward their eyes.

The head and the arms dissociate when people are not totally in agreement and when they are uncomfortable or embarrassed in front of someone. However, the atmosphere is not always negative.

No one really pays attention to messages related to the axis of the head and the hand. Yet they clearly indicate emotional states. And this is without a doubt one of a baby's first benchmarks! In fact, babies will eat less if the head of the person holding the baby's bottle does not lean in the direction of the arm holding the baby!

In negative situations, the hand and the head naturally dissociate. The negativity of the exchange is reinforced, but here it is very logical.

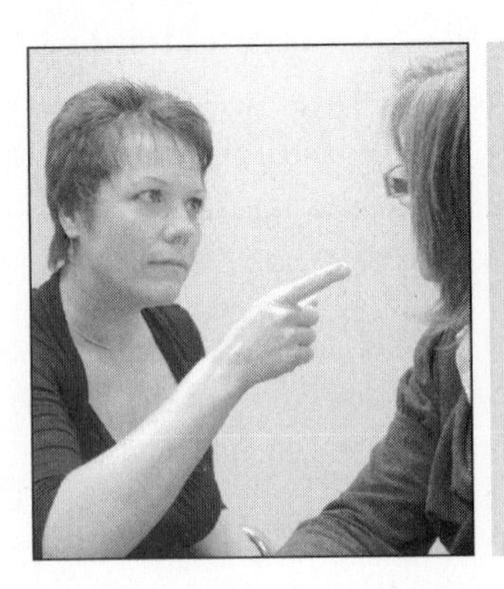

In this negative situation, the head does not move toward the direction of the chosen hand. This is completely logical.

Each time that the axis of the head and the hand are in opposite directions, we must ask ourselves why. If uneasiness is verbally expressed, the situation is normal. If, on the other hand, the person is trying to communicate a message of harmony, this is more surprising...

Someone who fidgets in his chair, who moves around, or who wavers, has a problem with the content of his message or with the person he is talking to. In these moments, the head's axis is never very straight, and his arms go in one direction while his head goes in another.

The hand expresses the state of thought: The left hand is used more when a person relaxes, while the right hand is used more when a person is trying to stay in control of the situation.

The axis of the head compared to that of the hand evokes the harmony of the exchange:

- **When a person's face and hand are turned in the same direction, he is in agreement with what he is saying and with the other person.**
- **When a person's face and hand go in different directions, he is expressing ambivalence, in relation to what he is saying or to the person he is talking to.**

CHAPTER 18

Our Gestures Speak of Our Values

Two people who are conversing with each other punctuate their words with gestures, trying to convince the other of the validity of their statements. Moving their hands around allows them to give their ideas concrete form. Their arms unfold in an incessant back-and-forth motion, one to the other, but a more meticulous observation shows us that they also move from right to left and outline imaginary points in space. Unconsciously, they are thereby revealing their deepest values, simply because to be consistent with themselves, they must place what they like and what they reject in the space in front of them.

The Part Education Plays in a Gesture

Reading the world takes place at the same pace as our education. A child learns that the future is "later," "tomorrow," "after." We tell him, "We will go to Mamie's house in three beddy-byes," and he understands that that is not right away. The past is "behind," "over," "before". . . The past and the future loom more clearly in space over the course of learning to write. A child forms letters that glide one after the other, from left to right in the West. Naturally, because his hand moves to the right as he writes, he places the past on the left of his paper and the future on the right. When he draws ladders, he will find this principle again on his ruler.

In the western world, writing goes from left to right, so the past is written at the beginning of the line on the left and the future at the end on the right.

In the Aramaic world, the past is written at the beginning of the line on the right and the future at the end on the left.

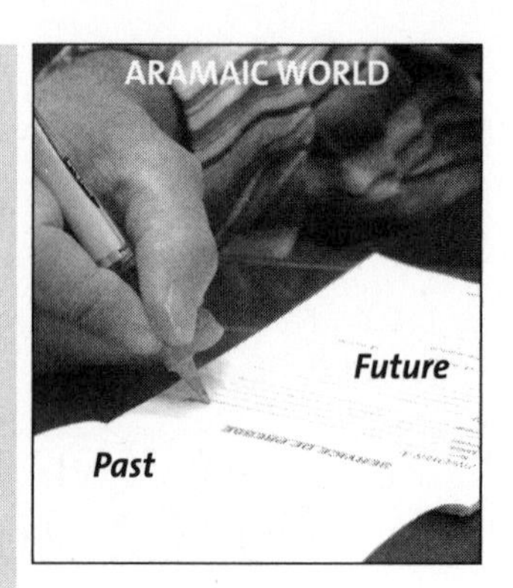

Psychologists, used to deciphering drawings, work with this reality every day. The location of an object on a piece of paper is an unconscious reality that concretely conveys itself by the fact that the past is drawn at the beginning of the paper to the left and the future to the right.[1] This reality is also found in gestures! We unconsciously place spatially, in our minds, the past to the left and the future to the right.

"What are you expecting tomorrow?"

Future.

For Westerners, the past and the future are spatially placed, respectively, from the left to the right.

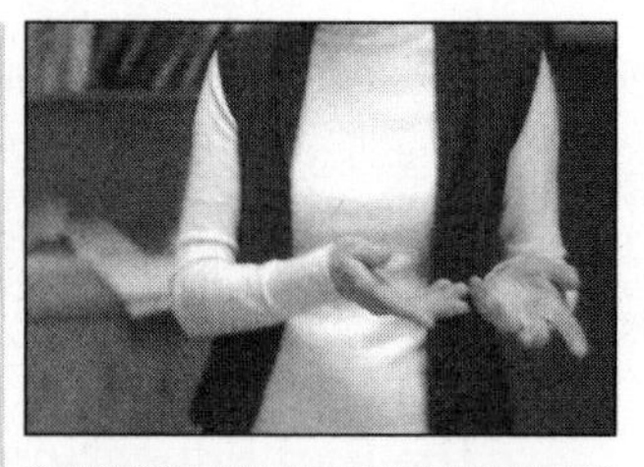

"In the past, human relations had a very particular form, more traditional..."

Past.

This sequence lasts three seconds.

When gestures accompany speech, it is as if space becomes a large, imaginary canvas.

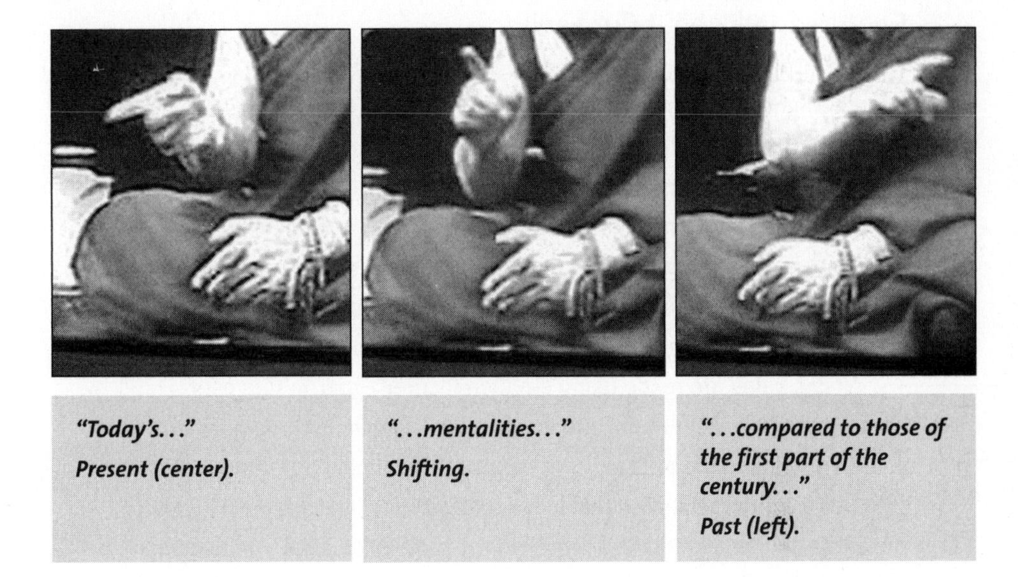

"Today's..."	***"...mentalities..."***	***"...compared to those of the first part of the century..."***
Present (center).	***Shifting.***	***Past (left).***

On this canvas, gestures addressed to the other person are not deciphered consciously, but they further support our speech. Remember eye movements. The same rules of deciphering apply here.

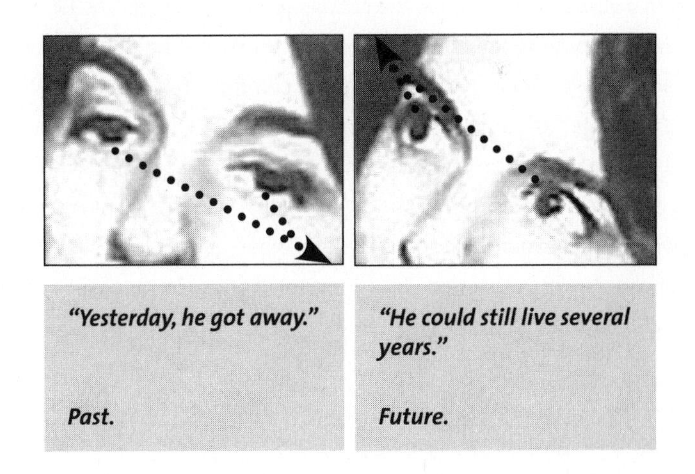

"Yesterday, he got away."	***"He could still live several years."***
Past.	***Future.***

The conception of time is thus encoded in the brain. Observing this rule[2] will allow us to integrate another reality that is even more interesting.

Gestures Talk About Our Feelings

The past is placed to the left and the future to the right. OK . . . but in everyday life, you might rightly object that most gestures are performed without evoking either the past or the future. If someone says to you, "I just read a book on string theory," there is no question of past or future, but the spatial position of his arms conveys a much more profound part of his personality.

Thought is almost always binary. It always requires choosing between this and that, this rather than that, this before that, or this after that.[3] This fact is without a doubt nothing less than a question of survival!

All decisions are made using emotional criteria and, in this context, all words, even the most neutral, are emotionally charged. Body language is not an exception to this rule. When two things are evoked at the same time, two gestures are often performed that are spatially distinct and that equally convey preferences.[4] The observation of the gestures' direction allows us to read the nature of emotions! Let's take, for example, the person who is talking to a colleague and asks him: "In order to finish this job more quickly, would you prefer to work with Donald or with Raynal?" The colleague responds: "For this project, you know, either Donald or Raynal, it doesn't make a difference to me!"

From a verbal point of view, the colleague is not engaged. As he does not formulate any preference, it is legitimate to think that he doesn't have one. However, the observation of the sequence of communication showed that with two everyday gestures, he placed Donald to his left and Raynal to his right. Without saying it, he expressed a preference. He prefers to work with Donald! When a person is relaxed, his gestures move spatially to the left when talking about what he likes more and to the right for what he likes less.[5] Gestures can be made with one or both hands: This does not change the process in any way.

This sequence lasts four seconds.

Here, a man considers scientists to be closed off, but the one he mentions is "open," to the philosophies of life. His gestures go from negative values, which he places to the right, toward positive values, which he places to the left.

What is fascinating with gestures is that they translate for the other person values that only make sense to ourselves. They do not reflect societal values but rather individual feelings, that which is personal and intimate. Words speak, gestures support them, and sometimes can do without the words.[6]

In the same vein, see here as a psychologist expresses herself speaking about relationships between couples on a Portuguese television show.[7]

"For couples, there are several ways to move away from each other..."

(Outside universe, to the right.)

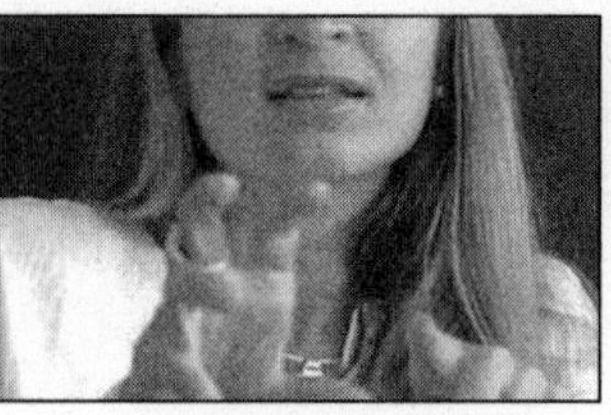

"...some do it through an adulterous relationship..."

(Outside universe, to the right.)

"...others by overprotecting their children..."

(Interior universe, to the left.)

This sequence lasts a total of seven seconds.

"...others by succeeding at work..."

(Outside universe, to the right).

"...still others through their hobbies..."

(Interior universe, to the left.)

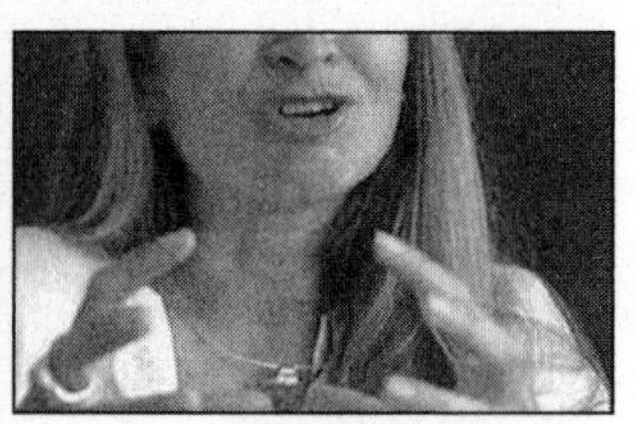

"...so much so that there is no more energy for the couple."

(Hands in the center.)

This phenomenon was observed before we were able to explain it.

It is the comparison with Aramaic gestures that has allowed us to understand the logic of gestural dynamics. See how an Aramaic person—in this case, an Algerian woman—places her world in relation to the outside world.

ARAMAIC LOGIC

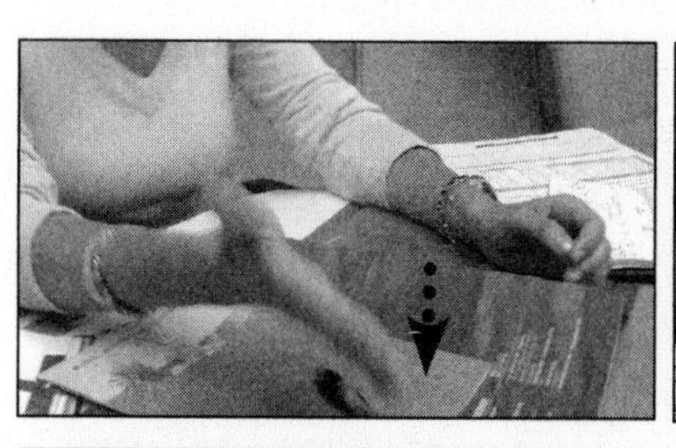

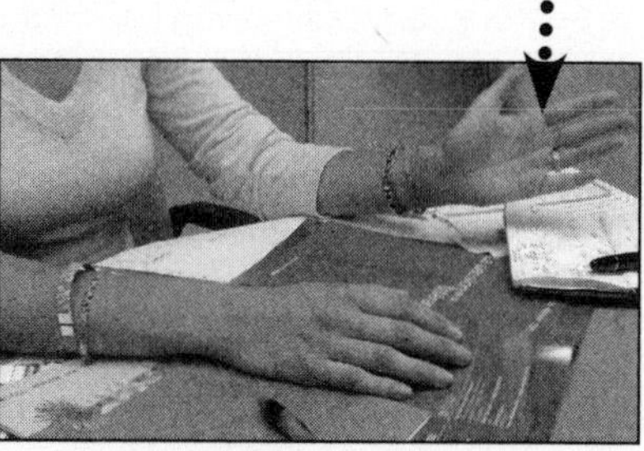

"Each one of our books leaves us with a seed of reflection . . ." (The interior world is placed to the right.)

". . .that refers us back to other books." (The outside world is placed to the left.)

Now observe the direction of the gaze of this other person from an Aramaic culture.

ARAMAIC LOGIC

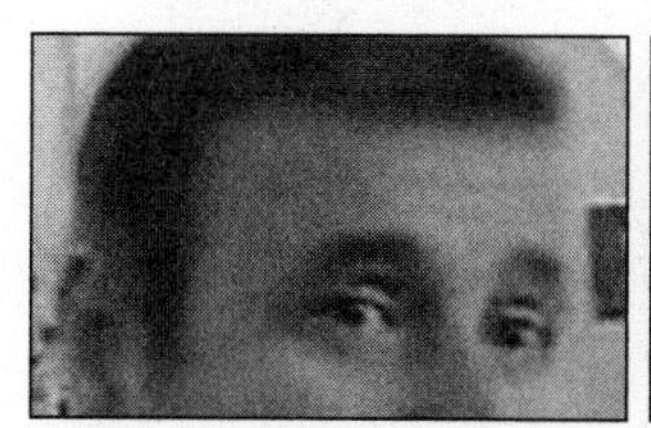

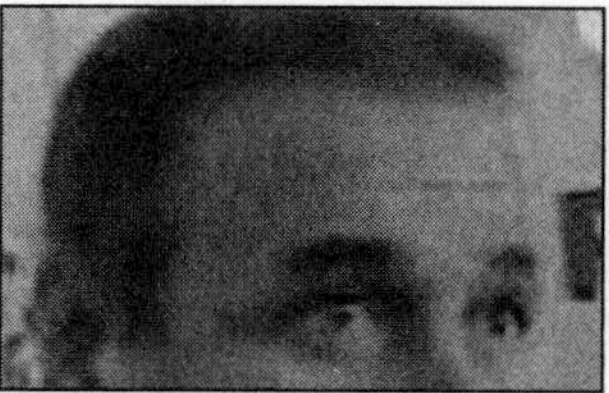

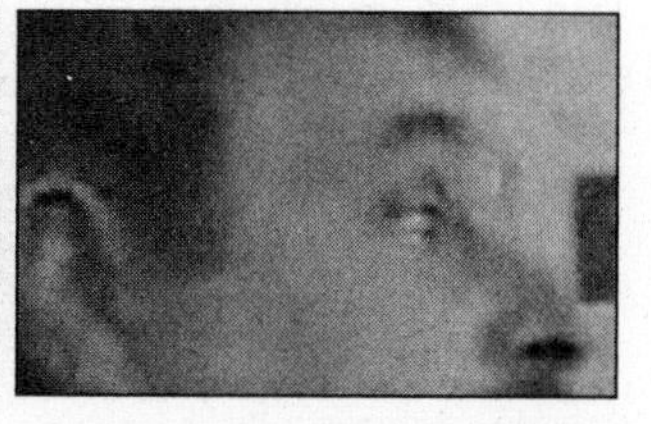

"You have true professionals (he is one of them), and people who come from the outside."

This sequence lasts five seconds.

For these two people, past and future read from right to left, like positive values (to the right) and negative values (to the left). Israeli values in the same dynamic read the same way.

Images like these are sufficient to persuade us that the values expressed by gestures have to do with basic education, but it is the gestures performed by people without writing that have really allowed us to understand what underlying phenomenon explains the connection between gestures, emotions, and values.

The Self, the Other, and the Awareness of Self

Westerners place what they like to the left and what they dislike to the right. Semetic people, for their part, when they speak Arabic or Hebrew, invert this process, according to how they learned to write. They speak about things that they like by placing them to the right and about what they dislike by placing them to the left.[8] But what about preliterate people?

"Me and my people know that there is progress."

"He left; I don't know if I will see him again."

This sequence lasts five seconds.

Through their gesture and gaze, preliterate people show that they place the interior world to the left and the exterior world to the right.

Here, unconscious spatial mapping brings this man who has no system of writing to place the clan to the left and what is outside of him to the right. People without writing place—this is, in any case, the most likely explanation in the current state of knowledge—their interior world to the left simply because the seat of self-awareness[9] in their right hemisphere leads them back to the left, to their interior world. They place to the right what is connected to the exterior.[10]

Self-awareness moves to the left, which refers to the self and intimacy, which is in opposition to that which belongs to the other on the right. The human being places what he likes in his interior world to the left and what he rejects to the right. Only different types of education can reverse this dynamic. That is what happens with the direction of Semitic writing, for example.

At this point in the book, a fact has perhaps intrigued you—the one of the connection between the gestures on the body (like when there is an itch) and those in the space in front of it among Western people. A person feels an itch on the left side of his face and his body when a subject that touches him positively is evoked; he performs spatial gestures to the left when he speaks of a prized value. This relationship explained by the theory of self-awareness should help a lot in reading movements on the body and spatial movements.[11]

Spatial gestures are not always made in the same place.

In the Western world, when people are relaxed because they feel positively, whether they are referring to the past or whether they are talking about things they appreciate or love, gestures are made to the left.

In the Western world, gestures that are connected to the future, to that which is exterior or despised and therefore rejected, are made to the right. These points are reversed in the Easterm world.

In stressful situations, the spatial references are different and these essential points are reversed.

CHAPTER 19

At What Point Is Body Language Universal?

Hundreds of centuries of exchange, of sharing, of attempts to better understand one another and make ideas clearer and more accessible have shaped a gestural heritage that is present today in every human being. But paradoxically, though gestures are universal, individual gestural heritage is influenced by culture! These two ideas seem contradictory . . . Here, therefore, are several clarifications.

Our Gestural Heritage Is, Above All, Genetic

All field observations agree and lead to the same conclusion: The nature of the gesture is universal. Wherever on the planet images of human beings communicating have been deciphered, their gestures look astonishing alike! If you doubt this, look at all the ethnological films referring to the Japanese, Chinese, Korean, Aramaic, Indonesian, or African languages, etc., and you will soon realize that there is no gesture made that is not universally understood!

This rule is true for societies with writing as well as for those without writing, which have evolved away from so-called developed societies. When these people that we call "primitive" are observed through "civilized" lenses, their movements, their gestures, their relationships to objects or to delicate motor skills never seem incongruous or even bizarre. The way they dress, their relationship with intimacy, and their way of transmitting knowledge differs from those of so-called evolved societies, but their gestures seem, however, to be the same, attesting to their universal foundations.

It takes just asking a stranger how to get somewhere before realizing that barriers of spoken language are not unavoidable and that everyone has at their disposal, in their genetic makeup, the necessary background to understand and to make themselves understood across cultures.

When by chance I meet people at conferences who are incredulous at this discussion (I was myself before compiling so much information), I tell them, if I am in Canada, for example: "Here we are in Canada. Compared to France and England, more than 400 years of history, an ocean, and a continent on which the American Indians lived for millennia separate us. Your history and your culture are definitely not French or English. But try to think of a gesture that a French person would not be able to understand before the end of the conference, about two hours from now." And sometimes I add, to stir up a taste for competition: "I offer a meal in the best restaurant in town to anyone who thinks of one!" Not one person has yet taken my offer up. I know, however, that it will happen one day, and if no hand goes up it is because people are caught off guard. There are, in fact, about ten gestures that can come from a country, from a sociocultural background, or from a professional field, that are not universal.[1]

The most complex elements of our motor skills are innate, inscribed in our genetics. A savage child will end up, for example, getting on his two legs and walking, even if he has never seen a human do so. He will simply do it later than a child who has been encouraged to do it. A child blind from birth will nod his head to say "yes" just like a sighted child does, for example.[2] He has, however never seen a person do this. His movements are perhaps less elaborate than those of a sighted child, but he has the same patterns and makes the same movements.[3] Life is teeming with examples that allow us to understand that a certain number of our body attitudes are written into our cells.

The recent discovery of a certain category of cerebral cells clarifies nonverbal language in a new way and results in these cells being rooted in a universal framework.

Our Brain Works the Same Areas as Those of Other People's Brains

Human gestural heritage is universal because empathy[4] has universal roots. Human beings understand each other by looking at each other! Thanks to the action of mirroring neurons,[5] when a human being is interested in another, he unconsciously activates the same cerebral areas as those activated in the other person's brain, just by looking at him. A person who is looking at another person can therefore understand what that person is feeling and can access, since she is performing the same cerebral processes, a certain number of his thoughts.[6] This observable phenomenon is apparently unconscious but everyday gestures are engraved in all human brains because the brain's general architecture is universal.

This illustration of body language's universality will have convinced the least skeptical among you. However, if you turn on your television, if you channel-surf from one country's stations to another's, you will probably get the feeling that you certainly understand all the gestures but that "it's not quite the same." Italians, for example, do not communicate entirely, from a nonverbal perspective, like the Japanese do. Is it possible that body language is not entirely the same everywhere and yet is universal at the same time?

Our Gestural Heritage Becomes Enriched by a Cultural Fluency

Gestural heritage is innate and develops as a function of the society in which it exists.

The role of gestures is connected to the place attributed to emotions in a society.[7] That is why making gestures was once a sign of bad manners in several cultures.[8] People in the elite took courses on eloquence and their bodies were carefully disciplined. Gestures were prohibited, repressed: "Do not point your finger!", "Stop moving!", "Stand up straight!" The only people who were recognized as having the right to gesture were the uneducated, forced to use the mechanisms of childish language, and thus their bodies, to make themselves understood.[9]

Gestures are eloquent where emotions are taken seriously! Italians, for example, are not afraid to make gestures to convey their states of mind as well as facts of everyday life, because they place emotions at the heart of any relation. An Italian actress living with a French actor explained on a primetime television show the difference between the atmosphere of Rome and that of Paris: "When I argue with my lover in Paris, we close our windows. In Rome, we open them!" How better to repress an emotion than with a rigid body, the head lowered, and the voice muted, and how better to make it come alive than by making our faces and bodies its resonance chambers.

We intuitively get the feeling that gestures are different from one people to another. In fact, it is their **amplitude** that we are considering and not their **frequency**. Europeans, for example, have the impression that Asians make fewer gestures and that Arabs make many of them. Now, if we establish criteria for comparing gestures of North Africans and those of Asians, we observe that the latter are not less frequent, yet on the other hand, their range is not as large.

When an Italian begins to talks a little loudly because he is dissatisfied, a Japanese person who has never left his country will think that this man is hysterical. The Japanese feel anger like Italians do, so they make exactly the same gestures, but the "noise level" of the gestures—that is to say, their range—will be smaller because range is cultural.[10]

Culture intervenes more with conscious gestures than with those that are unconscious. It does not transform unconscious gestures. Arms open spontaneously to welcome a loved one and close to protect oneself. This unconscious reality, in effect since the dawn of time, is still true, from the most evolved human being to the most frustrated ape.

On the other hand, culture intervenes in all conscious activities. The rules of politeness and of good manners, for example, are different from one nation to another. But conscious attitudes do not interest us because they can be fabricated, invented in every way. Let us take a look . . .

"All is well!" (Conscious gesture.)

Someone who wants to lie to you can, for example, make a nice gesture like this, which allows him to avoid telling you how he really feels. That is the case here. This woman's smile is forced: The corners of her lips do not go up. What's more, she is looking at us with her right eye.

It is impossible to believe this gesture. It replaces speech, and, like it, it can hide the truth. When someone makes conscious gestures, we don't generally analyze them. We prefer to rely on other signs (the position of the head and the shoulders, the openness of the eyes) to know if the person is being sincere.

Body language, in its unconscious dimension, goes well beyond appearances and cultural veneer. From brain to brain, by unconsciously conforming to the movements of the other and by understanding them, men and women with good intentions prove every day that unconscious universal gestures, deposited in everyone's brains and bodies, really exist. It is from this that we all find the heritage of our body's eloquence.

Our Gestural Heritage Is Partly Individual

Genetic gestural heritage is enriched by learned cultural codes,[11] but to leave it at that would mean that these unconscious body movements would be about the same from brother to sister, or between parents and their children. Yet we are compelled to recognize that this is not the case. Children have their own body language that is different from their parents'. Each person has a body dynamic that is his own.

Above and beyond the universal bodily references and independent of all cultural truths, there exist individual realities related to gestures.[12] A father who clears his throat when he doesn't know what to say, an uncle who scratches his chest with both hands when he is content, a mother who takes large steps when she is not in a hurry, an aunt who touches the tip of her nose when she does crossword puzzles all act as beacons in a child's development. This is half-cultural, half-individual. But there is another reason why human beings do not all make the same gestures: They do not have all the same emotions. Some are more sensitive than others, overwhelmed by outbursts, thrills to which their gestures bear witness. If an emotion that passes is stronger, it instantly leaves visible traces and **the frequency** of a gesture will increase.[13]

The difference in emotional experiences is fundamental to understanding that the body does not always transmit information with the same intensity. Other conditions are more individual, like the health of a person; for example, an older person who is tired and sick will not have the same "natural" tonicity as an adolescent—who is in some ways a "ball of hormones"—in good health. These factors have forced us to create a theoretical gestural equation that accounts for the level of general tonicity attributable to each human being, so that we can be sure sure that we are talking about the same thing.

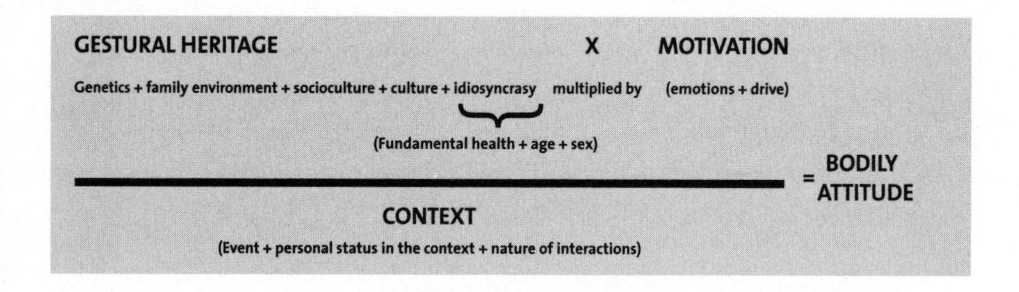

It is not a question here of returning to the logic of this theoretical equation, but simply of understanding, through it, that a human being has a gestural heritage that he puts to work according to his motivations. But even if motivation levels are equal, certain people have mastered them better, in the conduct of their actions [a Quebecois expression, borrowed from English, expresses this reality: We say that those people have *drive*] while others will be less focused on their objectives. Body expressions of motivation are not the same. We must also consider that the exact context of the event in which this heritage expresses itself is another factor to be weighed in. A person who is extremely motivated to present a project that he holds dear to his heart will not have the same body dynamic depending on whether he opens up about his ideas to his friends during lunch, during a very formal meeting, or near a metro station; and depending on whether he is executing orders or meting them out.

Fortunately, if our body expressions are specific to each one of us, the way we read them is universal. Let's look at an example that better illustrates our hypothesis.

The Kiss of an Initial Contact

Human beings use conscious gestures integrated in their bodily heritage and intended to facilitate first contact. When a stranger approaches us, we don't say to ourselves: "What should I do? Oh, yes, shake his hand!" Our hands "naturally" go toward the other person.

The hug is, among the ways to greet someone, more tender, and also more mischievous. Almost universally the small child kisses the adult by making a "pout," and giving a "peck," a "smack". . . Adapting the act of suckling, he tends to kiss his parents goodbye on the mouth. Then he understands that "pecks" are given on the cheek—he is learning what a kiss is—but no one, in the West, will tell him which cheek to start with, but it doesn't matter as long as the kiss is on the cheek. But each of us finds ourselves confronted from time to time by a situation in which we find ourselves nose to nose rather than cheek to cheek with the person we are kissing. Surprised, our heads switch to the other side but like the other person who has had the same reaction, we find ourselves nose to nose a second time! It is generally shared laughter that ends this embarrassment that we have created, in spite of ourselves. In these particular times, what has happened, why has this simple act suddenly become so complicated? In fact, *consciously* we have learned to peck on the cheek and *unconsciously* we choose which cheek. Let's look at this again. Kissing is not a ritual like any other. The skin of our face meets that of the other, our mouths are about two inches apart, and it takes very little for this attitude that is completely conventional to become much less so. It is the cerebral hemispheres that guide us toward other people the moment we kiss. If we are more vigilant or respectful, the right part of our face, controlled by the left hemisphere, naturally leads us toward the right half of the other person's.

On the other hand, if we are more spontaneous and more relaxed, the left eye, and with it the left side of the face, will naturally lead us toward the left side of the other person's face.

The kiss that is made first on the left cheek and then on the right is always more relaxed, more abandoned, and more emotional than the one from the right to the left. The kiss made on the left cheek is less formal and shows more affection.

The relationship to the other person's body, depending on the state of intimacy, will shape the embrace. The other person is approached either respectfully or spontaneously, but it is impossible to have these two mental attitudes at the same time since they are so different. Each time that we find ourselves nose to nose rather than mouth to cheek, ready to bump into the other person, it is because our relationship with them is not clear at that exact moment. One of the two is more spontaneous, relaxed, while the other is more comfortable with a relationship that is distant and formal. This reality is specific to each interaction, but at the same time the collective unconscious cannot be ignored because the relationship with spontaneity and intimacy goes beyond the individual. The difference between specific cultures in each country allows us to understand this situation better. Thus, the Quebecois and the French, for example, although they originate from the same people, do not kiss each other in the same way! The French will generally kiss starting with the right cheek, while the Quebecois will start with the left![14]

This phenomenon is not obvious without remembering the lovers' kiss that we discussed in the first part of this work, which is done left eye to left eye in proportions significantly larger than right eye to right eye.

The observation of hugs seems to convey the fact that Quebecois people will be less formal than French people, more relaxed during the initial contact. This is not the most original conclusion but it allows us to illustrate the reality of a collective mentality, a collective unconscious that is inscribed in gestures that differ from one people to another.

Gestural heritage is universal. Almost all body attitudes are understood by all human beings.

On the other hand, body dynamics are specific to each person. They depend on cultural and individual data as much as genetics.

The universality of body language is integrated in everyone's bodily heritage and personal history is also readable because the criteria to read it are universal.

CONCLUSION

The Moral of This Story

Conceived as a theoretical work as much as a practical manual, this book opens the door to a series of questions, beginning with this one: How do we remain engaged in an exchange when we must observe so many nonverbal details? This question inevitably raises another: Is it possible to master one's own body language in order to become more efficient during important or strategic interactions? Finally, for all those who are working on becoming better human beings, ask yourselves THE question: Don't we lose spontaneity and candor in exchange for what we are trying to gain through observing other people? These questions should not be avoided.

How Do We Decipher a Language That Is So Elaborate Without Losing Quality of Presence?

This work has fallen into your hands because you were looking for a tool to better understand other people, and in terms of this objective, let's admit that it does its job. At the same time, if you are interested in improving your relationships, therein lies the inevitable paradox. *The Secrets of Body Language* allows us to become better observers but the quality of our relationships depends on our capacity to be actors, not observers! Aren't we in the midst of choosing between two irreconcilable roads: to watch but seem strangely absent in the interaction or to be actors but deprive ourselves of the benefits of observation? What should we do?

This problem is two-fold.

- How do we become good observers?
- Can we be good observers while also acting?

In fact, adopting a specific mental attitude itself settles these two difficulties. We are going to propose that you **never think of body language!** This method which at first seems absurd is by far the most effective.

The Theory of the Ball That Rolls By

Body language consists of a number of parameters to be taken into account comparable to the number that is necessary to drive a car! We are going to therefore propose that you approach nonverbal language in the same manner as you would drive a car. Let's go back a bit. You remember your first driving lesson . . . how complicated it was? The car, first of all, with the steering wheel that must be held in a precise way, the three pedals and your feet that had to gently move from one to the other at the risk of stalling the motor, the clutch, the gas, the turn signals, the three mirrors, not to mention the road, your speed, the speed limit, the traffic lights, the other cars, those in front, those behind, and those that risk cutting you off, any emergency vehicles, the unpredictable pedestrians, and the children who are at risk of crossing without warning! In short, when you got out of the car after your first driving lesson, you certainly said to yourself: "I will never get it!" Fortunately, you had without a doubt someone close to you who understood none of these things and yet who drove! You may have thought: "If this person can do it, I must be able to do it, too; there isn't any reason why not!" That was probably several years ago. Tomorrow you will return home by car and your various concerns will be, if there are no traffic jams, forgotten as you drive, taken care of without you even thinking about them. You will arrive at your home, surprised that you are already there. You will have coordinated, during the length of your journey, about 15 actions simultaneously without thinking about any of them. All you need is for *a ball to cross the road so* that all of a sudden your driving reflexes return to you all at once. You will say to yourself that behind this ball there could be a child and, consciously, you will instantly become more attentive to a great number of traffic details.

With nonverbal observation, it is appropriate to adopt the same state of mind. First of all, like driving an automobile, you must learn. This book can act as a driving manual. Read it, study its contents, tear it, dog-ear its pages. And then go practice by watching television, movies, observing conversations in which you do not have to intervene. But when you are actively communicating, in command of your brain and your body, and the people around you expect you to have good communication reflexes so that the conversation is constructive, agreeable, and it gets where it needs to go safely, **forget about nonverbal communication.**

During an exchange, only pay attention to what is said; concentrate on the words, which are already complicated enough as it is. But there again, it will be enough to see a ball cross the road (!)—a ball, that is to say, a gesture, a bizarre attitude, astonishing or particular to what you have learned to identify—to make your reflexes as an observer come back to you without stopping your role in the communication.

Life gives many occasions to sharpen these reflexes. So do not spoil your past experiences with the people who matter by becoming an observer of your relationships. Life is meant to be lived, not observed. You will see the balls that will cross the road. At first they will do so infrequently, then more often, then very often, and then all of your reflexes as a nonverbal driver will come back to you. Quicker than you think, you will learn to downgrade, to integrate the other person's gestures into your communication, to modulate your interactions and your confidence in taking into consideration his needs without forgetting your own path.

The most brilliant people in nonverbal deciphering all have the same distinctive feature. Their skills bring much less to them than the general quality of the communication, and they put themselves at its service.

Can We Master Body Language?

When we are able to decipher another person's body language, it is very tempting to try to have "perfect" body communication ourselves. But it is a mistake to think this way.

Cerebral energy must naturally be channeled so that we are attentive to the other person, and not to ourselves. To focus on our own gestures brings about a combination of two negative effects:

- First, we will appear very uncomfortable if we constrain our body to work against the tide of spontaneity.
- Then, we will neglect the relationship to the detriment of the other person.

Communication always becomes more fluid if it is directed toward another person rather than toward our "little" selves . . . "me." When the body is fluid, thought is as well. This is the case when we dare to speak plainly. We communicate well because we are not asking ourselves how well we are communicating.

A Critique of Prefabricated Attitudes in Communication

The truth about communication is not, in our opinion, about seeking absolute mastery of nonverbal behavior. Definitely not. People are only spontaneous when they stop looking at themselves. Nevertheless, the way of total body mastery in order to communicate better has a name: mirrored communication.

The main idea of mirrored communication is that an exchange is more harmonious when a person adopts the same postures as the other person in a conversation, and thus accesses his emotional state. This attitude is of course manipulative,[1] but is it effective?

1. Is the empathetic connection facilitated by mirrored communication?
2. Does the desired connection really give privileged access to the other person's thoughts?

Unfortunately, just because you decide to be empathetic does not mean that other people will automatically feel understood. Besides, that would be the worst thing that could happen, because that would show that you had given up who you were: your opinions, your ideas, your thoughts, your position about what was said. Even though we'd like to put ourselves in other people's shoes, this is a part of body communication that we cannot master: the extrapyramidal system situated in the limbic lobe. This area cannot be consciously restrained. For example, as we saw previously, a small eye muscle, called the lower palpebral ligament, contracts or expands involuntarily. If you agree with other people, the fissure has a tendency to rise up to hide the lower part of the eyes, while it will droop down if you disagree. Japanese authors call this phenomenon *sampaku* eye.[2]

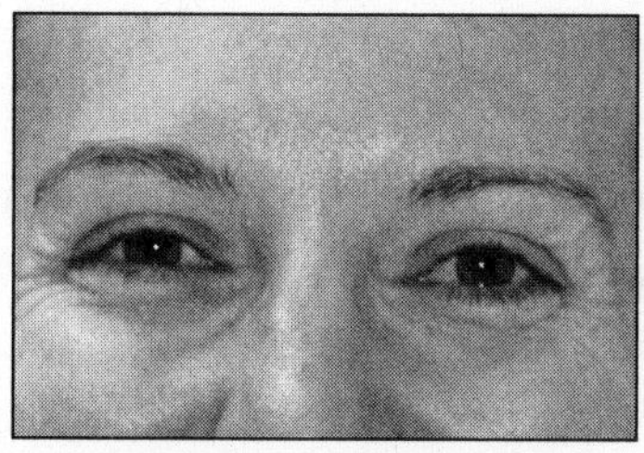

The lower eyelids rise up under the eye. The situation is positive.

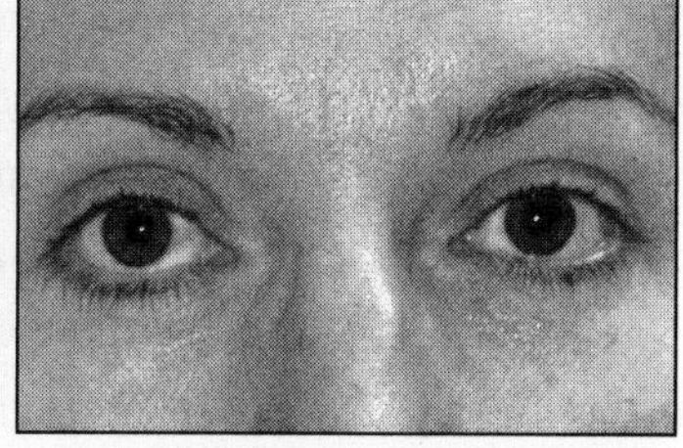

The white under the iris is visible. The situation is negative.

No one can voluntarily move this small muscle. We are without resources, powerless in face of it. Thus, whether you want to or not, if you do not like the other person, this muscle under the eye will droop slightly. You will have a nice smile, an attempt at mirrored communication . . . he will become more relaxed and you will show the white under your irises, and his brain will unconsciously decipher the phenomenon.

Do you now know what the principal characteristic is of people who we consider to be hypocrites? They are nice! Yes! They are people whose niceness seems fake. But hypocrites are not always someone else! We are hypocrites ourselves every time that we are not true to ourselves. A conscious part of our behavior shows one thing, while a part that we cannot control shows something else. The conscious part smiles while unconsciously a more negative message is sent.

Falsely empathetic people more readily say what we want to hear than what they are really thinking.[3] They say very little about their needs and their desires.[4] The only way to bypass this phenomenon so that someone "gives it to us straight" as far as his thoughts go, is to remain ourselves.

Do We Lose in Spontaneity What We Gain in Observation?

Upon entering into the communication profession, I thought that the principal obstacle of communication was shutting other people out. On the contrary, it is rather a lack of assertiveness. In fact, forced to say what another person wants to hear, some people are manipulated by their own interactions![5]

Understand that it is not a question of cutting oneself off from the advantages of a harmonious communication. It is harmony at any cost that we question. Going against everything you have read, we are not afraid to tell you that being yourself is to not be afraid to send honest messages, even if they might appear negative in the short term. This is a must for better quality in communication!

How can we attain our objectives if we do not give the other person the means to understand that something is bothering us? How many business meetings have we left shaking hands with the other party, satisfied with our professionalism in the relationship, without having adopted any concrete solutions? In these meetings, applying old methods like diplomacy and good faith, we strove to show our openness to the other person. Very much in control of ourselves, we hid our irritations and our disagreements, and the other party did the same! In fact, no one pointed out the unavoidable difficulties of the project at hand and how both parties faced insurmountable problems. In fact, it is the zeal and the seriousness and, even worse, the desire for things to go smoothly that prevented things from moving forward!

At certain times, our bodies could have turned away, fallen back; our hands could have disappeared under the table or covered our mouths; we could have discreetly cleared out throats, yawned, or detached our gaze from the other person's. Instead of that, we did not budge, acquiescing politely and continuing to present a foolproof, smooth face, a mastery worthy of the great martial arts masters. We do not know that, strangely enough, it is our openness somehow that has perhaps made the negotiation collapse. If the body had spoken and voiced its disagreement, if we had let it do that without constraint, it is quite probable that the other person would have seen it. He would not have deciphered it consciously, but his brain, his body, his mirroring neuron allies, would have helped him realize that there was a problem, that he was approaching a subject with which we were in disagreement. Our shutting down would have helped him take a step toward us to try to move deeper into a more delicate level of exchange.

One of my friends, a connoisseur of the good things in life, has a wine cellar with an extraordinary wine collection. He likes to surround himself with guests and receives many of them. To his new guests, he always serves a first bottle of very ordinary wine, explaining that it is of a lesser known vintage but still very good. If the guests fly into ecstasy over it, they will drink this wine, that is to say the cheap wine, throughout the whole meal. On the other hand, if they don't say anything and disappear behind their glass in a polite silence, he uses the warmth of the wine or the after-taste of the cork as an excuse, takes back the bottle, and serves great wine after great wine at his table. Set in his judgment, he is not afraid to think: "What quality of exchange and of sincerity could I have with someone who has decided to agree with me at the expense of their own taste?" He opts for authenticity and frankness over empathy and kowtowing.

The current fashion is not, however, about frank and direct speech, but rather magic formulas, a master key that is popularized by books on personal development and that proposes to eradicate all difficulties by breathing through the stomach and by cultivating such formulas as: *The solution is in me*. However, this concrete formula full of common sense and often accompanied by magical thinking, is inadequate in everyday relationships: *If the solution to all of my problems is in me, once I have gotten myself together, I will turn against the other person.* The person who applies this recipe has just cut himself off from relationship resources that are very real.

On the topic of recipes, let's not forget that the other person brings half of the ingredients to the exchange and that we never know in advance what they will be thinking, nor even what their tastes are. We do not even know if they have a good appetite, but if they choose to be up front with us, it is because they want to share their time with us. They bring 50 percent of the ingredients and 50 percent of the solution. Let's stop believing that the solution is in us!

The message of transparency is a matter of saying and showing, just, and even more so, when it is not convenient, to show our position to the other person, to reinforce it with him and thanks to him. In these circumstances, all the cerebral energy that we expend in attempting to agree, to be stupidly empathetic, we will turn toward the intelligent resolution of difficulties. *Authenticity and frankness over empathy and kowtowing . . .*

We send conscious and unconscious messages that other people receive. We look at them and respond to them. We build together. In the same way that we cannot be natural and spontaneous without stopping to think about it, we cannot hope to know who we are unless we stop watching ourselves communicate so that we can turn toward the other person and observe how he looks at us. The looks that he sends us and his body messages speak to us all the better if we are not afraid of looking at him and speaking to him about himself.

In terms of this book, we hope that it has given you a taste, if this attitude wasn't already natural to you, of a different interest you might take in other people, so that you may stop observing yourself in order to focus instead on the messages that are being sent to you by others.

We all live at the heart of a true paradox: *We would all like to be better understood and yet we are afraid of being deciphered*. This is not abnormal, but the more we reveal clear body messages and let others see them in us, the more we give keys to other people to understand us, and the more we will be recognized and be understood by them!

Being transparent is nothing more than giving all our keys to the other person to stir up in him the desire to open up. He can never understand us better if we do not give him a taste for sharing. The more he knows about us, the more we will take shape for him, the more solidly we will exist for him, and the more we will be understood.

Afterword

I am about to send the final corrections of this work to my publishing house. Fate has it that this is the day of Barack Obama's swearing in as the president of the United States and the television is turned on in front of me. Faced with the images that parade in front of me and that jump out at me, I cannot help adding these lines. Human beings who are watching the event, in the four corners of the planet, do not all speak English and do not understand all of the words that Barack Obama is saying to the two million people gathered before him in Washington, but they all feel like they can understand him. He is demonstrating the universality of body language.

Tuesday, January 20, 2009

The Face

Each point touched on the face corresponds to a video database code. Each time someone puts his hand on his face, wherever his hand lands, the sequence is classified according to the logic of these points. Databases of this kind also exist for the body, spatial gestures, and gestures that are made with or around objects. Each of the same gestures performed by people of all cultures is thus indexed many times.

In order to be taken into consideration, each one of these definitions proposed in this book were verified in at least 80 percent of the situations from images in the database. When it comes to scratching, they must be verified in at least 90 percent of cases.

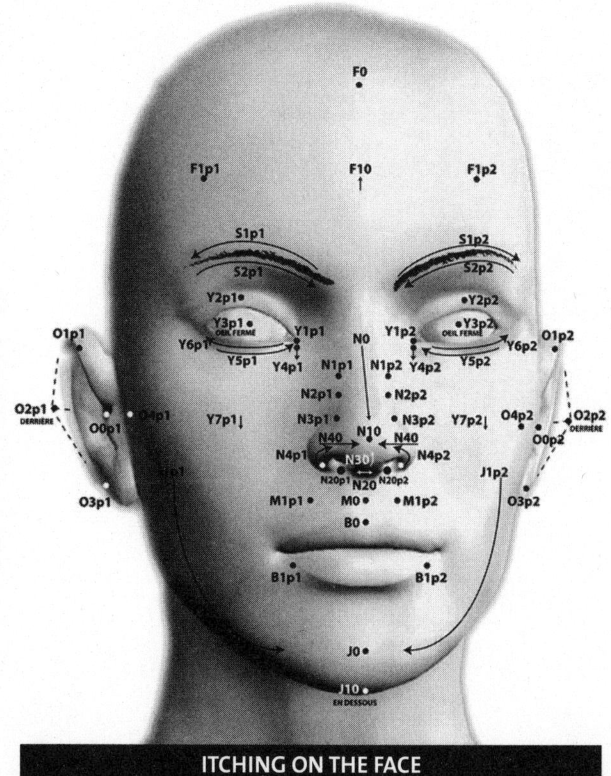

ITCHING ON THE FACE

APPENDIX 2

Scale of Overall Gestural Hypertonicity

Gestural hypertonicity is defined as a relationship between the magnitude and the frequency of a gesture; it allows for the establishment of a scale of cultural tonicity for all people. Thanks to this scale, we can understand that the feeling that we are leaving behind Western, Asiatic, and Oriental gestures will not be quite the same, since their intensity, their "sound" level, differs between countries and individuals. But ultimately, they are always the same gestures that are made by everybody.

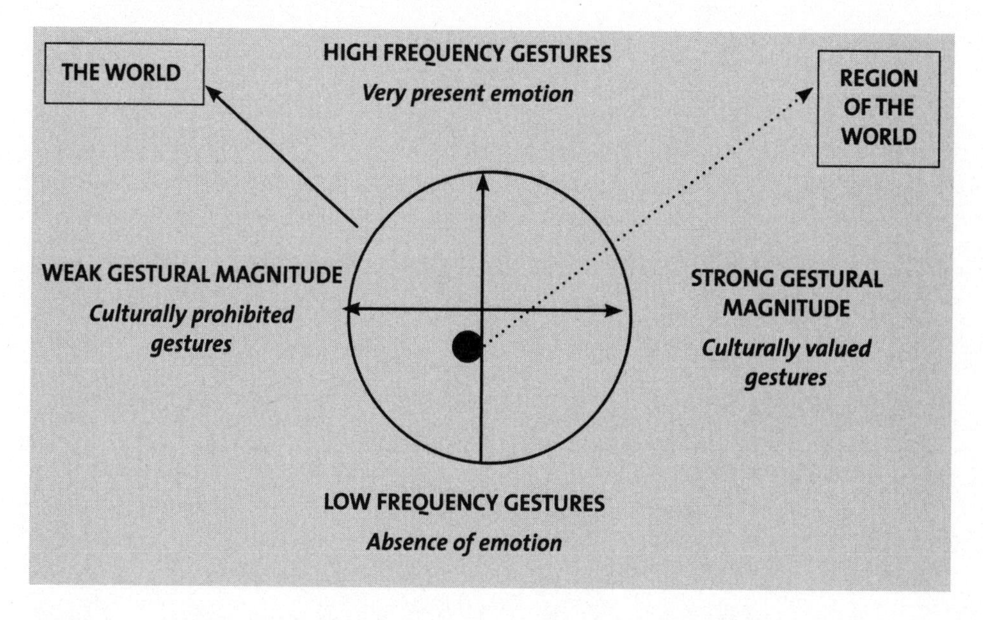

APPENDIX 3

Scale of Individual Gestural Hypertonicity

Each individual can also be positioned within his or her own culture.

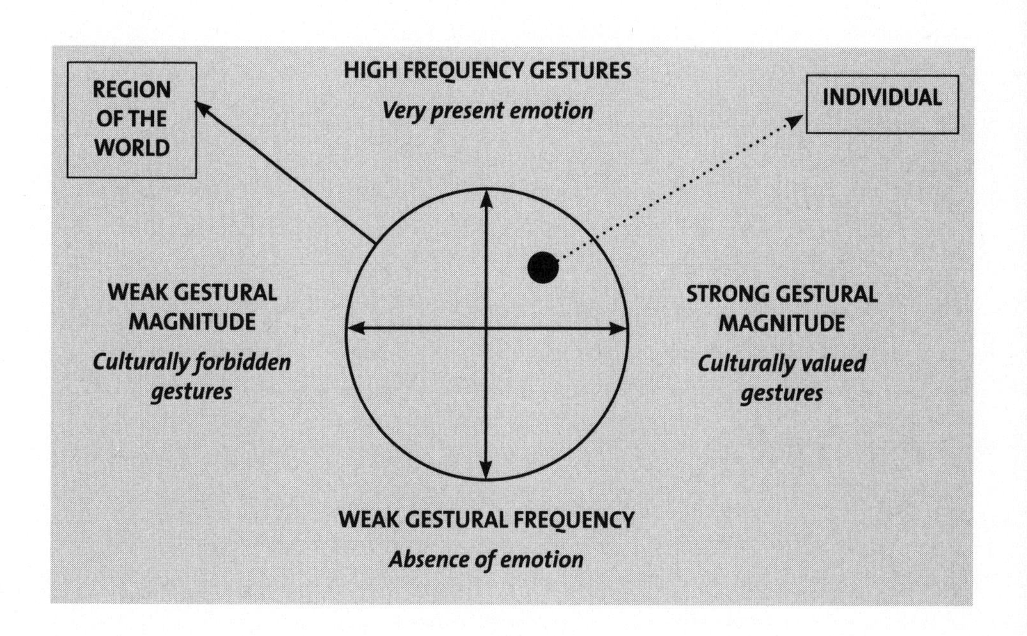

Glossary

Actor: The person at the center of an exchange. It is especially important not to become an observer of your own exchange.

Agreement: When two gestures go in the same direction in the same person; for example, they cross their arms (closing) and legs, turning away.

Analytical: What is defined in relation to oneself. In contrast to *systemic*.

Artifact: Secondary proposition presented as a postulate. It allows us to make the principal propositions coherent, but it cannot validate the current state of knowledge.

Behaviorism: In the context of the paradigm being used, behaviorism is considered to be the belief that the conscious modification of one's own nonverbal behavior will produce expected effects in the behavior of another. This is a dangerous illusion.

Behaviorist approach: In the field of nonverbal observation, a proactive attitude consisting of trying to change the behavior of another through the modification of one's own nonverbal behavior that poses a number of ethical problems that are not solvable.

Body of evidence: Simultaneous reading of several clues, also called items, that express the same reality.

Cerebral logic: The cerebral area at work will be read in the unconscious choice of which hand is used to communicate.

Chimera: A concept. The chimera is by definition an emotional state of very short duration (less than three-tenths of a second) visible by a surreptitious expression particular to the face which delivers information of a contradictory nature from the openly displayed facial expression.

Closing: It pits itself against movements of contraction or withdrawal.

Cognitive future: One of the four quadrants used to describe eye movement. It corresponds to a gaze unconsciously directed up and to the right.

Cognitive unconscious: Structuring of logical reasoning that leads to a decision that is not explicitly formulated.

Compassion: Emotional proximity to someone. The capacity to emotionally understand what another person is feeling, by feeling it ourselves and by helping to deepen this state through attentive listening.

Congruence: When the physical attitude of a human being corresponds to his mental attitude.

Convergence: Convergence occurs when the gestural attitudes of two people agree; they move a shoulder forward at the same time, for example. This attitude can be positive as well as negative.

Conscious gesture: Gesture that is indispensable to describing (e.g., "It is that way").

Corcept: Concept expressing the fact that the human body itself in a situation of communication, a producer of feelings, which the other person's brain unconsciously takes into account in the construction of the exchange.

Diachronic: Has to do with our unconscious representation of time, in respect to eye movement and gestural dynamics. This dimension is highly cultural.

Distal emotion: Takes into account the importance of the distance between two people and their special positioning to measure their empathy. It is particularly important to take the position of the head into consideration.

Egoloop: The movements in which the hand touches the left side of the body, referring to the idea that self-awareness housed in the right frontal cortex leads us to the left side of the body. This reality seems to be a universal law.

Emotion: Expression of a state readable in the interior attitude and identifiable on the face and through body movements. Emotions have three required characteristics. They are hyper or hypotonic, positive or negative, and turned toward the other or kept to oneself. An emotion that is not observable does not exist.

Primary emotions: The primary emotions were theorized by Charles Darwin before being labeled more precisely by other scientists.They are considered the six principal emotions and have two characteristics: They are recognizable after the first two years of life and they are universally recognized.

Secondary emotions: They are put in place, in a nuanced manner, throughout one's life.

Disguised emotions: Emotions that are not really felt but we try to believe in their existence.

Emotional future: One of the four synergologic quadrants used to describe eye movement. It corresponds to the gaze unconsciously directed to the bottom right.

Emotional intelligence: Concept founded in the 1980s that allows us to understand that emotions are essential to the foundation of rationality. Emotional intelligence intersects several kinds of information, allowing us to express the importance of emotion in the structuring of thought. Emotions can intuitively differentiate what is important from what is not, prioritizing information.

Emotional past: One of the four synergologic quadrants used to describe nonverbal eye movements, It corresponds to a glance positioned unconsciously down and to the left.

Empathy: Psycho-physiological process in which the another person's emotions are understood but not shared.

Engram gesture: Preverbal gesture that facilitates the production or the recall of the knowledge from "engraved" and stimulated resources in the brain. It participates in the development of thought and the formation of ideas in situations of exchange.

Falsifiability: See *refutability*.

Feeling: A state of being of long duration imprinted physically on the image (e.g., stooped shoulders, retracted neck).

Figurative gesture: Half-conscious gesture aimed at spatially describing an existing form (e.g., "a large house"). It is also called "descriptive."

Fusion: The process consisting of fully embracing the mental attitude of another.

Gesture: Position or movement—conscious or not—of the hands, made in front of oneself and not touching a part of the body nor an object nor any surface of any kind. If the hands hold an object, the nature of the gesture will be specified. It is a question of gripping. If the hand holds the other hand, this is a manual feedback loop; if the hand finds the body, this is a micro-movement.
Gestural category: Synergology defines three major categories of attitudes: conscious gestures, semi-conscious gestures, and unconscious gestures. Each category has its own gestural typology.
Gestural heritage: The gestural heritage is what we have available to use. It belongs to us. It constitutes the genetic form of a driving heritage and is influenced by our culture and by who we are individually.
Gestural refrain: Gestures that amount to a sustained frequency. Each person possesses certain refrains. They reveal background thoughts.
Half-conscious: Which is not conscious but can become so when we pay attention (e.g., almost all gestures).
Half-conscious gesture: Gesture made unconsciously but that can be identified by the person who performs it and by the one to whom it is intended.
Hemispheric symbolism: The symbolic universe peculiar to each person is rooted in his culture. It is integrated in the heart of the cerebral hemispheres. It is a question of becoming aware of them and then integrating them in reading nonverbal language.
History: In the sense of nonverbal observation, a concept expressing the fact that the history of a human being can be understood in its totality by observing the lasting characteristics recorded on the body. Utilized when one's image is evoked.
Horizon of meaning: Concept of synergology allowing us to evaluate and regroup items that go in the same direction.
Image: Technical term expressing the fact that a state of being or an emotion of very long duration ends up modifying the natural pathway of a feature or more considerably the general physical attitude. The smooth muscles are particularly involved in this neurophysiological modification resulting from the modification of a psycho-emotional state.
Impulse: State of very short duration which can transform an emotion or not and which is read in a micro-movement.

In-group: The movements made in space on the left side of the body that refer to the idea that we bring back into our world, that is to say to the left, what we value.
Incongruence: When a person's physical attitude does not correspond to his or her mental attitude.
Inductive: Reasoning that starts with an assumption. It is a matter of bringing an assumption to what one is trying to observe. It introduces the point of view that one is trying to show at the heart of the demonstration (e.g., "I think that this person is sad because I have observed this or that"). By taking it in this way, we refuse to read anything other than sadness. The induction immediately removes all pretention to scientific reasoning.
Inference: Reasoning from what one has observed. It is a question of a logical operation by which one accepts a proposition by virtue of its connection to another already held to be true. If we observe "this," it could mean "that." Reasoning must be inferred to be valid.
Interior attitude: Movement dictated by an emotion (e = exterior, motion = movement) and results in a change in the body.
Itching: Unconscious itching relieved by the tip of the finger or fingernail (the finger is therefore bent) in the absence of any integumental stimulus.
Item: A nonverbal item is the expression of an element of observation (e.g., the left eyelid that blinks). Synergology demands the observation of several items (assets) before being able to propose a reading of observations.
Kinesics: The first method of reading nonverbal communication, founded in the 1950s before the discovery of the distinct role of each cerebral hemisphere in communication. Kinesics developed the belief that nonverbal communication cannot be comprehensible unless it is associated with verbal speech. For us, this is an important methodological error. It is precisely because a gesture's horizon of meaning can be understood without any speech that gestures can sometimes seem to contradict speech. The unconscious understanding of another person's gestures is the basis of all communication. The recent discovery of the role of mirroring neurons in communication also validates this reality.
Lateral: What inclines to the side. Adjective that is particularly important in the analysis of head movements.

Lie: A lie corresponds either to the omission or the voluntary misrepresentation of one part or all of the truth. If no reason justifies it, some causes can explain it.

- ***The status of emotion:*** If certain emotions are favored (e.g., empathy, serenity, self-confidence), others are on the contrary censured (e.g., hate, fear). We will try therefore to silence their expression even more.
- ***The context:*** Laughter is a good example. When it is discreet, it conveys joviality and the company of cheerful people is sought out. On the other hand, it would be not genuine to laugh at a funeral, for example.
- ***The other person:*** There are moments when we feel that our emotions belong to ourselves and when we simply do not feel like confiding them to others because the type of intimacy that we share with the other person does not suit us. We can therefore be led to lie by omission if we are asked, for example, "Is everything OK?" and we answer, "Yes, and you?" In fact, things are not OK, but we inevitably do not feel like saying more. It is without a doubt that our social life is possible at this price.
- ***The facts:*** For reasons that belong to those who choose to lie, certain realities simply cannot be admitted. These lies begin with the first stolen candy.
- ***The denial:*** This is the last category of distortion of truth. It has a particular status since it is not conscious and can sometimes, because of this fact, not be considered a lie. Do we always experience the emotions that we speak of? No. For example, it is socially highly valued to leave on vacation and look forward to this moment of breaking away from traditional rhythms. At the same time, videos show people being questioned the evening before their departure that allow us to understand that this happy evocation is sometimes unconsciously faked. We are lying to ourselves. We can agree that this is not really a lie, but it constitutes the fifth category of reasons that prevent us from telling the truth.

Manipulation: In the context of nonverbal reading, the attitude that consists of modifying one's body expression to make another believe certain intentions or having the conscious objective of leading another to unconsciously modify his mental attitude.

Meta-language: Language situated around and beyond verbal language.

The idea of meta-language has been greatly highlighted by the Palo Alto movement.

Micro-attitude: That is one of two forms of micro-movements, the other form being micro-reactions. Micro-attitudes distinguish themselves from micro-reactions simply because the hand comes into play when the latter are expressed. We distinguish three types of micro-attitudes: itching, micro-caresses, and micro-fixations.

Micro-caress: A gesture of self-contact made by the pad of the finger. It is addressed to other people when it is done in front of them, with the desire to get them to come closer.

Micro-fixation: When the hand stops on the face or the body.

Micro-movement: A synergologic concept. Surreptitious movement. There are two types of micro-movements: micro-attitudes and micro-reactions.

Micro-reactions: It is a question of surreptitious facial and body movements. Micro-reactions are one of two categories of micro-movements. The other category is micro-attitudes.

Mimicry: Said about two bodies that communicate unconsciously by mirroring each other.

Mirroring neurons: Cerebral cells in our brain that cause us to unconsciously and very surreptitiously simulate, with the help of a mental process, other people's movements and to thus feel their emotions. This process only functions because it is performed unconsciously.

Neuro-symbolic: That which expresses the fact that our representation of the world is engraved in our neurons.

Nonverbal: Term used in the context of communication. Etymologically, nonverbal language represents that which is not within the meaning of the words. It consists of five dimensions:

the paraverbal dimension (*para* meaning "next to") includes that which supports words or are stuck to the words such as tone, timbre, and the intonation of the voice

the periverbal dimension (*peri* meaning "around") includes the space and distances in communication, notably

the preverbal dimension (*pre* meaning "before" and marking that which is prior) the other person's facial and body messages are decoded before speaking, notably

the infraverbal dimension (*infra* meaning "below") includes the nonverbal elements that unconsciously filter into the communication, like clothing, body odors, the colors of clothing

the supraverbal dimension (*supra* meaning "above") includes the unconscious interpretation of distinctive signs sent by other people, like distinctive marks of social status, for example

Nonverbal communication: Which excludes words. This expression appeared for the first time in English literature in 1956.

Nonverbal information: Synonym of *item*. Information is nonverbal when the body, the face, and the gestures, by their configuration, transmit information about a person. An emotion is a wealth of nonverbal information.

Out-group: The movements made to the right of the body that refer to the idea that we place outside of ourselves what we judge unconsciously as exterior.

Outloop: The movements in which the hand touches the right side of the body, referring to the idea that processed information is outside of us and that we reject it.

Palo Alto: Movement born in the United States, at the end of the 1950s, that introduced the central role of context in communication, which made the heuristic power of this group of ideas also its Achilles' heel. Concerned about not letting anything escape from the context in a communication, the Palo Alto researchers gradually turned away from the person, who is seen more as a symptom of the context than a productive authority of proper nonverbal language. A serious nonverbal approach cannot ignore the force and the contribution of this movement of fruitful ideas, but must equally acquire the tools to observe the human being in his dimension as an actor in the communication.

Passé cognitif : One of the four synergologic quadrants used to describe non-verbal eye movements. It corresponds to a glance unconsciously positioned up and to the left.

Primary feedback loop: Crossing of the arms or the legs. The body thus has a

tendency to make a loop of itself.
Projective gesture: Projection of states of being through body movements in order to integrate another person into the communication.
Proxemics: Analysis of nonverbal behavior taking into account distances. This is the periverbal dimension of nonverbal language.
Quadrant: Eye movement is divided into four quadrants.
Refutability: Also called falsifiability. Method of scientific logic developed by Karl Popper that distinguishes authentic sciences from those that are not. According to the principle of refutability, we will never be able to prove that something is true. We can only prove that it is not false. To be able to submit a proposition to the test of falsifiability grants a person scientific status or not. For example, 100 white swans on a lake will not let us say that the proposition "All the swans are white" is false. On the other hand, only one black swan on the lake will let us say it is false. A proposition is not truly scientific unless it is falsifiable. All nonverbal propositions set forth must be refutable. For that, they must be simple and clear.
Return-to-self: Synergologic time during which the human being returns to what he has observed. The return-to-self only takes place when one is truly alone. Otherwise, it is necessary to take care not to be the observer of one's own relationship.
Rotating: From right to left or from left to right, for movements of the neck or the ankles.
Sagittal: From front to back. Serves to describe certain movements of the neck.
Sampaku: Emotional state identifiable in the area of the eye above and below the iris.

***Sampuku* on top:** White of the eye that is visible under the upper eyelid.

***Sampuku* on the bottom:** White of the eye that is visible under the iris.

Secondary feedback loop: One hand around the other. The reading and interpretation of intention in the secondary feedback loop will vary depending on its nature.
Socio-emotional dimension: Gestures reflect emotions. They are born in a cultural atmosphere. This dimension takes this reality into account.

Standing full-length: Theoretical position of observing a human being in his totality. Synonym of image.
State of being: Synergology designates three states of being: impulse, emotion, and feeling, which are distinguished by their duration. Everyone can be read through their body expressions: the image, the interior attitude, and the micro-movements.
Subliminal: Movement performed unconsciously, that has not been detected by the "naked eye" by the one to whom it was addressed and which produces real effects in the attitude of the latter.
Symbolic gesture: Conscious cultural gesture representing what one is trying to designate (e.g., "It's OK.").
Sympathy: We understand the other person and we appreciate him, but we are not necessarily in agreement with him and we keep a distance from him. We can find a person to be nice without agreeing with him. This term needs to be distinguished from those of empathy, compassion, and fusion.
Synchronicity: Behavioral attitude that mimics the bodily attitude of another person in order to trigger empathy mechanisms. This attitude goes against the two following basic synergologic precepts:

1. We have become observers of our own communication, which is very detrimental in synergologic reading.
2. By putting ourselves in a situation of conscious synchronization, we register a conscious objective by intervening in the other person's mental attitude, which reveals manipulation.

Synergology: Discipline that can, through the observation and the decoding of nonverbal language, develop its own capacity to understand the human being.
Systemic: What defines something in relationship to another. As opposed to *analytical*.
Transparency: Totally fluid attitude of the body conveying the exact thought process, whether it be positive or negative. Transparency is the principal resource of a quality communication.
Truth: Concept that does not have a place in deciphering nonverbal language. Given the description of something to express a hypothesis on what it means, it is a question, from a body of evidence also called items, to specify a horizon of meaning.

Unconscious: Methodological concept. The unconscious is what we are not aware of, which is therefore unconscious. The definition is much more restrictive in synergology than the one used in psychoanalysis. For these reasons, the term "nonconscious" is often used in relation to the term unconscious.

Unconscious emotion: Unconscious decision making that does not meet specific cognitive logical criteria (e.g., some films will make us cry even though we know that it is a made-up story).

Working through: Concept borrowed from psychoanalysis. The capacity to analyze situations of shutting out, to work through them, that is to say to note all of the details relative to the context of their production. Working through is a cerebral mechanism performed unconsciously. It is a step in learning how to read nonverbal language that is indispensable to transparent communication. The trap in the context of another person shutting you out is to adopt a behaviorist attitude.

NOTES

Chapter 1

1. In a study that is referenced in the scientific community, it is estimated that in a conversation, the impact of words is 7 percent and that of tone, timbre, and intonation is 35 percent; body language takes the lion's share, with 55 percent. Cf. Mehrabian, A. (1972).
2. The only surveys that exist are the catalogs of cultural gesture stricto sensu. Cf. Morris, D. (1994); Caradec, F. (2005); or the intuitive collections. Messinger, J. (2002).
3. Let us also take note of deaf people who use a nonverbal language to communicate: sign language. They do not speak; they "sign." They are "signers." But neither the word "to sign," nor the word "signer," in this exact sense, are present in French dictionaries. There is not a simple and exact word to refer to these gestures; let us admit that the expression is missing. It is true these gestures made by deaf people can be eloquent, but we would never say that they are "good speakers"! Inscriptions on the Egyptian pyramids are also a type of sign language. Cf. Moody, B. (1998).
4. The Austrian doctor by the name of Hans Asperger, who in 1943, pointed out this form of autism at the highest level.
5. Cf. Ekman, P. M. O'Sullivan and Frank, M. G. (1999); Laplane, D. (2005).
6. Cf. Rosenthal, R. (1971).
7. Ibid.
8. The expression "nonverbal" appeared officially for the first time thanks to the title of a book, *Nonverbal Communication* by J. Ruech and W. Kess, published by the California Press of Berkeley in 1956. Since then, it has become an established expression in the academic world. Cf. Corraze, J. (1980); Barrier, G. (2008).
9. It is a matter of the discovery of mirroring neurons made by Rizzolatti and his team in 1996. Several teams in the world have since taken over this research. We will come back to this.

Chapter 2

1. Cf. Darwin, C. (1872).
2. Cf. Goleman, D. (1997).
3. Cf. LeDoux, J. (2005).
4. Paul McLean, who became a Nobel laureate for this construction, speaks of the triune brain, showing that, in the history of humanity, the archeocortex, paleocortex, and neocortex, also called the reptilian brain, limbic system, and frontal cortex, appeared one after the other, but also one above the other in three successive layers. He posits, in this theory, the supremacy of human beings and the human neocortex over animals. It is possible that the reign of this scheme lives its last days as emotions lodged in the limbic system participate in the functioning of reason. The scientific community today looks on the side of associative theories to counteract this line of localizationist thinking.
5. Cf. Damasio, A. R., Tranel, D., Damasio, H., and Bechara, A. (1993).
6. The expression was popularized by Daniel Goleman, doctor of psychology, journalist at *The New York Times,* and excellent popularizer. He carves out the work of specialists in theories of education like those of Howard Gardner on multiple intelligences, theories in fields like those of Joseph LeDoux on the role of the amygdala in emotional reactions, or those of Antonio Damasio in the prioritization of emotions. Cf. Goleman, Daniel, *Emotional Intelligence* (1997).
7. This is the theory of somatic markers from Damasio.
8. The words "facts" or "information" do have the same meaning here as legal science where the knowledge of facts is primordial. Here, fact is static and information circulates.
9. The amygdala allows for emotional reaction, and it is the hippocampus that has the function of storing information such that we can find it again. The amygdala is preformed at birth and the hippocampus forms at around the age of three years old. It is for this reason that we cannot have conscious memories before this age.
10. Cf. Rochat (2006).
11. Cf. Dimberg, U., Thunberg, M., and Elmehed, K. (2000).
12. People affected with Asperger's syndrome are incapable of reading other people's emotions. They treat nonverbal information provided by the face with the cerebral module, which normally specializes in dealing with the form of things, a bit like if we looked at a billiard ball while asking ourselves what it feels. A person affected by Asperger's syndrome must relearn how to read other people's emotions intellectually in order to understand them. Their performance in terms of emotional intelligence is greatly diminished by their weak capacity to decipher bodily information.
13. Cf. Darwin, C. (1872).
14. It is Carl Roger who, in the field of psychology, gave his acclaim to empathy, by devoting himself notably to the methodological virtues of the comprehension of others. Cf. Rogers, C. (1966).
15. Cf. Rochat, F. (2006); Meltzoff, A. N., and Moore, M. K. (1997).
16. That is one of the reasons that body language is universal and is not constructed socially according to personalities. A child deciphers emotions and not situations, facial expressions, or psycho-sociological realities.
17. Cf. Mineka, S. (1984).
18. Cf. Tokimura, H., et al. (1996).
19. This is an innate mechanism—it was notably described by Bradford Titchener. He differentiated it from the process of emotional attunement, also called the harmonization of emotions, according to which, after the second half of life, a child will emotionally become an adult, which will without a doubt allow him to attain intersubjectivity.

20. From the hour following birth, some babies are capable of imitating an adult who sticks out his tongue. Cf. Meltzoff, A.N., Borton, R. W., Greenberg, D., and Cohen, H., *Science*, no. 218.
21. See also, on the phenomenon of empathy at birth, Cyrulnik, B. (1989). At 14 months of age, an infant inclines his head if he is in agreement with someone. Hubert Montagner explains, and the statistics support this, that in 90 percent of cases, that is to say 619 times out of 678, inclining the head, if it is not preceded by a threatening gesture, establishes improvement and is a reinforcement of contact. Cf. Montagner, Hubert. *L'enfant et la communicaton,* Stock, 1978.
22. Cf. Montagner, H., et al. (1977).
23. Cf. Rizzollati, Giacomo, Fogassi, Leonardo, and Gallese, Vittorio (2001). These are called the mirroring neurons which have the specific function of carrying out the same task as those of the other person. They only work if the action of the other person has meaning for us. Cf. Stevens, J. A., et al. (2000) cited in Decety, J. and Jackson, Philip L. (2008).
24. This is the formula of the Kantian imperative.
25. After the critique of reason concealing emotions by Damasio (Cf. Damasio, 1995 and 2002), it is very possible that Kant's philosophy, constructed around reason rather than emotions, is also undermined and the current empiricism formed around Hume was rediscovered. Cf. Hume, D. (2001).
26. Certain emotional expressions do not stay on the face more than several hundredths of a millisecond, but this lapse of time is enough for the brain to decipher them and adapt to them without being conscious of it. In fact, we know today that this has been measured and that our brain can snap up emotions that are not held in place on the face more than 1/50,000 of a second. Cf. Kirouac, G. and Doré, F. Y., *Perceptual and Motor Skills*, no. 57.
27. Emotional experiences can take place outside of the awareness of stimuli. It is difficult in these conditions to evaluate the effects of messages on other people. Cf. Zajonc, R. (1980).

Chapter 3

1. There seems to be a reason why the connections of the cortical areas to the amygdala are less important than those of the amygdala to the cortical areas. This could explain why emotional information can so easily invade our conscious thoughts but why we have so much difficulty deciphering it.Cf. Amarai, D.G., et al., op.cit.
2. This distinction is established by Damasio. Cf. Damasio, A. (1999).
3. According to S. Epstein, for example, fear is tied to the outside and to self-anxiety. When fear cannot be mastered, it transforms into anxiety. Cf. Epstein (1972). Ohman, on his part, shows that the physiological responses observed among phobics who were exposed to objects that they were afraid of and patients affected by post-traumatic stress disorder (PTSD) reflect the activation of the one and the same response underlying anxiety. Cf. Ohman (1992).
4. The inter-rater method consists of saying that a proposal is serious and scientific if people separated from each other and observing the same scene come to the same conclusions. The method of deciphering emotions that we propose allows you to achieve this without any real difficulties.
5. The principal difficulty presented by emotions resides in the fact that they are used to fulfill different needs in different fields of knowledge. J. LeDoux, one of the major figures in neurobiology and a specialist in emotions, writes about the limbic system (the "emotional brain" par excellence): "Each year, we teach legions of neuroscience students where the limbic system is found and what it does. But there is a problem. That is that

this theory explains nothing about the emotional brain; some scientists even say that the limbic system does not exist." (Cf. LeDoux, J., 2005). For some, they are bodily responses that allow for the adaption of the human race over the course of life (Cf. Darwin, C., 1872). In this vein, for some, the principal emotions are universal (Cf. Ekman, P., 1993; Eibl-Eibesfeldt, I. 1976), while for others, they allow us to socialize; this is the socio-constructivist position (Cf. for example: Brunner, J. 1991; Vygotski, L., 1992; Fehr, F. S., 1984). Between the two, the cognitivist position encourages the thinking that it is mental illustrations that give meaning to experienced bodily states. Others lean toward the more physiological argument: emotions are mental states resulting from brain perceptions of bodily reactions (Cf. James, W., 1884), unless the brain generates emotions (Cf. Cannon, W. B., 1929). This last position is less fashionable today. Parallel to this series of questions is this one, which has become unavoidable since Freud added the unconscious to the sciences, which consists of wondering if unconscious forces trigger emotions. Certain writers speak therefore of an emotional unconscious (Cf. Zajonc, R. 1984). But there again, for some, the unconscious at the heart of the psyche cannot be unveiled consciously (Cf. Amaral, D. G., Price, J. L., Pitkanen, A., Carmichael, S. T., 1992), while for others the evaluation of conscious actions allows us to find the unconscious again (Cf. Arnold, M., who founded the concept of evaluation in 1960). The heterogeneity of these positions leads us to think that the best way to read emotions consists, without a doubt, of observing them and describing them systematically, in order to measure their coherence in relation to verbal speech. This is in any case the proposal of this book.

6. Cf. James, W. (1884).
7. Response proposed by a trend dominated by Cannon, W. B. (1929).
8. The works of J. LeDoux have allowed us to understand that it is the amygdala, situated in the subcortical structures (the emotional brain), that intervenes, summoning the body to react even before the cognitive brain has time to analyze the nature of the danger. Cf. LeDoux, J. (1997).
9. At the intrauterine stage, the baby knows the states and sensations that are embryonic of the most elaborate emotions; he must rediscover them upon coming into the world, because firm contact with his mother's stomach, on which he is placed after birth, hardly resembles the amniotic bath of his first residence. For him it is a matter of rediscovering emotions or rather letting them come back into being. Cf. Robert-Ouvray, S. (1997).
10. During this second stage, the baby announces behavioral tonalities that are more nuanced. Tiredness, hunger, and fear are timbered differently. The infant recognizes his mother when he sees her; he laughs and pronounces vocalizations. Cf. Jones, S. (1996).
11. This criterion of the pleasure/displeasure or positive/negative impulse is true for all living organisms. Thus, bacteria also protect themselves from danger. Their defensive mechanism leads them "naturally" to move far away from objects judged harmful. Cf. Gould, J. L. (1982). Emotions are said to be positive if they generate pleasure, negative if they engender displeasure.
12. What Jacques Vauclair calls the difference between "declarative" human gestures and "injunctive" gestures of the great apes.
13. Cf. Warneken, F. and M. Tomasello, *Science*, no. 311.
14. Cf. Johnson, S. C., Baxter, L. C., Wilder, L. S., Pipe, J. G., Heiserman, J. E., and Prigatano, G. P. (2002).
15. For Gallup, the recognition of self would be an essential prerequisite to the conception of self, which itself makes it possible to think about the mental state of others, an ability

that is called "theory of mind" (ToM for "Theory of Mind"). Cf. Gallup, G. G., Jr. (1998), et al. (2003).

16. The concept that Jean-Jacques Rousseau calls "the society that corrupts" appears between four and five years of age in a child, when he learns the difference between himself and the other, and becomes conscious little by little that his interests can be different from those of others.

Chapter 4

1. We will come back to gestural heritage in the last part of the book.
2. Western models try to make us forget time by hiding their wrinkles, as if they are trying to erase life. All this is very strange.
3. Deciphering emotions on the face is done thanks to the intersection of information of a dual nature: knowledge connected to cerebral functioning and visual observations. The observation of hundreds of sad or joyous faces reveals the constant, systematic signs that allow us to determine a body of traditional rules subject to statistical validation, which permits us to no longer make mistakes about the nature of emotion.
4. Sometimes they are called slow muscles. The autonomic nervous system does not act directly on the neuromuscular junction to trigger action, like the central nervous system does with the striated muscles, but through a chemical mediation. The system of triggering and reabsorption of the action is much slower in smooth muscles.
5. Let us take a caricature example that is quite vivid: If you are on vacation, relaxed, in a far away country, for example, and it takes three days for your metabolism to allow you to go to the bathroom, you say that certain smooth muscles of your stomach will take 400 times longer than your striated muscles (those charged with holding the glass of piña colada) before really going on vacation!
6. Our perspective obviously has nothing to do with Gall's phrenology (Cf. Gall, F. J., 1807), which is the opposite, the causal links being reversed; nor with morpho-psychology (Cf. Corman, L., 1991). If, by chance, the interpretations of facial features overlap, it is more than a happy accident.
7. It seems that it is the Purkinje cell, on the interior of the cerebral cortex, that is the central area implicated in this body-brain intervigilance. See Kahle, W. (2008) for more information on the role of the Purkinje cell. The defense responses are obtained by the stimulation of the central nucleus of the amygdala, the region communicating with the areas of the brain stem that regulate the responses governed by fear. Cf. LaBar, K. S., et al. (1995).
8. The most systematic work on emotions visible on the face due to muscular displacements is without a doubt that of Paul Ekman. Cf. Friesen, W., *The Facial Action Coding System Manual,* Palo Alto, Consulting Psychologist Press, 1982.
9. This proposal is scientifically refutable according to hard science criteria. 1. It is proven through observation. 2. Honest means of refuting it are proposed. For example, you can say that everybody plunged into a liquid will come out wet. If this is the case, if an object comes out dry, the proposition has been refuted. In the same way, synergological hypotheses are verifiable and refutable. Here, it is sufficient to look for negative emotions to see if they all have the presence of vertical wrinkles as characteristics. The proposal would be false if this were not the case. If, now, these same wrinkles were present during positive emotions (which is not the case), this would be proof that vertical wrinkles are not a discriminating feature. The theory had to be refuted, conforming to the rules of refutability also known as falsifiability. Cf. Popper, K., *La logique de la découverte scientifique, Payot,* 1978.

10. I quote from memory a study that was made of four book covers showing the faces of their authors that tend to demonstrate this.
11. It is extremely rare that we advocate this attitude, but it has been tested empirically with several groups converging on the images and shows that general impression is actually a better adviser than a systematic tracking of a solitary feature like the position of the chin.
12. It is important to succeed in deciphering emotions without going through procedures that ask the person what they feel, because it is definitively known today (Cf. LeDoux, J., 2005) that all these procedures have no scientific validity. They are impossible to control and even less so to restore unconscious feeling through speech. The apparent cause of an emotion is not always the real cause. The father who screams at his children about their botched homework does not necessarily know that the cause of his anger is perhaps his bad day at work.

Chapter 5

1. We are speaking here about gender identity, not sexual identity, because it would have been necessary to use the word "orientation."
2. On the issue of family secrets, see Tiseron, S. (1999) and Ancelin-Schutzenberger, A. (2003).
3. A guilty person and an innocent one who is afraid of police authorities send the same messages of fear, but those of the innocent person are devoid of vigilance, because he knows that he is not guilty, and this kind of spontaneity transmits itself on the body. We are beginning to master this subtlety. Some experts trained by us have, as validation of their training in deciphering body language, a test to detect lies.
4. Our methods permit the detection of 80 percent of lies in this test called "guilty/innocent." It is a matter of recognizing if a stranger in front of a camera does or doesn't fabricate a lie. The success rate is 90 percent when people work in a group. The pretested computer camera software should allow for the resolution of this 10 percent hiatus of lies that are extremely difficult to detect. In fact, the human eye cannot read a continuous emotional sign. We must identify several signs, and a machine that is properly set up can do so. Besides, it is very possible that this machine can never detect 100 percent of lies, but what is important to understand is that the machine only works with body language. This shows the precision of its messages!
5. During emotional activity, the right hemisphere is more active but in the left frontal cortex there is an inhibiting agent of the subcortical systems that allows us to conceal certain emotional expressions. It is very able to control the expression of the right half of the face, but this is less evident as far as the left half is concerned. (Cf. Rinn, W.). The left half of the mouth is less well controlled than the right because the central command of the mouth is seated in the left hemisphere. Thus, this hemisphere operates a control that is more instantaneous than what controls the right half of the mouth, and it is especially the left half, of which the corners are drawn up, that expresses the discrepancy of emotional expressions. It is the opposite for the right eyebrow, for which the dominant motor cortex is situated in the right hemisphere.
6. It is no longer clues delivered by the limbic system that are interesting, but the control put in place either at the level of the orbiculo-frontal cortex or at the level of the left anterior cingulated cortex. Thanks to this theory, methodological problems that have never been surpassed up to now can be; notably that of a lie detector like the polygraph test, which is otherwise extremely reliable, that reveals its limitations when faced with an emotional person.

7. Information is transmitted from one hemisphere to the other thanks to fibers in the corpus callosum. Each of the two hemispheres possesses its own specificities.
8. The triggering durations have been very rapid, too rapid for the wink to be done consciously (less than three-tenths of a second). The lower eyelid lifts up, as in this case, when the winks are unconscious. When the winks are conscious, it is the upper eyelid that begins the movement by moving down first.
9. Cf. for example, Pierre Feyereisen writes: "Most of us think that right-handed people, when they express themselves, make more gestures with their right hand than left-handed people who use their left hands more; this is false in both cases. Another conveniently conveyed belief would have left-handed people having both cerebral hemispheres reversed in relation to right-handed people, and saying that they are left-handed for this reason. This is also a misconception." Cf. Feyereisen, P. (1994).
10. This example is generalized for all people blind in one eye. It has been reproduced each time with the same success in men and women from different continents. In a situation of well-being, a person blind in the left eye looks with the left side of his face. A French politician of the extreme right, Jean-Marie le Pen, is blind in one eye. Go look at the images in the archives, and you will see that, depending on his interest at the time, he looks with one eye rather than the other, following the rules that have nothing to do with the fact that one of his eyes is more functional than the other.

Chapter 6

1. From the point of view of drive, the major hemisphere is almost always the left, but there are exceptions. Thus, for example, the eyelids' motor command is placed in the right hemisphere. For more information about the major and minor hemisphere, see Sperry, R.W., Zaidel, E., and Zaidel, D. (1979).
2. The crossing is made using pyramidal routes.
3. Serious debates present opposition to the community of ideas about whether the seat of the emotions is situated, according to researchers, either in the right hemisphere or in the limbic system. For a little clarity, halfway between the theory that says the emotions are lodged in the right hemisphere (as Gainotti and Gardner thought), and the other thesis that distinguishes, rather than the hemispheres, that the sub- and sub-cortical layers, in the theoretic lineage of Paul McLean, our sources of visual recordings bring us to believe that spontaneous emotions are without a doubt managed by the dominant motor cortex, whether the right motor cortex for the area of eyebrows and the left motor cortex for the area of the mouth, for example. Some paradoxical asymmetries are not presented as part of this work, pending further validation.
4. At birth, the right hemisphere of the baby is more developed than the left and will stay so during the first four months of life. Then, the left hemisphere will gradually catch up and, at about six months, the two hemispheres will separate information almost equally. The question of a child's cerebral development stages is complicated. Certain authors even suggest not referring to stages because cerebral advances are always followed by regressions, which are all the more specific to each child. On this issue, see notably Thelen, E. and Smith, L. B. (1994).
5. Cf. Sieratzky, J. S. and Woll, B. B. (1996).
6. Cf. Chateau, Peter de (1983), quoted by Vauclair, J. (2004).
7. In 1990, two English ethnologists, from the University of Liverpool, John Manning and Andrew Chamberlain, observed primates in a zoo and analyzed films and photographs of them in nature. They noted that 85 percent of chimpanzees, 82 percent of gorillas,

and 75 percent of orangutans carried their offspring on the left. This behavior would have appeared more than 6 million years ago. Cf. Damerose, E. and Vauclair, J. (2002).
8. Cf. Turchet, P. (2004).
9. At the movies, the violence of an action make it so that kisses are triggered from right eye to right eye (like in the image on the right), then, as the situation languishes, it is to the other eye, in fact the other side of the mouth and skin, that the kiss slides. Things go well four times more often this way than in the other direction.
10. Moreover, the left half of the face is more mobile that the right. Cf. Skinner, Mullen (1991).
11. Our experiments show that the public that was questioned was absolutely not conscious that the person in front of them was looking with the left eye, and this was true whether the person was present or they were viewing a recording 25 seconds long of someone who looked at them with the left eye. None of the people mentioned it in response to the question: What have you observed? This test was addressed to more than 3,000 people.
12. Cf. Gainotti, G. (1972); Heilman, K. and Satz, P. (1983). With regard to the origin of this hypothesis, specialists can consult Sperry, R. W. et al., and Winken, P. J. and Brun, G. W. (1969). Different experiments show that if the left somatosensory cortex is injured, people continue to succeed in tests where empathy is measured. Cf. Ralph, A. (2002 and 1999).
13. Which is why Suzanne Robert-Ouvray, specialist in psychomotor skills of newborns, says that it is not an accident if a child cannot hold his head up. She thinks or suggests that if he could do it before this age, it would be possible from him to confuse himself with the lamp, the handle of a door, or the wallpaper that is in front of him. Let us not forget that the brain, at that age, cannot conceive of a fusional stage.
14. Tomatis thinks that we talk like what we hear and Francoise Dolto, who followed this path for a time, thought that there is a voice particular to the child in whom the left hemisphere is dominant and a voice that is particular to the child in whom the right hemisphere is dominant. Cf. Dolto, F. (1985).
15. Gabor Maté, doctor and father of three left-handed children, makes the same analysis as Cyrulnik, who is also the father of three left-handed children. He thinks that at certain critical periods in a child's development, the presence of the father helps him to put to work the present mechanisms of the left hemisphere and that his absence prevents these mechanisms from being put in place. It is for him, like for Cyrulnik, one of the causes (it is not the only one!) of why children whose fathers were not present at critical periods are left-handed. Cf. Maté, G. (2003).
16. Cf. Cyrulnik, B. (1989).
17. Psychological propositions on the relationship between the two hemispheres recognize a certain number of Freud's propositions related to the concomitant dissociation of the self and the other. The creator of psychoanalysis realized, by 1925, that a baby does not discover things because they exist. For the baby, there is what interests him and what he rejects and what simply no longer exists for him. Winnicott explains, in 1962, that at this age the child shows during games that there is an "inside" and that things come from the "outside."
18. Cf. Peretz, I. and Morais, J. (1993).
19. Lanius shows, in 2004, that during emotional trauma, memories are stored in the right hemisphere among subjects who are affected by post-traumatic stress and in the left hemisphere by others. They put them into words, classify them by exteriorizing them, and get rid of them unconsciously.
20. Cf. Witling, Werner. "Brain asymmetry in the control of autonomic-physiologic activity," in Davidson, Richard J. and Hugdahl, Kenneth, *Brain Assymetry*, Cambridge and London, MIT Press, 1995.

21. Ressland, in 2000, shows that the left hemisphere is the one of stimulation. A mother who stimulates her baby rather than helping it fall asleep changes her intonation and intensity of voice, and she places her baby on her right side.
22. Cf. Borod, J. C. (1992), op. cit.
23. Skeptics of video footage. This concrete and detailed proposal contains all the terms of those used in hard sciences. Mastering nonverbal observation is learned. Certified training can be achieved. This is the object of our discipline: synergology.
24. Damasio constructed his work, *Descartes' Error*, in 1995, around the case of Phinéas Gage, a man whose mental capacities were intact but who could no longer make sound decisions because he did not feel empathy.

Chapter 7

1. I. Eibl-Eibesfeldt, in 1976, observed the eyebrow movements of members of Amazonian tribes.
2. It is the resources of the right hemisphere that allow us to recognize our own face among others (Cf. Platek, et al., 2004). The left hemisphere performs better when it is a matter of identifying strangers (Cf. Platek, et al., 2002). If a hemisphere is put outside of a circuit, the right hemisphere is much better at its own recognition and the left hemisphere at recognizing others. Other tests that highlight this reality show that people attribute themselves qualities more quickly when using the left hand to identify them in a written medium, whereas the right hand is faster at assigning qualities to others. (Cf. Platek, et al., 2003).
3. Dutel shows that in certain circumstances, a lie accompanies the raising of the right eyebrow. Being reserved is a personality trait and not an emotion. How is the shifting of direction of an emotion or a personality trait shown on the face? Certain emotions are more familiar to certain types of personalities. The left eyebrow marks personal distance. This attitude is not antithetical to reserve, which is also marked by raised shoulders and a lowered chin.
4. All the signs, therefore, assure us of the description that functions in 80 percent of cases. It is the combination of these signs that allow us to be certain of conceiving a horizon of acceptable meaning. The movement of the eyebrow can be coupled with attention paid to the eye that looks, even before deciphering the other expressions of the body.
5. See the glossary.
6. Witling, while working on the lateralization of neurotransmitters in the brain, showed that serotonin and norepinephrine are found principally in the right hemisphere, while dopamine, especially implicated in the exact control of the motor response, is found in the left hemisphere. Cf. Witling, Werner (1995).
7. Borod demonstrates that emotions do not interfere with the two halves of the face. It is the unconscious control that is responsible for tensions on the right side of the face. Cf. Borod, J. C. (1992).
8. Ray Birdwhistell founded, in the year 1950, kinesiology. This was the first rigorous attempt at nonverbal classification. The knowledge available at the time did not permit the differentiation, common today, between the left and the right hemispheres on the face. It is possible to express similar critiques of the more successful work of P. Ekman, whose methodological postulates of departure were established in the year 1970. Very present in the world of ideas, it remains, in our opinion, an unavoidable reference.
9. Because the white is equally visible underneath the eye in certain circumstances, as we will see further on. Cf. Oshawa, G.
10. When negative emotions are experienced, the left eyelid has a tendency to blink more than the right. We will come back to this a little later by addressing the blinking of the eyelids.

11. This phenomenon permits us to differentiate a real smile from a false one and was one of the first emotional mechanisms detected. It was discovered by a French doctor, Boulogne de Duchene, in 1862, and then was popularized by P. Ekman.
12. This observation, if it is made methodically, is like a questionnaire on self-esteem; as we have already said, we cannot consciously make the unconscious emerge. This is the unavoidable limit of all theories of self-evaluation. Cf. LeDoux, J. (2005).
13. On the other hand, when she loses control of herself and ultimately attacks you spontaneously, it is with the left side that she looks at you. One of the methods of validation consists of several overlapping—to avoid a possible induction—signs. If the other signs do not point toward the initial deduction, it cannot be made (e.g., the *sampaku* of the right eye corresponds to putting the other at a distance, but the eye that looks at us in a dominant way is the left and the head leans to the left: Our first reasoning is not valid).
14. This is all the difference between the action of the pyramidal system and the action of the extrapyramidal system, an absolutely indispensable connection in the expression of sincere emotion. Cf. Damasio, A. (1995).
15. This is not the objective of this work, and we will not explore this theme anymore, but between a human being and a dog, the similarities of nonverbal behavior are more than anecdotal.
16. It is not because we look at everything with our eyes that we pay attention to what our eyes rest on. For example, when we are "spacing out," we are looking but we are elsewhere and we do not see. This proposal, as logical as it is, is not scientific. One hundred white swans on a lake do not allow us to say that the proposal "all swans are white" is true. On the other hand, one black swan on a lake allows us to say that it is false. Cf. Popper, K. (1878). There are, in fact, moments when the eyes do not see.
17. They believed that it was to answer the demands of this or that hemisphere or to go looking for resources in one hemisphere rather than in the other that the eyes go to the left or to the right. Thus, they had remarked that the eyes go to the left when people refer to the past and go to the right when they think about the future, and I believe their theories were well corroborated by the facts, but that they were not tested in other parts of the world. Cf. Bandler, R. and Grinder, D. (1970).
18. The direction of the gaze, for reasons of protocol, has never really been taken into account in the world of scientific research, and that is a shame because eye movements are linked to our arms during speech and provide psycho-emotional indications of an individual's intentions (see Part Three). Orienting debates around protocols rather than for the sake of producing knowledge breeds a poverty of discoveries, and in a context where there is no ideal protocol, the theories of verbal evaluation (asking people what they feel when they make such a movement) have definitely challenged their limitations.
19. My thanks to Rabah Aiouaz for his work and his precise collaboration in the understanding of nonverbal language in places other than the West. His observations, taken from Aramaic records, allowed us to clarify and more definitively validate our earlier observations on the role of writing in relation to eye movement. But it is his deciphering of video footage, on which one observes preliterate people, that has permitted us in this case to understand that cerebral logic presides over eye movements (it is the same among these people as among Westerners) and that it can be distorted and reversed by the direction of writing (this is the case with Semitic people). A universal functioning presides over eye movements, but this functioning is modified by cultural specificities.

This discovery won him the 2007 Award of Excellence in synergology. Cf. Aiouaz, Raban. "La diachronie gestuelle: étude comparative entre peuples maghrébins et peuples occidentaux," 2007.

20. The direction of Asiatic writing (from bottom to top) contributes to the fact that Asian eyes never go to the left or very often to the right to find information, and they have more of a tendency to look above the person in front of them.
21. The lower left quadrant is the only one that is not dependent upon writing and establishes a universal reality. Self-consciousness finds its seat in the right hemisphere. This reality forces us to distinguish the moments during which the direction of writing is predominant from moments of contemplation. As for what concerns the relationship between the right hemisphere and self-awareness, see notably Keenan, J. P., et al. (2001).
22. In the brain, it is the area of the anterior cingulate cortex that makes this work.
23. Cf. Bergeron, S. and Mathieu, L. (2009). Beware: We must be in front of the person we are talking to in order to observe this phenomenon.
24. For the detector of bodily activation (D.A.C.), a lie becomes significant when eight signs or features go in the same direction. Other signs lead here to a lie in the general attitude of the body. It is impossible, even for a very well-trained person, to hide all these signs of control. More than one hundred among them are listed and it would be necessary to master all of them at the same time, but at least one will most likely not work.

Chapter 8

1. Annick de Souzenelle in 1991, identified the manner in which the great religions describe each body segment and concluded that, whatever the religion, the body segments play the same symbolic role. The work of Claude Lévi-Strauss expanded this reality to preliterate people. We construct the image of the world from our bodily experiences and if numerous universes pre-exist it is because our bodies are structured in the same way: a head to receive information, arms for grasping, legs for moving forward, a torso to express oneself.
2. Damasio shows that quadriplegic patients express muted emotions, simply because the messages from the body no longer go to the brain. From this fact, they are also less depressed than they could be. Cf. Damasio, A. (2002).
3. Cf. Ada, Abraham, *Le dessin d'une personne,* Delachaux and Niestlé, coll. Pedagogical and psychological activities, 1962.
4. A cat runs after his tail. If, by accident, he catches it, he treats it like an exterior object; he does not differentiate between "to be" and "to have." He does have a consciousness that it is a part of him, in the same way that he does not recognize himself in mirrors. He sees it like how a human being who carries crutches sees crutches: They are his and serve him to move but do not intrinsically belong to him.
5. Even if psychoanalysis does not consciously or explicitly refer to synergology, we would be mistaken to ignore what it proposes when it puts body space in relation to verbal space.
6. In the history of humanity, they have developed concurrently with the members themselves. The Cro-Magnon man, for example, did not have our long neck. His head was much closer to his shoulders. Joints introduced flexibility into the body, at the moment when the brain also acquired it and refined it.
7. It is for this reason that the sexual abuse of children is so easy. For them, someone who loves them cannot hurt them; sexual abuse is therefore not really conceivable. The subjectivity of the other is not perceived in the same way among adults. Cf. Robert, J. (2000).
8. Sociology even speaks of "voting with your feet" when talking about electoral abstention of the disaffection from public life and a return to individual spheres. Cf. Hirschmann, A. O.

(2006).

9. The eye is the only organ for which the right and the left are systematically dissociated in statistics.
10. This is what is called an artifact. We are not sure if this expression is the exact expression but this is the best possible explanation. In fact, it can be submitted to the criteria of refutability, which means that if it is not correct, it would be possible to find videos that show that the opposite—in fact, video footage showing the opposite makes up less than 5 percent of our database.
11. Timed, they last longer and this is true whether we are right-handed or left-handed.
12. Cf. Craig, A. D. (2000 and 2002); Andrew, D. (2001).
13. In the case of embarrassment, which is well identified and well documented, several phenomena take place. It is even possible to speak about a signature cardiovascular characteristic involving a rise in facial temperature as well as a flux in blood flow and a rise in blood pressure, thus a small tingling. Cf. Morow, et al.(1981).
14. The cerebral areas destined to treat emotions become less active when we scratch ourselves. G. Yosipovitch, of Wake Forest University, discovered the fact that scratching oneself (in this experiment, the participants had to scratch themselves mechanically; we are speaking here of itching) makes the emotional level go down. The cingulate cortex stops working. Now, this area is implicated in pain. At the same time, the prefrontal cortex areas that are involved in rewards or compulsive behaviors become reactive, which would explain why scratching oneself is so pleasant. Cf. Raymond, J. (2008).
15. Cf. Ramachandran, V. S. and Ramachandran, R. D. (1996).
16. "Researchers consider that scratching among chimpanzees is an indicator of negative emotional excitement, as much in social contexts as in nonsocial ones. For example, isolated apes in their cages scratch less often than those placed in groups. In their natural environment, vocalizations from rival groups (risking provoked clashes) will provoke itching. In a situation of performance evaluation during a difficult test versus an easy one, there is an increase in scratching, especially after a wrong answer. Similar results can also be seen among orangutans." Cf. Lachance, S. (2009).
17. Certain authors speak of self-contact gestures without separating itching, micro-fixations, and micro-caresses, but we distinguish these three categories. Cf. Freedman, N. and Steingart, J. (1975).
18. When emotions move through us and disturb us. They can bring about emotional reactions conveyed by very short itches, which Americans call arousal responses. We scratch ourselves because "it itches." And we do it more with the left hand, whether we are right-handed or left-handed. Cf. Kimura, D. (1976).

Chapter 9

1. The nature of the observations mentioned is labeled in tens of thousands of video footage, where they can be retrieved. The logic of itching on the face is shown in detail in Appendix 1.
2. Cf. Witling, Werner, op. cit.; Bourassa, M. (1997) concerning the active resources of the left hemisphere.
3. R. Ornstein has remarked that the cortical activity of individuals changes hemispheric mode when they undergo a logical activity or an intuitive activity. Cf. Ornstein, R. (1993).
4. The authenticity of a smile is measured by the juxtaposition of three items: the corners of the mouth going up, the orbicularis oculi muscles dilating (causing crow's feet), and the gaze going toward another person.
5. The path of the arms toward the head is not taken into account in this calculation performed on 100 micro-caresses of the right hand (0.3 sec.) and 100 micro-caresses of the left hand (0.9 sec.). These statistics have been elaborated from archived images

taken from video footage, television programs, etc.

6. This gesture must not be confused with the one of examining the ends of one's hair to evaluate its quality or the tips of one's fingers, or brushing dandruff off one's clothing while talking. Although it doesn't look like much, the person who makes these gestures introduces distance. The ambience of the communication is therefore not the same. The facial and body features are also different.
7. Concerning bodily heritage, see Part Three of this book.
8. The opposition between men and women, from a nonverbal point of view, is, according to us, an absurdity, with several close exceptions. We speak of these exceptions in the book *Pourquoi les hommes marchent-ils à la gauche des femmes?* (*Why Do Men Walk to the Left of Women?*)
9. Our observations indicate that we must not put too much value into which hand performs the gesture. In fact, there are too many examples to the contrary for us to establish that the choice of the hand that is used supplies supplementary information.
10. I remember a man who pulled his eyebrows. When he asked me what that could signify, I remained doubtful and told him that perhaps he was searching for an important hidden memory. To that, he answered, after some time, that he thought this attitude had appeared during the period when he had discovered that his father wasn't his real father. Unfortunately, my proactive attitude had made the value of this anecdote useless, for I had, without wanting to, proposed an injunction by suggesting in some way a path to the response. I had awkwardly asked him what he thought by proposing to him what I thought. Cf. for the process of autosuggestion: Megglé, D. and Erickson, M. (2002); Erickson, M. and Rossi, E. (1980).
11. Which is to say that the brain is a hundred thousand times better connected to internal information representing the connections between the neurons than to sensory and motor information. Cf. Rossi, E. (1993).
12. Itching that is felt under the left eye is four to five times more frequent than itching felt under the right eye.
13. During a meeting that lasted one hour and fifteen minutes, thirty-seven scratches were counted. Cf. Dalai-Lama (1999).
14. Today it is thought that blushing is an advantage of evolution. Cf. Harris (2007).
15. The connection between self-awareness and the right hemisphere is beginning to be very well documented. Cf. Keenan, J. P. (2000 and 2001); Platek (2003 and 2004).
16. The same scenario occurs again and again; that of something unspoken related to oneself, therefore a lie. And this is true, be it an angry actor explaining that he never gets angry, a lecturer contradicting himself and continuing as if nothing happened, a man explaining that one cannot buy justice shortly before being condemned for attempted bribery, or of a dishonest art dealer trying to convince us of his sincerity.
17. If the nose, as the olfactory sensor, sends its information to the heart of the brain without decussation, with respect to that which is motor and sensory, it is the left trigeminal nerve that takes charge of this activity and the activity is thus organized by the contralateral hemisphere.
18. The conductivity of the skin precedes the impression of experiencing a feeling. Cf. Damasio, A., et al. (2000).
19. To understand what the other feels necessitates tracing our own emotions. This mechanism allows for empathy and, consequently, adaptation. It is the somatosensory cortex that operates (Cf. Craig, A., 2000). This mechanism is unconscious. It is difficult to operate consciously because various phenomena of projection interfere with thoughts. Cf. LeDoux, J. (2005).
20. "All that belongs to me is me." It is on this proposition that the society of consumption is built. If it were no longer true, the society of consumption would collapse (Cf. Baudrillard,

J., 1968). Objects are a coherent system of signs that make us up (Cf. Baudrillard, J., 1970). They no longer lead to the satisfaction of needs, but rather to differentiating ourselves. Objects become self. With itching, objects end up being "corporeal." Example: "I scratch the left side of my nose if someone says something bad about my car!"

21. Jumbled-up images that are observed show us an important Tibetan dignitary speaking about China, a host denigrating a woman author that he bluntly calls a "whore," a man who talks about his father in rather harsh terms, and a host who rejects a guest with the tone of his humor. In all these videos, the common point is that the other person "irritates" the one who scratches. He therefore scratches this irritation. We would have never thought, much less said, anything of it if the solid base of video footage had not convinced us. Body language always requires corroborating statements and pictures.
22. For this proposal to be verifiable, we need two ingredients: 1. Clarity: Here, the hand comes back above the mouth when the person asserts his authority. 2. Providing honest means to control the proposal: This gesture is supposedly connected to authority in a conversation. This is the principle of the theory of refutability. Once these two prior criteria reunite, this video must be analyzed with an inter-rater method, that is to say, that the people must make the same analysis of the images without having communicated between themselves.
23. Women scratch their cheeks less than men do. It is difficult to know if this type of aggressiveness is typically masculine or if this gesture is considered more masculine, and is in fact more absent from their bodily heritage.
24. Cf. Keenan, J. P., et al. (2001). Researchers have shown their patients a photo of their face and one of a celebrity while asking them to memorize the latter one. One of their hemispheres was then anesthetized. When the left hemisphere was anesthetized (right hemisphere active), all of the subjects recognized their face more rapidly, and when the left hemisphere was the only active one, they recognized the face of the celebrity more rapidly.
25. When a person is positioned over the left arm, his state of being is often more lascivious, more abandoned, than when he is positioned over the right. Tucker and Williamson have identified that the actions performed with the left arm convey more openness than those made by the right arm. Cf. Tucker, D. M. and Williamson, P. A. (1995).
26. Tomatis identified, even before the MRI revolution, the differences between the left hemisphere and the right and established the connections between psychic integration and psychomotor development and issues with the integration of parental roles. His poorly understood work and especially the power issues surrounding the ownership of this knowledge have unfortunately contributed to his influence in the world of ideas remaining minor. Cf. Tomatis, A. (1976 and 1991).
27. This gesture, for example, is part of the gestural heritage of the French actor Fabrice Luchini. He is caricatured in this position by some comedians.

Chapter 10

1. Cf. Martineau, C. (2008).
2. In this video footage, we observe an actress who scratches her neck to defend herself because someone accuses her of saying anything to newspapers; a novelist who is accused of using his charms to succeed; a man who reproaches himself for having never gone to school; a politician who says he did not know how to make the right decision at a difficult moment.
3. G. Klein shows that people who are looking for a compromise always try to equalize difficulties in order to move forward. Their attitude is more an attitude of apparent submission (in *The Prince*, Machiavelli details numerous equalizer strategies), while others

on the contrary think that they are much more effective in combat; for them it is a driving force to advance and they do not disdain the need to show aggressiveness. He calls them "the sharpeners." If these categories are adequate, let us admit that itching on the back left side of the body is well-suited to equalizers.

4. Several authors have noted that in professional relations, as soon as there are superior hierarchical, collaborative relationships, the collaborators' hands generally become moist.
5. Cf. Aiouaz, Rabah, "Ines Ego", Personal Synergology Video Library, 2007.
6. The horizon of meaning of these images is quite clear so that the gestures of these animals cannot be confused with itching caused by insects or resulting from food allergies. Even with animals, the context (e.g., the case of aggression) is sometimes so eloquent that it is possible to interpret "beyond all reasonable doubt." Cf. Lachance, S. (2008).
7. It is the nature of this communication that allows us to draw conclusions. Thus, some will experience the desire to make connections between the domain of communication and that of pathology. The fact that the breast is an external organ leads us there quite naturally. However, we do not risk establishing connections as directly, because they demand other disciplines outside of our field of study, notably the medical disciplines in this case.
8. Within the strict context of itching.
9. The exact discovery of cerebral areas where mirroring neurons officiate allows us to understand this.
10. The clear and conscious awareness of the body before that of the mind is at the heart of our current work and the setting up of the concept of corcept to which we will have to return another time.
11. Cf. Robert, J. (1999).
12. This is not a metaphor. Video footage attests to this.

Chapter 11

1. Common sense has more trouble conceiving that the body can know one thing of which the brain is not completely conscious. Cf. Amaral, D. G., Price, J. L., Pitkanen, A., and Carmichael, S. T. (1992).
2. The reactions that we are talking about are achieved on the prefrontal level. As in hemiplegia, the side of the face that is touched is the same as the side of the body that is affected. There is therefore no crossing over on the level of the face. For non-specialists, the crossing over corresponds to the phenomenon that the cerebral decussation establishes itself on the body and not on the face.
3. Let us not forget that the cerebral areas destined to treat emotions become atonic when we scratch them. Cf. Yosipovitch, G. (2003).
4. For example, a pretty television host says to an actor all the good things that she thinks about his work: "You are good!" He is in front of her, satisfied, and his body seems to want to get closer to hers. The signs of openness are visible in the eyes of the two protagonists.
5. Cf. Yosipovitch, G. (2005), op. cit.
6. From a methodological point of view, this itching is interesting. If the side where she feels it is looked at from a spatial perspective, the person would scratch herself on the left to leave, because she would thereby differ physically from the person who is speaking and who is to her right on the television. But the interpretation of itching is analytical, preconstructed in her cerebral organization. If she feels like leaving, in order to not participate in the discussion, she will scratch herself on the right, no matter the context.
7. In all cases, this situation is observed in this context and this is the explanation that makes the most sense. The observation adheres perfectly to the theory of the archaic

Freudian stages that didn't have this research input. It has superimposed itself on this explanation.

Chapter 12

1. The eyebrows move when we communicate our emotions, but they do it most of the time in connection with the shoulders, to reinforce their messages. This is so true that in situations of apraxia, when a neurological impairment makes movement difficult, a person to whom you have asked to lift her shoulders can raise her eyebrows without her shoulders moving! Cf. Lebrun, Y. "Apraxie de la parole et apraxie bucco-faciale," in Le Gall, D. and Aubin, G., Apraxie, Marseille, Solal, 2004.
2. Cf. Hubel, D. and Livingstone, M. (1987).
3. Which is also not without raising a certain number of theoretical questions among researchers who have observed this phenomenon, notably this one: What remains of our freedom to act if we act before even being consciousness of acting? Does our freedom resume simply when we become capable of stopping the action? In these conditions, can we still make a choice that is truly free? (Cf. Libet, 2004). This theoretical puzzle provides, however, a certain number of paths to decipher itching. They are the mark on the body of inhibited action.
4. Cf. de Souzenelle, A. (1991).
5. Tucker, D. M. and Williamson, P. A. (1991), op.cit.
6. Cf. Witling, Werner, op.cit.
7. Is it also a coincidence that the relation to spoken language is situated more in the left hemisphere and the right wrist is more mobile than the left (Kimura, D. and Humphrys, C. A., 1981)? If this affirmation is true regarding conscious movements (made because of an order), it is not true for those that are unconscious (half-conscious), made without paying attention, because with the latter, the same areas of the brain are not at work.
8. Acupuncturists know, for example, that a particular point on the ankle must not be touched under the pretext of provoking the childbirth of a pregnant woman. Reflexologists are also very vigilant.

Chapter 13

1. At the age of eight years old, only 31 percent of children draw fingers on "snowmen." Ada Abraham thus describes the works of Terman in *Le dessin d'une personne,* op. cit.
2. Cf. Cyrulnik, Boris (1989).
3. Suarez and Gallup have shown, in 1981, that orangutans, unlike gorillas, were capable, like chimpanzees, of passing the mirror test.
4. This is the principle of falsifiability (or refutability). It is a matter of finding visible examples that can contradict a theory to refute it.
5. During an observation of a professional environment, a person scratched his right index finger while one of his collaborators was greeted by the head of the company. She seemed (according to other items of hypertonic emotion kept to oneself) to fear that this person took a symbolic place of too much consequence in the heart . . . the reason for his entourage.
6. A gorilla whose dominance is contested by a man is filmed, during an experiment, and scratches his right index finger. See Lachance, Sylvie. *Enregistrement*, Zoo de Granby, Montréal, 2006.

Chapter 14

1. This is the principle of elevation. Cf. Martineau (2008).
2. The gorilla stands taller and strikes his chest to show that he is stronger. The dominant

dog places his paw on the dominated dog that sleeps by his side. Bears stand to fight and to seem bigger than their adversaries. We do not need to be afraid, if we come across the most aggressive among them, the polar bears, and raise our arms and stand up on any object that might make us seem larger. This is the first instruction given by the guards of national parks in the Rocheuses. If we seem larger, we will appear stronger, and there will be a greater chance that the bear will go peacefully on his way.

3. In the photograph on the right, if a modern man looks, his gaze risks seeming displaced and if he does not look, we might believe that he is oblivious of femininity. Whatever his attitude is, it will not be good. Here we are at what the specialists call a double constraint. Cf. Bateson, G. (1977).
4. Different from itching, explained in detail in Part One, these movements are called micro-caresses. As you have come to understand, these gestures are not the same. During an itch, the hand responds to the desire of the body; it is only the executor. Here, the hand is the master of the action; it is the hand that goes looking for the other person's gaze to lead it to a part of the body.
5. The cries of nonhuman primates are organized around the Sylvian fissure, while those of humans are in the cingulate cortex, an area that appeared more recently (Cf. Jurgens, U., 1989). The area called "Broca's area" in which words are stored, connects to the AMS, the supplementary motor area that is indispensable to body language in the parietal cortex. From the body language of a great ape to that of man, an area in the brain seems to have mutated. Broca's area, which manages verbal production, developed, encroaching on the area which, in apes, manages gestural motor functions. This evolution occurred, according to researchers, about 40 million years ago.
6. Moreover, linguists, like some paleontologists, are beginning to defend the idea that the larynx and the pharynx positioned higher in the throat would not have prevented *Homo erectus* from speaking, long before *Homo sapiens.* Cf. notably Boe, L. J., et al. (2000).
7. Concerning the gestural origin of the word, see Rizzolati, G. and Sinigalalia, C. (2008).
8. This was already the hypothesis expressed by André Leroi-Gourhan. Discoveries made thanks to the MRI, which reveals the secrets of the brain, reinforcing the theory completely. Cf. Leroi-Gourrhan, A. (1971); and more recently Noble, W. and Davidson, L. (1996).
9. A gene could be responsible for the emergence of language (see the work of Svante Pääbo and his team at the Max Planck Institute on the gene FOXP2). This hypothesis does not compete with others. There is no reason to think that the genetic mutation isn't linked to the modification, among *Homo sapiens*, of their reproduction conditions.
10. The most intelligent apes can learn hundreds of words and show that they have understood them by identifying them thanks to pictograms, but they are incapable of creating, whether it be through pictograms or something else, a sentence with a subject, a verb, and a complement, as simple as that is! Language is not a cry that is transformed thanks to the organ of speech. At least, it is not just that. Asking is one thing that apes can do by crying; sharing a relationship is another thing they can do. The difference between injunctive language and declarative language is made explicit by Vauclair, J. and Michaud, Y. (2002).
11. As we have seen, before he is four years old, a child is certain that his parents know his thoughts. He believes the parent who says to him: "I know what you did . . . it is my pinkie finger that told me!" Then he discovers that his parents cannot know his thoughts. He thereby learns progressively that the little finger does not speak!
12. Cf. Damasio, A. (1999).
13. This is a classic gesture that we call injunction. It means "Be quiet!" and even a dog can understand it if he is trained to. A child of eighteen months also understands it.
14. From a cerebral point of view, it is the appearance of the neocortex that allowed the human

being to acquire the capacity to make choices that integrate more parameters. He gains a freedom in relation to his body because he can, in a certain way, watch himself act. It is also completely possible that, thanks to his vertical position, he was able to watch his hands work and that his neocortex was developed and permitted the great leap forward. It's all about the gesture . . .

15. The citation, as elsewhere in this general discussion on metaphors, borrows a great deal from the minds of (again a metaphor) Lakoff and Johnson. Cf. Lakoff, G. and Johnson, M., *Les métaphores dans la vie quotidienne,* Paris, Editions de Minuit, 1980.
16. According to Lakoff and Johnson, "Metaphors of spatialization are rooted in our physical and cultural experience. They are not attributed by accident. A metaphor can only serve to understand a concept by virtue of its basis in experience." Cf. Lakoff and Johnson, op. cit.

Chapter 15

1. Moreover, the cerebral apparatus that allows the brain to make gestures in order to be better understood is the location of a particular kind of intelligence. Three gestures out of four among nonhuman primates are the result of immediate imitation, but that is not the case among humans. Cf. Vauclair, J. (1998).
2. Ekman and Friesen speak on this occasion of emblematic gestures, which put all of human body language into four categories, where we distinguish seven categories (figurative, symbolic, projective, engram gestures, micro-caresses, itches, and micro-fixations). In our opinion, they did not want to see, according to McNeil, that gestures are producers of speech and are made in conjunction with emotional messages produced through dialogue, thanks to gestures. By reducing the logic of body language to a socio-constructivist paradigm, they have forbidden the interpretation of it and have closed themselves off to the possibility of understanding it.
3. The techniques of hypnosis are based on this principle: bringing a person back to an initial state so that the emotions that are tied to that physical state will return.
4. This research was in part carried out by Desmond Morris, in 1994.
5. This continues to exist, even if we are not visually accessible to each other. Bekdache observed that on the telephone, for example, we make fewer gestures, but we do in fact make them.
6. Language production passes through two forms of cerebral configurations. One of them has a relationship with interior language. It does not interact with motor activities in dialogue. Gestural production in the brain is situated in an area connected to Broca's area. The stimulation of this area helps, without a doubt, the production of certain ideas, when our conversation is addressed to someone.

Chapter 16

1. See the glossary. We will come back later to the notion of bodily heritage.
2. We see here that, contrary to what popular common sense sometimes tells us, we do not show the palms of our hands to try to get closer to other people.

Chapter 17

1. Cf. Kimura, D. and Kimura, A. (1981).
2. Cf. Iaccino, J. (1993). Iaccino shows that the nerve fibers that control the hand and the arm develop more rapidly in the left hemisphere than in the right. Moreover, the left hemisphere controlling the movements of the right hand is more directly operational (Cf. Joseph, R. 1992). Language is also controlled by an area contiguous to the one that

manages the movement of the right hand. For all of these reasons, the right hand, as soon as it is a matter of taking control or of deciding something, is the more operational hand.

3. It is also in the left hemisphere, at the level of the left anterior cortex, that we find the area controlling principles and value judgments. Thus, the right hand is in direct connection with this hemisphere. Cf. Gazzaniga, M. S. and LeDoux, J. (1978).
4. Scientists who are less productive in the domain of nonverbal language never forget to say that nonverbal language is very complicated and that we can never be certain of having observed it well. That is generally the gist of what they say. Of course, and then? These sermonizers are generally quite clever at explaining what one must not do; they are much less eloquent at describing exactly what one must look for. In face of the wilderness of discovery in this field, it is the questioning of scientific production that we must look at one day. In order to avoid arguments about following rules, we must point out objective criteria for validating observations, and we must especially agree on a body of knowledge that is transferable to all other human sciences. In this perspective, a detector of body activation (D.A.C) capable of deciphering nonverbal language without human intervention should demonstrate that the objective criteria of deciphering and the interpretation of body movements are defined using the same norms that exist in the hard sciences. To philistine researchers who ask how the question of context can be ignored, it must be said that it never is. An individual integrates the context of each one of his actions; they are transformed by the brain that takes them into account systematically. The context is in the right arm that someone raises, for example, which conveys his vigilance. If his right eye is more active at that time, this person shows that he is placing the person he is talking to at a distance. If the head leans to the right, if he stiffens, if his right upper lip is raised . . . etc. In short, one must be aware that the human being is himself the expression of the context that he has integrated.
5. Cf. Tucker, D. M. and Williamson, P. A.
6. Cf. McNeil, D. (1986) op. cit.
7. This type of knowledge (right hemisphere = spontaneity) is integrated into pedagogical strategies (Cf. Vandergift, L., 1995). A student having great difficulty learning seems sometimes surprisingly fast. In fact, if he is fast, it is not because he is spontaneous, but because he botches what he doesn't understand. He flees. Incapable of flexibility, he favors a systematic type of responses—by nature simultaneously right—at the expense of the work of more profound integration, which is characteristic of the left hemisphere.
8. Patrick Vertischel works on diagnostic apraxia, what happens when the two hemispheres no longer communicate with each other and the two hands seem to act in an uncoordinated manner. He writes: "In diagnostic apraxia, everything happens as though the left hemisphere (the right hand) acts in full consciousness, responding to the subject's intentions, while the right hemisphere (the left hand) becomes autonomous, expressing a different individuality. [. . .] We can see here an illustration of good or bad, or even the psychoanalytic unconscious: The left brain benefiting from a double dominance in gesture and language decides and acts in full consciousness. It knows how to define what it will do and report what it has done. On the other hand, the responses of the right brain are more implicit, often automatic, when the context is typical. These actions are sometimes not conscious, not having reached the stage of consciousness." Cf. Vertischel, P. (2005).
9. For further information on this question, see Das, J. P. (1988), op. cit.

Chapter 18

1. In the same way that children write from left to right, they draw their family from left to

right, beginning with the most important references (sometimes they place themselves first) going toward the least important. This is often ultimately the dog or the cat. Projection into the drawing espouses the same logic as that of body movement. We say that this reality is neuro-symbolic.

2. We know that the past and the future have to do with the direction of writing because Aramean people, notably Arabs and Israelis, for whom writing is reversed, also invert the past and future in their unconscious body movements in relation to the West. The direction of their gaze is also reversed. This reality is of a neuro-symbolic order. It is associated in our neurons without our knowing it. It is largely unconscious.
3. Different realities can be located as gestures in the same spatial location, but in reality they are not the same. People will not say, "During our vacation, we went to Paris and Florence" while making gestures in exactly the same spot. Emotions and values intertwine and are located spatially to the right or to the left.
4. Antonio Damasio talks about somatic markers. Cf. Damasio, A., et al. (1991).
5. Research on competitiveness can reverse the process. Individuals who research competition will have a tendency to enter into confrontation, to become extremely focused and attentive, and use neurotransmitter resources more present in the left hemisphere, like dopamine (Cf. Witling, W., 1995). They will take control of the environment with their right hand and will reject the left. This phenomenon ALWAYS disappears in a relaxed situation. This observation was made after watching tens of thousands of videos showing people experiencing various levels of stress, from the lowest to the most elevated.
6. Jacques Chirac, for example, during his last interview as president of the French Republic that he granted to the journalist at France 2, Arlette Chabot, spoke about two of his ministers, Prime Minister Dominique de Villepin and Interior Minister Nicolas Sarkozy. The fact that he granted more trust to de Villepin than to Sarkozy was hardly a secret, but behind a veneer of impartiality, he placed de Villepin to the left and Sarkozy to the right with his body language, revealing to us what he did not say. Beware that stress when the climate seems hostile can overturn this phenomenon (but people do not speak with both hands). In a trusting situation, the phenomenon is ALWAYS visible.
7. Synergology is a young discipline and the use of video footage taken from television for purposes of validation permits us therefore to obtain images without any suspicion that they might have been manipulated.
8. We are talking here about the movement of the gesture and not of the arm which is used.
9. See the theory of self-awareness in the first part of this work
10. This could very well explain why, in a difficult situation, some children have a tendency to freeze in a way, retreating to their inner world and creating a bubble. In the vocabulary of educational theories, these are the children said to be "right hemisphere dominant." These dominances remain in adulthood. Cf. Das, J.P. (1988).
11. The deciphering of gestures made by Aramean or Asiatic people cannot be done with the same facility. An Aramean person will feel an itch on the left side of his face and body when a subject that touches him positively is evoked, but he makes the gesture spatially to the right when he speaks about a popular value. Spatial gestures are a neuro-symbolic representation, that is to say they are managed by our education, while itches are of a logical, cerebral origin. Our brains are constructed in identical ways. Five thousand or 10,000 years of writing have not deeply transformed what was created between 10 and 350 million years ago . . .

Chapter 19

1. Desmond Morris is without a doubt the first to have systematically tracked these cultural

gestures. Unfortunately, and not for nothing, because he documented cultural gestures, it has been assumed that gestures are cultural. In fact, he has made it such that the exception is the rule. Cf. Morris, D., *Bodytalk: The Meaning of Human Gestures*, London; Cape, Jonathan and Caradec, F., *Dictionnaire des gestes,* Fayard, 2005.

2. Cf. Laplane, D. (2005).
3. Cf. Galati, D. and coll. (1997).
4. In psychology, it is possible to say that Carl Rogers elevated the technicality of provoked empathy to the rank of therapeutic techniques. (Cf. Brunel, M., 2004). However, the discovery of mirroring neurons requires us to fully review the approach to empathy in this discipline because it is no longer a mental state to be constructed but a reality de facto, the same as eating or drinking (yes!). A new question is therefore asked: Empathy being a given, is it the therapist who is important or his capacity to show that he feels? Is it still empathy in these conditions? Cf. Rogers, C., *L'approche centrée sur la personne*. Anthology of texts presented by Kirschenbaum, H. and Henderson, V., Land, 2001.
5. Cf. Rizzolati, G., et al., "Premotor Cortex and the Recognition of Motor Actions," *Cognitive Brain Research,* op.cit.
6. These neurons were identified by chance in apes. Their existence was not revealed until later in human beings. We are talking about universality . . .
7. It is an issue between social classes in countries that we call "civilized." The sociology of Pierre Bourdieu and notably the concepts of ethos d'hexis and of habitus take this reality into account. Cf. Bourdieu, P. (1989).
8. Today, the left hand still experiences this discredit in regions of the world where religion governs private life. Muslims, for example, make gestures with both hands while speaking, but as soon as they must perform noble tasks, it is forbidden to use the left hand, the soiled hand. Thus, Allah possesses two right hands (Cf. Chebel, M., 1995). The Catholic religion is less repressive about body language, but the Bible is not much more positive regarding the right hand: "The heart of a wise man is in his right hand and the heart of a fool is in his left hand."—Ecclesiastes, X, II.
9. This fact was responsible, notably, for the repression of sign language (Cf. Itard, I.) and for the inability to create, for a very long time, a nonverbal deaf alphabet worthy of this name. The oral methods that were in vogue in the world (and in a lesser way in the United States) constrained deaf people to learn to speak even though they could not hear what they were saying, rather than learning sign language (gestural method), which would have allowed them to effectively overcome the barrier of silence. This attitude required them to develop between themselves, far from their professors, a natural language using signs. Cf. Moody, B. (1998); Cuxac, C. (1987).
10. Gestural logic is coded in synergology according to precise rules. On a gestural scale from one to ten, Italian is eight and Japanese will never exceed five. In fact, they make the same gestures, but their intensity is different. Each gesture is incorporated in a classification. Example: G_M_C_56_M4_A_F_12. G: we consider that this is a gesture (the hands move outward), four other categories of bodily attitudes are possible; M: the gesture is semi-conscious (which means it is not essential to understand the situation); C: the configuration of the hand that interests us; 56: it is the right hand being considered; M4: the general position of the wrist; A: the direction of the fingers, pointing upward here; F: the fingers (here the hand is closed, eight different positions of the fingers are possible); 12: the thumb and the index finger point away from the hand). If we were interested in the direction of the gesture, we could have, for example, (G_M_D_N_D_ PAGA). G: gesture; M: semiconscious; D: direction of gesture; N: the phrase used while the gesture makes reference to an "engraved" symbol (neuro-symbolic); D: if time that is evoked is

taken into account ("Yesterday it was nice"); PAGA: the gesture is made toward the left while evoking the past. Twelve codes of this type are possible here. Each gestural sequence is thus listed in the video footage database in multiple languages that are compared to each other.

11. We have, for simplicity's sake, avoided addressing the question of ideational ideograms and verbo-motors. In fact, words and gestures are made jointly. If someone says to you "cork screw," it is probable that you imagine your hand turning to uncork a bottle. Our gestural heritage is nourished by numerous ideational ideograms or verbo-motors that are rendered unconsciously and that help us situate ourselves. You can, for example, use the word "barrier" and make the gesture to create a barrier completely unconsciously while speaking. If you say "chalk on the board," it is possible that you hear the chalk screech in your head. If someone gives you a comb, you are not going to ask what it is used for . . . however some patients suffering from ideomotor apraxia use their combs to spread butter on their bread! This apraxia makes it so the gesture corresponding either to the word or to the object is lost. For more information on ideational apraxia, see Le Gall, D., et al. (2000).
12. The exact technical word is "idiosyncratic."
13. See the scale of gestural hypertonicity in Appendix 2 and 3.
14. The Quebecois are, of all the people who were observed, those with whom the percentage of kisses made on the left is the highest. The Quebecois distinguish themselves, on this point, from English Canadians who come from Anglophone provinces.

Conclusion

1. A person is manipulative from the moment that he takes on physical postures that allow him to approach another with ulterior motives in order to lull them into trusting him under false pretensions.
2. Literally means: "three white spots in the eye."
3. People who are very empathetic are, from a nonverbal point of view, quite easy to spot because their heads are permanently inclined when they communicate. There are, without a doubt, psycho-cognitive causes for this, on which we have worked but we will not come back to as this is not the purpose of this book.
4. Empathy is a technique that can produce miracles in psychotherapy, precisely because therapists do not have, with respect to their patients, a need or a particular expectation. They are focused on the other person's healing only and have no messages of their own to pass on. This situation is very different from the traditional exchange of ideas, which is much more interesting when the points of view expressed are different.
5. In the psychological domain, Sigmund Freud had, from the creation of his psychoanalytical theory, identified this phenomenon particularly well. To remedy this difficulty, he had introduced a kind of communication in which he did not look at his patients and left them free to weave their own association of ideas.

Bibliography

ADA, Abraham. *Le dessin d'une personne,* coll. Activités pédagogiques et psychologiques, Delachaux and Niestlé, 1962.

AGGLETON, J. P. *The Amygdala: Neurobiological Aspects of Emotion, Memory and Mental Dysfunction*, New York, Wiley-Liss, 1992.

AIOUAZ, Rabah. "La diachronie gesturelle: étude comparative entre peoples maghérebins et peuples occidentaux," *Annales synergologiques,* Lausanne, 2008.

ALLPORT, Gordon W. *Pattern and Growth in Personality,* New York, Holt, Rinehart and Winston, 1937.

AMARAL, D. G., J. L. Price, A. Pitkanen and S. T. Carmichael. "Anatomical Organization of the Primate Amygdaloid Complex," in AGGLETON, J. P. (dir.). *The Amygdala: Neurobiological Aspects of Emotion, Memory and Mental Dysfunction,* New York, Wiley-Liss, 1992, p. 1–66.

AMIEL-TISON, Claudine and Albert GRENIER, *La surveillance neurologique au cours de la première année de la vie,* Paris, Masson, 1984.

ANDERSON, Steven W. and Daniel Tranel. "Awareness of Disease States Following Cerebral Infarction, Dementia and Head trauma: Standardized Assessment," *The Clinical Neuropsychologist,* vol. 3, no. 4, November 1989, p. 327–339.

ANDREW, D. and A. D. Craig. "Spinotalamic Lamina, Neurons Selectively Sensitive to Histamine: A Central Neural Pathway for Itch," *Nature Neuroscience,* no. 4, 2001, p. 72–77.

ARGYLE, Michael. "Nonverbal Communication in Human Social Interaction," in HINDE, Robert A. *Nonverbal Communication,* Cambridge, Cambridge University Press, 1975, 458 p.

ARGYLE, M., L. Lefevre and M. cook. "The Meaning of Five Patterns of Gaze," *European Journal of Social Psychology,* no. 4, 1974, p. 125–136.

ARGYLE, M., P. Trower and B. Bryant. "Explorations in the Treatment of Personality Disorders and Neuroses by Social Skills Training," *British Journal of Medical Psychology,* vol. 47, no. 1, March 1974, p. 63–72.

ARNOLD, Magda B. *Emotion and Personality,* New York, Columbia University Press, 1960.

BALDWIN, James Mark. *Le développement mental chez l'enfant et dans la race: 1895–1897,* L'Harmattan, 2006, 464 p.

BARRIER, Guy. La communication non verbale: comprendre les gestes, perception et signification, 4e édition, Issy-les-Moulineaux, ESF, 2008, p. 191.

BANDLER, Richard and John Grinider. *Les secrets de la communication,* 3e édition, Les Editions de L'Homme, 2005, 307 p.

BATESON, G. *Vers une écologie de l'esprit,* Tome 1, Paris, Seuil, 1977.

BATESON, G. *Vers une écologie de l'esprit,* Tome 2, Paris, Seuil, 1980.

BATESON, G., D. D. Jackson, J. Haley and J. Weakland. "Toward a Theory of Schizophrenia," *Behaviorial Science,* no. 1, 1956.

BAUDRILLARD, Jean. *La societé de consommation* Paris, Gallimard, 1970.

BAUDRILLARD, Jean. *Le système des objets,* Paris, Gallimard. 1968.

BEKDACHE, K. *L'organisation verbo-viscéro-motrice au cours de la communication verbale selon la structure spatiale ou proxémique, Thèse de psychologie (3e cycle),* Université Lyon-II, 1976.

BEKOFF, M., C. Allen and G. M. Burghardt. *The Cognitive Animal: Empirical and Theoretical Perspectives on Animal Cognition,* Cambridge, The MIT Press, 2002.

BELZUNG, Catherine. *Biologie des Emotions,* Brussels, De Boeck, 2007, 480 p.

BERGERON, S. and L. Mathieu. "Les quadrants des yeux dans la maladie d'Alzheimer," *Synergologie,* vol. 1, 2009.

BERRY, D. S. and L. Z. McArthur. "Perceiving Character in Faces: The Impact of Age-Related Craniofacial Changes on Social Perception," *Psychological Bulletin,* vol. 100, no. 1, July 1986, p. 3–18.

BERTHOZ, S. and G. Kedal. "Les traces cerébrales de la morale," *La recherche,* vol. 30, 2008.

BERTRAND, Pierre-Michel. *Dictionnaire des gauchiers,* Paris, Imago, 2004, 298 p.

BILAND, C., J. Py and S. Rimboud. "Evaluer la sincerité d'un témoin grace à trios techniques d'analyse verbales et non verbales," *European Review of Applied Psychology,* vol. 49, no. 2, 1999, p. 115–122.

BILAND, C. *La psychologie du menteur,* Paris, Odile Jacob, 2004.

BIRDWHISTELL, Ray. *Kinetics and Context: Essays on Body Motion Communication,* Philadelphia, University of Pennsylvania Press 1970, 338 p.

BLAKE, Robert R. and Glenn V. Ramsey. *Perception: An Approach to Personality,* New York, Ronald Press, 1951, 442 p.

BLANCHARD, D. C. and R. J. "Ethoexperimental Approaches to the Biology of Emotion," *Annual Review of Psychology,* vol. 39, January 1988, p. 43–68.

BOE, L. J., L. Menard and S. Maeda. "Adaptation of Control Strategies During the Vocal Tract Growth Inferred from Simulation Studies with an Articulatory Model," *Proceedings of the 5th Seminar on Speech Production: Models and Data,* Munich, 2000, p. 277–280.

Borod, J. "Interhemispheric and Intrahemispheric Control of Emotion: A Focus on Unilateral Brain Damage," *Journal of Consulting and Clinical psychology,* vol. 60, no. 3, 1992, p. 339–348.

Bourassa, Michelle. "Les difficultiés d'apprendissage. Le profil functionnel: les apports de la neuropsychologie à l'adaptation scolaire," *Education et francophonie,* vol. 25, no. 2, automne-hiver 1997.

Bourdieu, Pierre. *La distinction,* Paris, Les Editions de Minuit, 1979.

Bourdieu, Pierre. *La domination masculin,* Paris, Seuil, 1998.

Bourdieu, Pierre. La *réproduction.* Paris. Les Editions de Minuit, 1970.

Bourdieu, Pierre. *The sens pratique,* Paris, Les Editions de Minuit, 1980.

Braten, S. *Intersubjective Communication and Emotion in Early Ontogeny,* Cambridge, Cambridge University Press, 1998.

Bremner, J. D., T. Randall. T. M. Scott, R. A . Bronen, J.-P. Seibyl, S. M. Southwick, R. C. Delaney, G. McCarthy, D. S. Charney and R. B. Innis. "MRI Based Measurement of Hippocampal Volume in Patients with Combat-Related PTSD," *American Journal of Psychiatry,* vol. 152, 1995.

Brunel, Marie-Lise and Cynthia Martiny. "Les conceptions de l'empathieavant, pendant et après Rogers," *Carriérologie*, vol. 9, no. 3–4, 2004, p. 473–500.

Bruner, J. *Car la culture donne forme à l'esprit. De la révolution culturelle à la psychologie cognitive,* Paris, Eshel, 1991.

Bruner, J. *Comment les enfants apprennent à parler?,* Paris, Retz, 1987.

Burghardt, G. M. Bekoff and C. Allen. *The Cognitive Animal: Empirical and Theoretical Perspectives on Animal Cognition,* Cambridge, The MIT Press, 2002.

Buser, Pierre. *Cerveau de soi, cerveau de l'autre.* Paris, Odile Jacob, 1998.

Butler, A. *Learning and teaching style in theory and practice,* Maynard, Gabriel Systems Inc., 1984.

Cacioppo, J. T., R. E. Petty and L. G. Tassinary. "Social psychophysiology: A new look," *Advances in experimental social psychology,* vol. 22, 1991, p. 39–91.

Caine, R. N. and G. *Teaching and the human brain,* Alexandria (E.-U.), ASCD, 1991.

Calbris, G. "Espace-temps: Expression gestuelle du temps," *Semiotica,* vol. 55, nos. 1–2, 1985. p. 43–73.

Calbris, G. *L'expression gestuelle de la pensée d'un homme politique,* preface of J. Cosnier, CNRS, 2003.

Carlson, J. S. *Advances in Cognition and Educational Practice,* vol 1, A. *Theoretical Issues: Intelligence, Cognition, and Assessment,* Greenwich (E.-U.), London, JAI Press, 1992.

Cannon, W. B. *Bodily Changes in Pain, Hunger, Fear and Rage,* 2nd edition, New York, Appleton, 1929.

Caradec, Francois. *Dictionnaire des gestes,* Fayard, 2005, 305 p.

Casanova, G. *Histoire de ma vie,* Paris, Robert Laffont, 1993.

Chartrand, T. L. and J. A. Bargh, *Journal of Personality and Social Psychology*, vol. 76, 1999, p.893

CHEBEL, M. *Dictionnaire des symboles musulmans*, Paris, Albin, Michel, 1995.

CHRISTIE, R. and F. L. Geis. *Studies on Machiavellianism,* New York, Academic Press, 1970.

CHRISTOPHE, A., "L'apprentissage du langage," in Michaud, Y. L'Université de tous les savoirs. *Le cerveau,lelangage, le sens* vol. 5, Paris, Odile Jacob, 2002.

COLE, J. K. *Symposium on Motivation,* Lincoln, University of Nebraska Press, 1971, p. 163–206.

CORMAN, L. *Visages et caractères,* Paris, PUF, 1991.

CORRAZE, J. *Les communications non verbale,* Paris, PUF, 1980.

CORSON, Samuel A. and E. O'Leary Corson. *Ethology and Nonverbal Communication Mental Health,* Oxford, Pergamon Press, 1980 p. 231–258.

COSNIER, J. *La communication non verbale,* Delachaux and Niestlé, 1992.

COURAGE, M. L. and M. L. Howe. "From infant to child: the dynamics of cognitive change in the second year of life," *Psychological Bulletin,* vol. 128, no. 2, 2002, p. 250–277.

CRAIG, A. D. "How Do You Feel?" Interoception: The Sense of Physiological Condition of the Body," *Nature Review Neuroscience,* no. 3, August 2002, p. 655–666.

CRAIG, A. D., K. Chen, D. J. Bandy and E. M. Reiman. "Thermosensory Activation of Insular Cortex," *Nature Neuroscience,* vol. 3, 2000, p. 184–190.

CUXAC, C., "La langue des signes: construction d'un objet scientifique," *Revue du collège des psychoanalystes,* no. 46–47, 1993, p. 97–115.

CYRULNIK, Boris. *Sous le signe du lien,* Paris, Hachette, 1989.

DALAI Lama, *His Holiness the 14th Dalai Lama: Ethics for the New Millenium,* 1999.

DAMASIO, Antonio R. *L'erreur de Descartes: La raison des emotions,* Paris, Odile Jacob, 1995.

DAMASIO, Antonio R. *Le sentiment meme de soi,* Paris, Odile Jacob, 1999.

DAMASIO, Antonio R. *Spinoza avait raison,* Paris, Odile Jacob, 2002.

DAMASIO, Antonio R., Antoine Bechara and Hanna Damasio. "Insensitivity to future consequences following damage to human prefrontal cortex," *Cognition,* vol. 50, 1994, p. 7–12.

DAMASIO, Antonio R. Thomas J. Grabowski, Antoine Bechara, Hanna Damasio, L. Laura, L. B. Ponto, Joseph Parvisi and Richard D. Hichwa. "Subcortical and Cortical Brain Activity During the Feeling of Self-Generated Emotions," *Nature Neuroscience,* 2000, p. 1049–1056.

DAMASIO, A. R., D. Tranel and H. Damasio. "Somatic Markers and the Guidance of Behavior: Theory and Preliminary Testing," in Levin, H. S., H. M. Eisenberg and A. L. Benton, *Frontal Lobe Function and Dysfunction,* New York, Oxford University Press, 1991, p. 217–229.

DAMASIO, A. R., D. Tranel, H. Damasio and A. Bechara. "Failure to Respond Autonomically in Anticipation of Future Outcomes Following Damage to Human Prefrontal Cortex," *Society for Neuroscience,* vol. 19, 1993, p.791.

DAMASIO, A. R. and G. W. Van Hoiesen. "Emotional Disturbances Associated with Focal Lesions of the Limbic Frontal Lobe," in Heilman, K. M. and P. Satz *Neuropsychology of human emotion,* New York, The Guilford Press, 1983, p. 85–110

DAMEROSE, E. and J. Vauclair. "Posture and Laterality in Human and Non Human Primates: Assymetries in Maternal Handling and the Infant's Early Motor Assymetries," in Rogers, L. and

M. Andrew. *Comparative Vertebrate Lateralization*, Cambridge, Cambridge University Press. 2002.

Darwin, Charles. *The Expression of Emotions in Man and Animals,* New York, Philosophical Library, 1872.

Das, J. P. "Simultaneous-Successive Processing and Planning: Implications for School Learning " in Schmeck, R. *Learning Strategies and Learning Styles, Perspectives on Individual Differences,* New York, London, Plenum Press, 1988.

Davidson, Richard J. "Prolegomenon to the Structure of Emotion: Gleanings from Neuropsychology," *Cognition and Emotion,* vol. 6, no. 3–4, 1992, p. 245–268.

Davidson, Richard J., P. Ekman, S. Senulius and W. Friesen. "Emotion Expression and Brain Physiology: Approach/Withdrawal and Cerebral Asymmetry," *Journal of personality and Social psychology,* vol. 58, 1990.

Davidson, Richard J. and K. Hugdahl. *Brain Asymmetry,* Cambridge, The MIT Press, 1995, p. 121–134.

Davidson, Richard J., D. C. Jackson and N. H. Kalin. "Emotion Plasticity Context and Regulation: Perspectives from Affective Neuroscience," *Psychological Bulletin,* vol. 126, no. 6, 2000.

Decety, J. "Simulation and Knowledge of Action," in Dokic, J. and J. Proust. *Advances in Consciousness Research,* Philadelphia Publishers, 2002, p. 53.

Decety, J. and Philip L. Jackson. "Le sens des autres," *The Research Papers,* vol. 30, 2008.

Dimberg, U. "Facial Electromyography and Emotional Reactions," *Psychophysiology,* vol. 27, no.5, September 1990, p. 481–494.

Dimberg U., M. Thunberg and K. Elmehed. "Unconscious Facial Reactions to Emotional Facial Expressions," *Psychological Science,* vol. 11, no. 1, January 2000, p. 86–89.

Dixon, N. F., *Preconscious Processing,* New York, Wiley, 1981.

Dixon, N. F., *Subliminal Perception: The Nature of Controversy,* London, McGraw Hill, 1971.

Dokic, J. and E. Pacherie. "On the Very Idea of a Frame of Reference," in Hickmann, M. and S. Robert. *Space in Languages, Linguistic Systems and Cognitive Categories,* Amsterdam, Benjamins, 2006.

Dolto, F. *La cause des enfants,* Paris, Pocket, 1995.

Dolto, F. *L'image inconsciente du corps*, Paris, Seuil, 1984.

Duchenne, B. *Mécanisme de la physionomie humaine ou analyse electrophysiologique de l'expression, Paris, Baillere, 1862.*

Dunn, R. and K. *Productivity Environmental Preference Survey,* Lawrence Kansas, Price Systems, Inc., 1978.

Dutel, O. "Le mensonge à travers les items signifiants," Archives synergologiques, Montréal, 2006.

Efron, D. *Gesture, Race and Culture,* New York, King's Crown Press, 1941.

Eibl, Eibesfeldt, Irenauss. *L'homme programmé,* Paris, Flammarion, 1976.

Ekman, P. "An Argument for Basic Emotion," *Cognition and emotion,* vol. 6, 1992, p. 169–200.

Ekman, P. *Emotion in the Human Face,* Cambridge, Cambridge University Press, 1982.

EKMAN, P. "Facial Expression of Emotion: New Findings, New Questions," *Psychological Sciences*, vol. 3, 1992, p. 34–38.

EKMAN, P. *Manual for the Facial Action Coding System*, Palo Alto, Consulting Psychologist Press, 1978.

EKMAN, P. "Strong Evidences for Human Emotions," *Psychological Bulletin*, vol. 115, no. 2, 1994.

EKMAN, P. *Telling Lies*, New York, Norton, 1985.

EKMAN, P. and R. J. Davidson. "Voluntary Smiling Changes Regional Brain Activity," *Psychological Science*, vol. 4, no. 5, September 1993, p. 342–345.

EKMAN, P. and W. V. Friesen. "Hand Movements," *Journal of Communication*, vol. 22, p. 353–374.

EKMAN, P., W. V. Friesen and P. Elsworth. *Emotion in the Human Face: Guidelines for Research and a Review of Findings*, New York, Pergamon Press, 1972.

EKMAN, P., R. W. Levenson and W. V. Friesen. "Autonomic Nervous System Activity Distinguishes Among Emotions," *Science*, vol. 221, no. 4616, September 1983, p. 1208–1210.

EKMAN, P., M. O'Sullivan and M. G. Frank. "A Few Can Catch a Liar," *Psychological Science*, vol. 10, no. 3. May 1999, p. 263–266.

EPSTEIN, S. "The Nature of Anxiety with Emphasis Upon its Relationship to Expectancy," in Speilberger, Charles D. *Anxiety: Current Trends In Theory and Research*, New York, Academic Press, 1972.

ERICKSON, M. and E. Rossi. "The Indirect Forms of Suggestions" in Rossi, E. *The Collected Papers of Milton Erickson on Hypnosis*, vol. 1, Newton Irvington, 1980.

ERMIANE, R. and E. Gergerian. *Album of Expressions of the Face*, Paris, Universal Thought, 1978.

ETCOFF, Nancy L., P. Ekman, J. J. Magee and M. G. Frank . "Lie Detection and Language Comprehension," *Nature*, vol. 405, no. 139, May 11, 2000.

EXLINE, R. V. "Visual Interaction: The Glances of Power and Preference," in Cole, J. K. *Nebraska Symposium of Motivation*, Lincoln, University of Nebraska Press, vol. 19, 1971, p. 163–206.

EXLINE, R. V., J. Thibault, C. B. Hickey and P. Guimpert. "Visual Interaction in Relation to Machiavellianism and an Unethical Act," in Christie, R. and F. Geis (dir.), *Studies on Machiavellianism*, New York, Academic Press, 1970.

FEHR, B. and J. A. Russell. "Concept of Emotion Viewed from a Prototype Perspective," *Journal of Experimental Psychology:* General, vol. 113, 1984, p. 464–486.

FEUERSTEIN, Reuven, Ya'cov Rand and Mildred B. Hoffman. *The Dynamic Assessment of Retarded Performers: The Learning Potential Assessment Device: Theory, Instruments, and Techniques*, Baltimore, University Park Press, 1979.

FEYERSEN, Pierre. *Le cerveau et la communication*, Paris, PUF, 1994.

FEYERSEN, Pierre and J. D. de Lanndy, *Psychologie du geste*, Mardaga, 1985, 364 p.

FIELD, T. M., R. Woodson, R. Greenberg and D. Cohen. "Discrimination and Imitation of Facial Expression by Neonates," Science, vol. 218, no. 4568, p. 179–181.

FILLIOZAT, Isabelle. *L'intelligence du coeur*, Alleur, Marabout, 2007, 341 p.

Freedman, Norbert and Irving Steingart. "Kinesic Internalization and Language Constuction," *Psychoanalysis and Contemporary Science*, vol. 4, 1975, p. 355–403.

Freud, Sigmund. "La négation, (1925) in LaPlanche, Jean (dir.). Résultats, idées, problèmes, tome 2 (1921–1938), coll. Bibliothèque de psychanalyse, Paris, PUF, 1985, p. 135–139.

Frey, Siegfried. "Tonic Aspects of Behavior in Interaction" in Kendon, A., R. M. Harris and M. Ritchie. *Organization of Behavior in Face-to-Face Interaction,* Walter de Gruyter, 1975.

Frey, S., U. Jorins and W. Daw. "A Systematic Description and Analysis of Nonverbal Interactions Between Doctors and Patients in a Psychiatric interview," in Corsion, E. and E. Oleary. *Ethology and nonverbal Communication in Mental Health,* New York, Pergamon Press, 1980, p. 231–258.

Fruda, N. H. "The Place of Appraisal in Emotion," *Cognition and Emotion,* Vol. 7, no. 3–4, 1993, p. 357–387.

Gadamer, Hans-Georg, *Verité et méthode. Les grandes lignes d'une herméneutique philosophique,* Paris, Seuil, 1996.

Gainotti, G. "Emotional Behavior and Hemispheric Side of the Lesion," *Cortex*, vol. 8, no. 2, March 1972, p. 41–55.

Galaburdia, A. M. "Anatomic Basis of Cerebral Dominance," in Davidson, Richard J. and Kenneth Hugdahl, *Brain Assymetry,* Cambridge, London, The MIT Press, 1995, p. 51–73.

Galati, D., K. R. Scherrer and P. E. Ricci-Bitti. "Voluntary Facial Expression of Emotion: Comparing Congenitally Blind with Normally Sighted Encoders," *Journal of Personality and Social Psychology,* vol. 73, no. 6, p. 1363–1379.

Gall, Franz Joseph. *Craniologie; ou découvertes nouvelles concernant le cerveau, le crane, et les organes,* Paris, 1807.

Gallup, G. G. fils, J. R. Anderson and D. J. Shillito. "Chimpanzees: Self-Recognition," *Science*, vol. 167, 1970, p. 86–87.

Gallup, G. G. fils, J. R. Anderson and D. J. Shillito. "The Mirror Test," in Bekoff, M., C. Allen and G. M. Burghardt. *The Cognitive Animal: Empirical and Theoretical Perspectives on Animal Cognition,* Cambridge, The MIT Press, 2002, p. 325–333.

Gallup, G. G. fils, J. R. Anderson and D. J. Shillito. "Self Awareness and the Evolution of Social Intelligence," *Behavioral Processes,* vol. 42, 1998, 239–247.

Gardner, H. *Frames of Mind: The Theory of Multiple Intelligences,* New York, Basic Books, 1983.

Gardner, H. *The Mind's New Science: A History of the Cognitive Revolution,* Basic Books, 1987, 448 p.

Gardner, H., H. Brownell, W. Wapner and D. Michelow. "Missing the Point: the Role of the Right Hemisphere in the Processing of Complex Linguistic Materials," in Pericman, E. *Cognitive Processes and the Right Hemisphere,* New York, Academic Press, 1983.

Gazzaniga, M. S. *Le cerveau social,* Paris, Robert Laffont, 1982.

Gazzaniga, M. S. and J. E. Ledoux. The integrated mind, New York, Pienum, 1978.

Gazzaniga, M. S., R. B. Ivry and G. R. Magun, *Neurosciences cognitives la biologie de l'esprit, De Boeck, 2001.*

Gebauer, G. and C. Wulf. *Jeux, rituels, gestes: Les fondements mimétiques de l'action sociale, préface by R. Hess, Anthropos, 2004.*

George, P. A. and G. J. Hole. "The Role of Spatial and Surface Cues in the Age Processing of Unfamiliar Faces," *Visual Cognition,* vol. 7, no. 4, 2000, p. 485–509.

Geschwind, N. and A. M. Galaburdia. "Celebral Lateralization: Biological Mechanisms, Associations, and Pathology. III: A Hypothesis and a Program for Research," *Archives of Neurology,* vol. 42, no. 7, 1985, p. 634–654.

Gibbs, F. "Les positions sur la chaise," *Revue of synergologie,* Paris, 2009.

Goffman, Erving. *Asiles,* Paris, Editions de Minuit, 1968.

Goffman, Erving, *Behavior in Public Places,* The Free Press, 1966.

Goffman, Erving. *La mise en scène de la vie quotidienne, les relaltions en public,* tome 2, Paris, Les Editions de Minuit, 1973.

Goffman, Erving. *The Presentation of Self in Everyday Life,* New York, Anchor Books, 1959.

Goffman, Erving. *Les rites d' interaction,* Paris, Les Editions de Minuit, 1974.

Golay, K. *Learning patterns and temperamental styles,* Newport Beach, Manas-Systems, 1982.

Goleman, Daniel. *L' intelligence émotionelle,* Paris, Robert Laffont, 1997, 481 p.

Golse, Bernard. *L'etre bébé,* Paris, PUF, 2006.

Gordon, R. "Folk Psychology as Stimulation," *Mind and Language,* vol. 1, 1986, p. 158–171.

Gosselin, P. *Qualités expressives et communicatrices des configurations faciales émotionelles, thèse de doctorat,* Québec, University Laval, 1989.

Gould, J. L. *Ethology. The Mechanisms and Evolution of Behavior,* New York, Norton, 1982.

Gregorc, Anthony F. *An Adult's Guide to Style,* Maynard (E.-U.), Gabriel Systems Inc., 1982.

Guasch, Gérard. *Quand le corps parle. Pour une autre psychanalyse,* Vannes, Sully, 2002, 239 p.

Hall, Edward T. *La dimension cachée,* coll. Points Essais, Seuil, 1966.

Hall, Edward T. *The Silent Language,* New York, Double Day, 1959.

Harris, C. "L'embarras, un atout en societé," *Pour la science,* vol. 354, 2007, p. 52–58.

Hauser, M. D., N. Chomsky and W. T. Fritch. "The Faculty of Language: What Is It, Who Has It and How Did It Evolve?," *Science*, vol. 286, p. 2526–2528.

Harwood, H. and Harvey, N. Switzky, "Ability and Modifiability," in Carlson, Jerry S. *Advances in Cognition and Educational Practice,* vol. 1, part A, *Theoretical Issues: Intelligence, Cognition, and Assessment,* Greenwich, JAI Press, 1992.

Heilman, K. M. and P. Satz, *Neuropsychology of Human Emotion,* New York, The Guilford Press, 1983.

Heilman, K., R. T. Watson and D. Bowers. "Affective Disorders Associated with Hemispheric Diseases" in Heilman, K., and P. Satz, *Neuropsychology of Human Emotion,* New York, Guilford Press, 1983.

Hess, E. H. "Attitude and Pupil Size," *Scientific American,* vol. 212, 1965, p. 46–54.

Hickmann, M. and S. Robert. *Space in Languages, Linguistic System and Cognitive Categories,* Amsterdam, Benjamins, 2006.

Hide, R. A. *Non Verbal Communication,* Cambridge, University Press of Cambridge, 1972.

Hirschmann, A. O., *Bonheur privé, action publique,* coll. Pluriel, Hachette Literature, 2006.

Hobson, J. *The Chemistry of Conscious States: How the Brain Changes Its Mind,* Boston, Little Brown, 1994.

Hohmann, G. W. "Some Effects of Spinal Cord Lesions on Experienced Emotional Feelings," *Psychophysiology,* vol. 3, no. 2, p. 143–156.

Honey, P. and A. Mumford. *The Manual of Learning Style,* Maidenhead (R.-U.), Ardingly House, 1986.

Hubel, D. and M. Livingstone. "Segregation of Form Color and Stereopsis in Primate Area 18," *The Journal of Neuroscience,* vol. 7, 1987, p.3378–3415.

Hume, D. *Essais, moraux, politiques, et littéraires et autre essais,* intro. by Gilles Robel, Paris, PUF, 2001.

Iaccino, James. "Left Brain–Right Brain Differences, Inquiries, Evidence, and New Approaches," *Hillsdale,* Lawrence Eribaum Associates Publishers, 1993.

Itard, J. M. G. *Traité des maladies de l'oreille et de l'audition,* 2 tomes, Paris, Méquignon Marris, 1821.

Iverson, J. M. and E. Thelen. "Why People Gesture when They Speak?" *Nature*, vol. 396, p.228.

Jackson, D. D. *The Etiology of Schizophrenia,* New York, Basic Books, 1960.

James, W. "What Is an Emotion?," Mind, vol. 9, 1884, p. 188–205.

Jeannerod, M. "The Representing Brain: Neuron Correlates of Motor Intention and Imagery," Behavioral Brain Sciences, vol. 17, 1994, p. 187–245

Johnson, S. C., L. C. Baxter, L. S. Wilder, J. G. Pipe, J. E. Heiserman and G. P. Prigatano, "Neural Correlates of Self-Reflection," *Brain*, vol. 125, 2002, p. 1808–1814.

Jones, S. S. "Imitation or Exploration? Young Infants Matching of Adults Oral Gesture," *Child Development*, vol. 67, no. 5, 1996, p.1952–1969.

Joseph, R. *The Right Brain and the Unconscious, Discovering the Stranger Within,* New York, London, Plenum Press, 1992.

Jurgens, U. "Neural Pathways Underlying Vocal Control," *Neuroscience and Biobehavioral Review,* vol. 26, no. 2, 2002, p. 235–258.

Kahle, W., H. Leonhardt and W. Platzer, *Anatomie 3. Système nerveux* Flammarion, 1998.

Kant, E. Critique de la raison pure, Paris, Gallimard, 1980.

Keenan, J. P., S. Freund, R. H. Hamilton, G. Ganis and A. Paschal-Leone. "Hand response differences in a self-face identification task," *Neuropsychologia,* vol. 38, n. 7, 2000, p.1047–1053.

Keenan, J. P., B. McCutcheon, S. Freund, G. G. Gallup fils, G. Sanders and A. Pascual-Leone. "Left Hand Advantage in a Self-Face Recognition Task, *Neuropsychologia,* vol. 37, 1999, p. 1421–1425.

Keenan, J. P., A. Nelson, M. O'Connor and A. Pascal-Leone. "Self-Recognition and the Right Hemisphere," *Nature*, vol. 409, 2001, p. 305.

Keenan, J. P., M. A. Wheeler, S. M. Platek, G. Lardi and M. Lassonde. "Self-Face Processing in a Callosotomy Patient," *European Journal of Neuroscience,* vol. 18, 2003, p. 2391–2395.

Kendon, A. "Some Functions of Gaze Direction in Social Interactions," *Acta Psychological,* vol. 26, 1967.

KIMURA, D. "The Neural Basis of Gesture," in Whitaker, H. and Harry A. *Studies in Neurolinguistics,* vol. 2, Academic Press, 1976, p. 145–156.

KIMURA, D. and C. A. Humphrys. "A Comparison of Left and Right Arm Movement During Speaking," *Neuropsychologia,* vol. 19, 1981, p. 807–812.

KIRCHER, T. T. J., C. Senior, M. L. Phillips, P. J. Benson, E. T. Bullmore, M. Brammer, A. Simmons, S. C. R. Williams, M. Bartels and A. S. David. "Towards a Functional Neuroanatomy of Self Processing: Effects of Faces and Words," *Cognitive Brain Research,* vol. 10, 2000, p. 133–144.

KIROUAC, Gilles and F. Y. Doré. "Judgment of Facial Expressions of Emotion as Function of Exposure Time," *Perceptual and Motor Skills,* vol. 59, no. 1, p. 683–686.

KLEIN, G. S. "The Personal World Through Perception" in BLAKE, R. R. and G. V. Ramsey. *Perception, An Approach to Personality,* New York, Ronald Press, 1951, p. 328–355.

KOLB, D. A. *Experiential Learning: Experience as the Source of Learning in and Development,* Englewood Cliffs, Prentice-Hall, 1984.

KOLB, D. A., *Learning Style Inventory,* Boston, McBer and Company, 1976.

KOSKI, L., M. Iacoboni, M. C. Dubeau, R. P. Woods and J. C. Mazziota. "Modulation of Cortical Activity During Different Imitative Behaviors," *Journal of Neurophysiology,* vol. 89, no. 1, p. 460–471.

KOSSLYN, S. M. and O. Koenig. *Wet Mind: The New Cognitive Neuroscience,* New York, McMillan, 1992.

LABAR, K. S., J. E. Leddux, D. D. Spencer and E. A. Phelps. "Impaired Fear Conditioning Following Unilateral Temporal Lobectomy in Humans," *Journal of Neurosciences,* vol. 15, no. 10, 1995.

LABORIT, H., *L'aggressivité détournée,* U.G.E. 10/18, 1970.

LABORIT, H. *L'éloge de la fuite,* Paris, Robert Laffont, 1976.

LABORIT, H. *La légende des comportements,* Paris, Flammarion, 1994.

LABORIT, H. *La nouvelle grille,* Paris, Robert Laffont, 1974.

LACHANCE, Sylvie. "Du singe à l'homme, les synchronies gestuelles," Revue de synergologie, no. 1, Paris, 2009.

LA GARANDERIE (DE), A. *Pour une pédagogie de l'intelligence,* Paris, Le Centurion, 1990.

LAING, R. D. and D. G. Cooper. *The Divided Self: An Existential Study in Sanity and Madness,* London, Tavistock, 1960.

LAKOFF, G. and M. Johnson, *Les métaphores dans la vie quotidienne,* trad. De l'américan by Michel de Fornal, Paris, Les Editions de Minuit, 1980.

LANE, H. "Histoire chronologique de la repression de la langue des signes en France et aux Etats-Unis," *Langage*, vol. 56, 1979.

LANG, W., L. Petit, P. Hollinger, Peitrzyk, N. Tzourio, B. Mazoyer and A. Berthoz. "A Positron Emission Tomography Study of Oculomoteur Imagery," *Neuro Report*, no. 5, p. 921–924.

LANIUS, Ruth, Pour la science, no. 317, March 2004, p. 11

LAPLANE, Dominique, *La pensée d'outre-mots,* Editions Les Empecheurs de penser en rond, 2000.

LAUTREY, J. and H. Rodriquez-Tomé. "Etudes interculturelles de la notion de conservation" in Reuchlin, M. *Cultures et conduites,* Paris, PUF, 1976.

LAZARU S, R. and S. Folkman. "Coping and Adaption," in Gentry, W. D. *Handbook of Behavioral Medicine,* New York, Guilford, 1984, p. 282–325.

LEBRUN, Y. "Apraxie de la parole et apraxie bucco-faciale," in LeGall, D. and G. Aubin. *L'Apraxie,* Marseille, Solal, 1994.

LECOURS, A. R. and F. Hermite. *L'Aphasie,* Paris, Flammarion Médicine-Sciences, 1979.

LEDOUX, J. E. Le cerveau des émotions. *Les mystérieux fondements de notre vie Emotionelle,* préface de J. D. Vincent, Paris Odile Jacob, 2005.

LEDOUX, J. E. "Emotion, Memory and the Brain" in *Scientific American,* numéro special, New York, vol. 7, no. 1. 1997, p. 68–75.

LEDOUX, J. E. *The Emotional Brain: The Mysterious Underpinnings of Emotional Life,* New York, Simon and Schuster, 1996.

LEDOUX, J. E. "Emotional Memory Systems in the Brain," *Behavioral and Brain Research,* vol. 58, no. 1–2, 1993.

LE Gall, Didier and Ghislaine Aubin. *L'Apraxie.* 2nd edition, coll. Neuropsychologie, Marseille, Solal, 2004.

LE GALL, D. T. Morineau, Etcharry and Bouyx. "Les apraxies: forms techniques et méthode d'évaluation" in Leroi-Gourhan, André. *Le geste et la parole,* tome 1, Paris, Albin Michel, 1964, 326 p.

LEVINSON, C. S. *Space in Language and Cognition. Explorations in Cognitive Diversity.* Cambridge, Cambridge University Press, 2003.

LIBET, B. "Mind time: The Temporal Factor in Consciousness," *Perspectivesin Cognitive Neuroscience,* Cambridge, Harvard University Press, 2004.

LICHTENBERG, Georg, Christophe. *Le couteau sans lame et autres textes satiriques,*Corti, 1999.

LINDEN, M., X. Seron and A. C. Juillerat. *Traité de neuropsychologie clinique,* tome 1, Marseille, Solal, 2000.

LOWENFELD, V. "Tests for Visual and Haptical Aptitudes," *The American Journal of Psychology,* vol. 58, no. 1, 1945, p. 100–111.

MARTINEAU, C. "Les gestes de préhension," *Archives synergologiques,* Montréal, 2006.

MATE, Gabor. *L'esprit dispersé: comprendre et traiter les problèmes de la concentration,* Montréal, Les Editions de l'Homme, 2001, 386 p.

MCCARTHY, B. "A Tale of Four Learners: 4MAT's Learning Styles," *Educational Leadership,* vol. 54, no. 6, 1997, p. 46–51.

MCEWEN, B. S. et al. "Paradoxical Effects of Adrenal Steroids on the Brain: Protection versus Degeneration," *Biological Psychiatry,* vol. 31, no. 2, January 1992, p. 177–199.

MCGAUGH, J. L., I. B. Introini-Collision, L. F. Cahill, C. Castelano, C. Dalmaz, M. B. Parent and C. L. Williams. "Neuromodulatory Systems and Memory Storage: Role of the Amygdala," *Behavioral Brain Research,* vol. 58, no. 1–2, December 20, 1993, p. 81–90.

MCGUIGAN, F. J., *The Psychophysiology of Thinking,* London, Academic Press, 1973.

McNeill, D. *Hand and Mind: What Gestures Reveal About Thought,* Chicago, University of Chicago Press, 1996, 423 p.

McNeill, D. "So You Think Gestures Are Nonverbal?" *Psychological Review*, vol. 92, no. 3, 1985, p. 350–371.

Meggle, Dominique. *Erickson, hypnose et psychothérapie.* 2nd edition, Paris, Retz, 2000.

Mehrabian, Albert. *Nonverbal Communication*, New York, Walter de Gruyter Inc., 1972.

Meltzoff, A. N. and R. W. Borton. "Intermodal Matching by Human Neonates," *Nature*, vol. 282, no. 5737, November 22, 1979, p. 403–404.

Meltzoff, A. N. and M. K. Moore "Explaining Facial Imitation: A Theoretical Model," *Early Development and Parenting,* vol. 6, 1997, p. 179–192.

Meltzoff, A. N. and M. K. Moore. "Infant Intersubjectivity: Broadening the Dialogue to Include Imitation, Identity and Intention," in Braten, Stein. *Intersubjective Communication and Emotion in Early Ontogeny.* Cambridge, Cambridge University Press, 2006, 471 p.

Meltzoff, A. N. and M. K. Moore. "Imitation of Facial and Manual Gestures by Human Neonates," Science, vol. 198, no. 4312, 1977, p. 75–78.

Michaud, Y. (dir.) *Le cerveau, le langage, le sens,* coll. L'université de tous les saviors, vol. 5, Paris, Odile Jacob, 2002, 362 p.

Mineka, S. M. Davidson, M. Cook and R. Keir. "Observational Conditioning of Snake Fear in Rhesus Monkeys," *Journal of Abnormal Psychology,* vol. 93, no. 4, 1984, p. 355–372.

Montaginer, Hubert. *L'enfant et la communication: comment les gestes, des attitudes, des vocalisations deviennent des messages,* Paris, Stock, 1978.

Montaginer, H., J. C. Henry, M. Lombardi. "Etudes étho-psychologiques de groupes d'enfants de 14 mois à 5 ans à la crèche et à l'école maternelle," *Psychologie médicale,* 9, 11, 1977.

Montessori, M. *L'enfant,* Desclée de Brouwer, 1963.

Montoya, P. and R. Schandry. "Emotional Experience and Heartbeat Perception in Patients with Spinal Cord Injury and Control Subjects," *Journal of Psychophysiology,* vol. 8, 1994, p. 289–296.

Moody, Bill et al. *La langue des signes,* édition revue et augmentée, Vincennes, Editions IVT, 1997–1998.

Morin, G. *Les rèves et le langage du corps,* Devry, 1989.

Morow, L., P. B. Vrtunski, Y. Kim and F. Boller. "Arousal Responses to Emotional Stimuli and Laterality of Lesion," *Neuropsychologia,* vol. 19, no. 1, 1981, p. 65–71.

Morris, D. *Bodytalk: A World Guide to Gestures,* London, Jonathan Cape, 1994, 231 p.

Morris, D. *The Naked Ape,* Delta, 1999, 256 p.

Myers, Briggs, I. Myers and C. Briggs. *Myers-Briggs Type Indicator,* Palo Alto, California, Consulting Psychologist Press, Inc. 1943–1976.

Nallet, Lionel et al. "Stimulation or Subterritories of the Subthalamic Nucleus Revealed that It Integrates the Emotional and Motor Aspect of Behavior in PNS of the USA," *Cerveau et psycho, Pour la science,* no. 22, 2007.

Nasio, J.-D., *Mon corps et ses images,* Paris, Payot, 2007, 263 p.

NAVILLE, Ferdinand. "Mémoire d'un médecin aphasique. Auto-observation et contes psychologiques sur le D'Saloz père, de Genève, atteint d'aphasie totale suivie de guérison," *Archives de psychologie*, no. 17, 1918, p. 1–57.

NISBETT, R. E. and T. D. Wilson. "Telling More Than We Can Know: Verbal Report on Mental Processes," *Psychological Review*, vol. 84, no. 3, May 1977, p. 231–259.

NISHITANI, N. and R. Hari. "Temporal Dynamics of Cortical Representation for Action," *Proceedings of the National Academy of Sciences*, vol. 97, no. 12, January 18, 2000, p. 913–918.

NOBLE, W. and L. Davidson, *Human Evolution, Language and Mind,* Cambridge, Cambridge University Press, 1996, 284 p.

OHMAN, A. "Fear and Anxiety as Emotional Phenomena: Clinical Phenomenology, Evolutionary Perspectives, and Information-Processing Mechanisms," in Lewis, M. and J. M. Haviland (dir.) *Handbook of Emotions,* New York, Guilford, 1993, p. 1–30.

ORNSTEIN, R. *The Roots of Self: Unraveling the Mystery of Who We Are,* San Francisco, Octagon Press, 1995.

O'SULLIVAN, M. "Measuring the Ability to Recognize Facial Expressions of Emotion" in Ekman, P. *Emotion in the Human face,* Cambridge, Cambridge University Press, 1982.

PAGET, J. H. *Le pouvoir de l'illusion,* Plon, 2005.

PASK, G. "Styles and Strategies of Learning," *British Journal of Educational Psychology,* vol. 46, 1976, p. 128–148.

PASK, G. "Learning Strategies, Teaching Strategies, and Conceptual or Learning Style," in Schmeck, Ronald R. (dir.). *Learning Strategies and Learning Styles,* New York, Plenum Press, 1988, p. 83–89.

PENFIELD, W. and Rasmussen, *The Cerebral Cortex of Man,* New York, The MacMillan Company, 1950, 248 p.

PERETZ, I. and J. Morans. "Music and Modularity," *Contemporary Music Review,* vol. 4, 1993, p. 279–293.

PERICMAN, E. *The Cognitive Processes and the Right Hemisphere,* New York, Academic Press, 1983.

PETERS, G. "Left-Handedness and Cerebral Dominance" in Davidson, Richard J. and K. Hugdahl, *Brain Asymmetry,* Cambridge, The MIT Press, 1995, p. 121–134.

PICO, P. "L'humain à l'aube de l'humanité" in Pico, P. M. Serres and J.-D. Vincent. *Qu'est-ce que l'humain?*, Paris, Le Pommier, 2003.

PLATEK, S. M., S. R. Critton, T. E. Myers and G. G. Gallup fils. "Contagious Yawning: The Role of Self-Awareness and Mental State Attribution," *Cognitive Brain Research,* vol. 17, 2003, p. 223–227.

PLATEK, S. M., S. R. Critton, T. E. Myers and G. G. Gallup fils. "A Left-Hand Advantage for Self-Description: The Impact of Schizotypal Personality Traits," *Schizophrenia Research,* vol. 65, no. 2–3, December 15, 2003, p. 147–151.

PLATEK, S. M., J. W. Thompson and G. G. Gallup fils. "Cross-Modal Self-Recognition: The Role of Visual, Auditory, and Olfactory Primes," *Consciousness and Cognition,* vol. 13, no. 1, March 2004, p. 197–210.

Popper, Karl R. *La logique de la découverte scientifique,* Paris, Payot, 1978.

Povinelli, D. J., K. R. Landau and H. K. Perilloux. "Self-Recognition in Young Children Using Delayed Versus Live Feedback: Evidence of a Developmental Asynchrony," *Child Development,* vol. 67, no. 4, August 1996, p. 1540–1554.

Premack, D. G. and G. Woodruff. "Chimpanzee Problem-Solving: A Test for Comprehension," Science, vol. 202, no. 4367, November 3, 1978, p. 532–535

Prinz, W. and B. Hommel. *Common Mechanisms in Perception and Action,* Oxford University Press, 2002, p. 62–119.

Rainville, P., G. H. Ducan, D. D. Price, B. Carrier and M. C. Bushnelle. "Pain Affect Encoded in Human Anterior Cingulate but Not Somatosensory Cortex," *Science*, vol. 227, no. 5328, 1997, p. 968–971.

Ralph, Adolphs. "Neural Mechanisms for Recognizing Emotion," *Current Opinion in Neurobiology,* vol. 12, 2002, p. 169–178.

Ralph, Adolphs. "Social Cognition and the Human Brain" *Trends in Cognitive Sciences,* vol. 3, no. 12, 1999, p. 469–479.

Ramachandrian, V. S. and R. D. "Synaesthesia in Phantom Limbs and Induced with Mirrors," *Proceedings of the Royal Society of London,* vol. 263, 1996, p. 377–386.

Raymond, J. "It Feels Good and Everybody Does It. Scientists are Using State-of-the-Art Technology to Look at What Happens in the Brain when a Person Scratches an Itch. There's More Going on than You Might Think," *Newsweek*, January 31, 2008.

Ressland, Nadja. "The Cradling Bias in Relation to Pitch of Maternal Child-Directed Language," *British Journal of Developmental Psychology,* vol. 18, no. 2, 2000, p. 179–186.

Reuchlin, M. *Cultures et Conduites,* coll. Psychologie d'aujourd'hui, Paris, PUF, 1976.

Rinn, W. "The Neuropsychology of Facial Expressions: A Review of the Neurological and Psychological Mechanisms for Producing Facial Expressions," *Psychological Bulletin,* vol. 95, no. 1, p. 52–77.

Rizzolatti, Giacomo et al. "Premotor Cortex and the Recognition of Motor Actions," *Cognitive brain research,* vol. 3, no. 2, 1996, p. 131–141.

Rizzolatti, Giacomo, L. Fadiga, L. Fogassi and Vittorio Gallese. "Resonance Behaviors and Mirror Neurons," *Archives italiennes de biologie,* vol. 137, no. 2, 1999, p. 85–100.

Rizzolatti, Giacomo, Leonardo Fogassi and Vittorio Gallese. "Neurophysiological Mechanisms Underlying the Understanding and Imitation of Action," *Nature Reviews Neuroscience,* vol. 2, 2001, p.661–670.

Rizzolatti, Giacomo and C. Sinigaglia, Les neurons miroirs, Paris, Odile Jacob, 2008.

Robert, J. *Parlez-leur d'amour et de sexualité,* Montréal, Les Editions de L'Homme, 1999.

Robert, J. *Le sexe en mal d'amour, de la révolution sexuelle à la régression érotique,* Montréal, Les Editions de L'Homme, 2005.

Robert, J. *Te laisse pas faire. La sexualité expliquée aux enfants,* Montréal, Les Editions de L'Homme, 2000.

Robert-ouvray, S. *Integration motrice et développement psychique, une théorie de la psychmotricité,* 2e edition, Paris, Desclée de Brouwer, 1997.

Rochat, P. *Le monde des bébés,* Paris. Odile Jacob, 2006.

Rochat, P. "Self-Perception and Action in Infancy," *Experimental Brain Research,* vol. 123, no. 1–2, 1998, p. 102–109.

Rochat, P. and S. J. Hespos. "Tracking and Anticipation of Invisible Spatial Transformation by Four to Eight-Month Old Infants," *Cognitive Development,* vol. 11, no. 1, 1996, p. 3–17.

Rogers, C. *L'approche centrée sur la personne,* anthologie de texts présentée par Howard Kirschenbaum and Valerie Land Henderson, Lausanne, Randin, 2001.

Rogers, C. *Le développement de la personne,* Paris, Dunod, 1968.

Rogers, L. J. and M. Andrew. *Comparative Vertebrate Lateralization,* Cambridge, Cambridge University Press, 2002.

Rolls, E. T. *The Brain and Emotion,* Oxford University Press, 1999.

Rorty, A. O. "Explaining Emotions" in Rorty, A. O. *Explaining Emotions,* Berkeley, University of California Press, 1980.

Rosenfeld, Joelle "Emotion ressentie, émotion transmisse" in Lebovici, Serge and Philippe Mazet, *Emotions et affects chez le bébé et ses partenaires,*Paris, Eshel, 1992.

Rosenfeld, Israel. *The Strange, Familiar, and Forgotten: An Anatomy of Consciousness,* New York, Knopf, 1992.

Rosenfeld, R. and L. Jacobson, *Pygmalion à l'école,* Paris, Casterman, 1971.

Rosenthal, R. "The PONS Test: Measuring Sensitivity to Non Verbal Cues," in MacReynols, P. *Advances in Psychological Assessment,* San Francisco, Jossey-Bass, 1977.

Rossetti, Y. and L. T. PISELLA "Several 'Vision for Action' Systems: A Guide to Dissociating and Integrating Dorsal and Ventral Function," in Prinz, W. and B. Hommel. *Common Mechanisms in Perception and Action,* Oxford University Press, 2002, p. 62–119.

Rossi, E. *The Collected Papers of Milton Erickson on Hypnosis I,* Newton Irvington, 1980.

Rossi, E. *The Psychobiology of Mind-Body Healing. New Concepts in Therapeutic Hypnosis,* New York and London, W. W. Norton and Company Inc., 1993.

Ruesch, J. and W. Kress. *Non Verbal Communication: Notes on the Visual Perception of Human Relations,* Berkeley, University of California Press, 1956.

Russell, J. A. "Is There Universal Recognition of Emotion from Facial Expression? A Review of the Cross-Cultural Studies." *Psychological Bulletin,* vol. 115, 1994, p. 102–141.

Rutter, D. R. and G. M. Stephenson "Visual Interaction in a Group of Schizophrenic and Depressive Patients," *British Journal of Clinical Psychology,* vol. 11, p. 57–65.

Scherer, K. R. "Neuroscience Projections to Current Debates, in Emotion Psychology," *Cognition and Emotion,* vol. 7, no. 1, 1993, p. 1–41.

Scherer, K. R. "Studying the Emotion-Antecedent Appraisal Process: An Expert System Approach," *Cognition and Emotion,* vol. 7, 1993, p. 325–355.

Scherer, K. R. and H. G. Walbott. "Evidence for Universality and Cultural Variation of Differential Emotion Response Patterning," *Journal of Personality and Social Psychology,* vol. 66, no. 2, 1994, p. 310–328.

Schmeck, R. R. *Learning Strategies and Learning Styles, Perspectives on Individual Differences,* New York and London, Plenum Press, 1988.

SCHUTZENBERGER-ANCELIN, A. *Aie mes aieux, liens transgénérationnels, transmission des traumatismes et pratique du génosociogramme,* Paris, Desclée de Brouwer, 1993.

SCHUTZENBERGER-ANCELIN, A. *Ces enfants malades de leur parents,* Payot, 2003.

SCHWARTZ, C. E. et al. Inhibited and Uninhibited Infants 'Grow Up': Adult Amygdalar Response to Novelty," *Science*, vol. 300, 2003.

SHAPIRO, J. "Multi-Bacteria as Cellular Organism," *Scientific American,* vol. 256, No. 6, June 1988, p. 84–89.

SIERATZKI, J.-S. and B. B. Woll. "Why Do mothers Cradle Babies on the Left?," *The Lancet,* vol. 347, 1996, p. 1746–1748.

SINGER, T., B. Seymour, J. O'Doherty, H. Kaube, R. J. Dolan and C. D. Frith, "Empathy for Pain Involves the Affective but Not the Sensory Components of Pain," *Science*, vol. 303, p. 1157–1162.

SKINNER, Mullen. "Facial Assymetry in Emotional Expression a Meta-Analysis Research," *British Journal of Psychology,* vol. 30, 1991, p. 113–124.

SOUZENELLE (DE), Annick. *La Symbolique du corps humain,* Paris, Albin Michel, 1991.

SPERRY, R. W. "Lateral Specialization of Cerebral Function in Surgically Separated Hemispheres," in McGurgan, F. J. and R. A. Schoonover. *The Psychophysiology of Thinking,* New York, Academic Press, 1973.

SPERRY, R. W., M. S. Gazzanigga and J. E. Bogen. "Interhemispheric Relationships. The Neocortical Commissures: Syndromes of Their Disconnection," in Winken, P. J. and G. W. Bruyn, *Handbook of Clinical Neurology,* vol. 4, Amsterdam, North Holland Publishing Company, 1969.

SPERRY, R. W., E. Zaidel and D. Zaidel. "Self-Recognition and Social Awareness in the Disconnected Minor Hemisphere," *Neuropsychologia,* vol. 17, 1993, p. 153–166.

STERN, D. *Le monde interpersonal du nourrisson, une perspective* psychoanalytique *et développementale, Paris, PUF, 1989.*

STERNBERG, R. J. *The Triarchic Mind. A New Theory of Human Intelligence,* New York, Viking Penguin, 1989.

STEVENS, J. A. et al. *Neuro report,* vol. 11, 2000, p. 109–115.

SUAREZ, S. D. and G. G. Gallup fils. "Self-Recognition in Chimpanzees and Orangutans, but Not Gorillas," *Journal of Human Evolution,* vol. 10, 1981, p. 109–115.

SULGER, F. *Les gestes-vérité,* Sand, 1991.

TARDE, Gabriel. *Les lois de l'imitation,* 1890 pour la 1re édition, Paris, Editions Les Empecheurs de penser en rond, 2001.

TARDIF, Jacques. *Pour un enseignement stratégique, L'apport de la psychologie cognitive,* coll Théories et pratiques en enseignement, Montréal, Logiques, 1992.

TEMPLE, C. *The Brain: An Introduction to the Psychology of the Human Brain and Behavior,* London, Penguin Books, 1993.

THELEN, E. and L. B. Smith, *A Dynamic Systems Approach to the Development of Cognition and Action,* Cambridge, The MIT Press, 1996.

TISSERON, S. *Nos secrets de famille. Histoire et mode d'emploi,* Paris, Ramsay, 1999.

Tokmura, H., Y. Tokmura, A. Oliverio, T. Asakura and J. C. Rothwell. "Speech-Induced Changes in Corticospinal Excitability," *Annual of Neurology,* no. 40, 1996, p. 628–634.

Tomatis, Alfred. *L'oreille et le langage,* nouvelle edition, Paris, Seuil, 1991.

Tomatis, Alfred. *L'oreille et la vie,* Paris, Robert Laffont, 1977.

Tomkins, S. S. and C. E. Izard. *Affect, Cognition and Personality,* Tavistock, 1966.

Torrance, E. P. and Z. L. Rockenstein. "Styles of Thinking and Creativity," Schmeck, Ronald. *Learning Strategies and Learning Styles,* New York and London, Plenum Press, 1988.

Trocme-Fabre, H. *J'apprends donc je suis,* 2e édition, Paris, Les Editions d'Organisation, 1994.

Tucker, D. M. and P. A. Williamson "Asymmetric Neural Control Systems in Human Self-Regulation," *Psychological Review,* vol. 91, 1991, p. 185–215.

Turchet, Philippe. "Clignements de paupières et détente émotionelle, *Archives synergologiques,* Montreal, 2006.

Turchet, Philippe. *Les codes inconscients de la séduction,* Montréal, Les Editions de l'Homme, 2004.

Turchet, Philippe. *La synergologie. Pour comprendre son interlocuteur à travers sa gestuelle,* Montréal, Les Editions de l"Homme, 2000.

Turchet, Philippe. "Qu'est-ce que la synergologie?," Revue de synergologie, no. 1, Paris, 2009.

Turchet, Philippe. *Pourquoi les hommes marchent-ils à la gauche des femmes?Le syndrome d'amour,* Montréal, Les Editions de l'Homme, 2002.

Vandergift, Laurens. "Language Learning Strategy Research: Development of Definitions and Theory," *Journal of CAAL (Association canadienne de Linguistique Appliquée), vol. 17, no. 2, 1995, p. 87–104.*

Varela, F. J. *Invitation aux sciences cognitives,* trad. de Pierre Lavoie, Paris, Seuil, 1989.

Varela, F. J. *L'inscription corporelle de l'esprit. Sciences cognitives et expérience humaine,* en collaboration avec Thompson, E. and E. Rosch, coll. La couleur des idées, Paris, Seuil, 1993.

Varela, Jacques. *L'homme et le singe, Psychologie comparée, Paris,* Flammarion, 1998.

Vauclair, Jacques. "L'intelligence de l'animal" in Michaud, Y. *L'Université de tous les saviors. Le cerveau, le langage, le sens,* vol. 5, Paris Odile Jacob, 2002.

Vauclair, Jacques. "Porter son bébé à gauche?," *Cerveau et Psycho,* no. 4, 2004.

Vauclair, Jacques. *Psychologie compare de l'homme et du primate non humain: cognition, langage et dévéloppement, questions approfondies et dévéloppement, apprentissage et cognition,* école doctorale "Norme, cognition et culture," conference internationale invitée, Université catholique de Louvain, Louvain-la-Neuve, Belgique, June 2006.

Veer (de), M. W., G. G. Gallup fils, L. A. Theall, R. van den Bos and D. J. Pownell. "An 8-Year Longitudinal Study of Mirror Self-Recognition in Chimpanzees (Pan troglodytes)," *Neuropsychologia,* vol. 4, no. 2, 2003, 229–234.

Vertischel, Patrick. "La main du diable," *Cerveau et psycho,* vol. 6, p. 68–72.

Vincent, Jean-Didier. *Biologie des passions,* Paris, Odile Jacob, 1986.

Vincent, Jean-Didier. *Le voyage extraordinaire au centre du cerveau,*Paris, Odile Jacob, 2007.

Vygotski, L. *Pensée et langage,* Paris, Editions sociales, 1992.

WALLON, Henri. *Les origins du caractère chez l'enfant,* Paris, PUF, 1934.

WARNEKEN, F. and M. Tomasello. "Altruistic Helping in Human Infants and Young Chimpanzees," *Science*, vol. 311, no. 5765, March 3, 2006, p. 1301–1303.

WATZLAWICK, P. and J. H. Beavin. *Pragmatics of Human Communication,* New York, W. W. Norton and Company, 1967.

WATZLAWICK, P., J. H. Beavin and D. D. Jackson. *La logique de la Communication*, Paris, Seuil, 1979.

WEAKLAND, J. H. "The Double-Bind Hypothesis of Schizophrenia, and Three-Party Interaction" in Jackson, Donald D. *The Etiology of Schizophrenia*, New York, Basic Books, 1960, 456 p.

WEISZ, D. J., D. G. Harden and Z. Xiang. "Effects of Amygdala Lesions on Reflex Facilitation and Conditioned Response Acquisition During Nictitating Membrane Response Conditioning in Rabbit," *Behavioral Neuroscience*, vol. 106, no. 2, April 1992, p. 262–273.

WILLIAMS, Terrence J., Michelle E. Pepitone, Scott E. Christensen, Bradley M. Cooke, Andrew D. Huberman, Nicholas J. and Tessa J. Breedlove, Cynthia L. Jordan and S. Marc Breedlove. "Finger-Length Ratios and Sexual Orientation." *Nature,* vol. 404, March 30, 2000, p. 455–456.

WINKIN, Yves. *La nouvelle communication,* Paris, Seuil, 1981.

WINNICOT, Donald W. "L'integration du moi chez l'enfant," in *Processus de maturation chez l'enfant*, Paris, Payot, 1970.

WITKIN, H. A., C. A. Moore, D. R. Goodenough and P. W. Cox. "Field-Dependent and Field-Independent Cognitive Styles and Their Educational Implications," *Review of Educational Research,* vol. 47, no. 1, winter 1977, p. 1–64.

WITLING, Werner. "Brain Asymmetry in the Control of Autonomic-Physiologic Activity" in Davidson, Richard J. and Kenneth Hugdahl, *Brain Asymmetry,* Cambridge and London, The MIT Press, 1996, p. 305–357.

ZAJONC, R. B. "Feeling and Thinking: Preferences Need No Inferences," *American Psychologist,* vol. 35, 1980, p. 151–175.

ZAJONC, R. B."On the Primacy of Affect," *American Psychologist,* vol. 39, no. 2, February 1984, p. 117–123.

ZAZZO, René. *Reflets de miroir et autres doubles,* Paris, PUF, 1993.

ZOCCOLOTTI, P., D. Scabini and C. Violani. "Electrodermal Responses in Patients with Unilateral Brain Damage," *Journal of Clinical Neuropsychology,* vol. 4, no. 2, July 1982, p. 143–150.

Index

D

E

F

G

H

I

J

K

L

M

N